LONDON'S
EAST END
LIFE AND TRADITIONS

LONDON'S
EAST END
LIFE AND TRADITIONS

JANE COX

SEVEN DIALS

First published in the United Kingdom in 1994 by
George Weidenfeld & Nicolson

This paperback edition first published in 2000 by
Seven Dials, Cassell & Co
Wellington House, 125 Strand
London, WC2R 0BB

Distributed in the United States of America by
Sterling Publishing Co., Inc.
387 Park Avenue South,
New York, NY 10016-8810

A CIP catalogue record for this book is available
from the British Library

ISBN 1 84188 101 5

Edited, designed and typeset by Playne Books
Editor: Gill Davies
Designer: David Playne
Printed in Italy.

Photograph opposite title page: Stepney in 1936
Contents page photograph: Bow in 1912

For Sue

ACKNOWLEDGEMENTS

I must thank, firstly, my own family, headed
by my aunt, Violet Short, they are East Enders
with long memories.
Secondly, Madge Darby and Ray Newton of the
Wapping Historical Trust and Julie Hunt of my own
Stepney Historical Trust for inspiring and informing
me. Also, thank you to all the people who have come
to lecture to the Stepney Historical Trust.
Chris Lloyd, the local history librarian of Tower
Hamlets must come next — along with vastly
increasing numbers of genealogists with East End
connections — I am most grateful to them all and
to Chris for his particular support.
By the endlessly patient and well-informed staff at
the Guildhall library I am, as usual, astonished, as
by the archivists at the Greater London Record Office.
At my second, or possibly first home, the dear old
Public Record Office, there are some special people to
be thanked: Sue Lumas, Elizabeth Hallam and my son,
Oliver Hoare. At St Dunstan's, Stepney, once the parish
church for the whole of the East End, my sincere
thanks must go to the Rector and the Curate.
On a more personal level, there are a list of people who
have sustained me through a labour of undoubted love
— one that, for private reasons, has had its painful
moments: my sister Sue, Noel and Stuart MacDonald,
Paul Conrad, Yvonne Hughes, Catriona Ross
Treacher, Diane Smith, my son Charles (born in
Whitechapel) and Lyttleton Springer.
If I didn't want you to take my book seriously,
I would add that the spirit of Ramsay MacDonald
had hovered over my word processor.

Jane Cox May 1994

The author and publishers
would like to thank the
following institutions and
photographers for permission
to reproduce illustrations
and for supplying photographs:

James Bartholomew
Paul Berkshire
The British Museum
Fox Photographs
Godfrey New Photographics
Greater London Record Office
Guildhall Library, London
Halifax Photographs
Nigel Henderson
History of Wapping Trust
Horton Picture Library
John Topham Picture Library
Lambeth Palace Library
The Museum of London
Port of London Authority
St Dunstan's, Stepney
The Salvation Army
Stepney Historical Trust
Rosemary Taylor
Topical Press
Tower Hamlets Local History Library

Line drawings and maps by
Barbara Mainwaring and David Playne

The publishers have taken all possible care to trace
and acknowledge the source of illustrations.
If any errors have accidentally occurred, the publishers
will be happy to correct these in future editions,
provided they receive sufficient notification.

Contents

PREFACE
8

INTRODUCTION
9

THE EARLY DAYS
Celtic twilight to the Middle Ages
12

STEPNEY
The church and village at the heart of it all
21

ALONG THE ROAD TO THE EAST
Aldgate and Whitechapel
35

EAST OF THE TOWER
St Katharine's and East Smithfield
54

SHOREDITCH
In company with Shakespeare
68

WAPPING, SHADWELL,
RATCLIFF AND LIMEHOUSE
The riverside hamlets
74

BETHNAL GREEN, SPITALFIELDS
AND MILE END NEW TOWN
If it weren't for the weaving,
what should we do?
106

MILE END, BOW AND
BROMLEY
The commuter belt
121

POPLAR AND THE ISLE OF DOGS
From cattle pasture to
Canary Wharf
134

THE TRANSIT CAMP
A world of strangers: influx and immigration
142

SLUMS AND DEPRIVATION
'Not a wery nice neighbourhood'
151

MORE FRIENDLY THAN IT IS NOW
The East End remembered
165

SELECT BIBLIOGRAPHY
188

INDEX
190

ACKNOWLEDGEMENTS
192

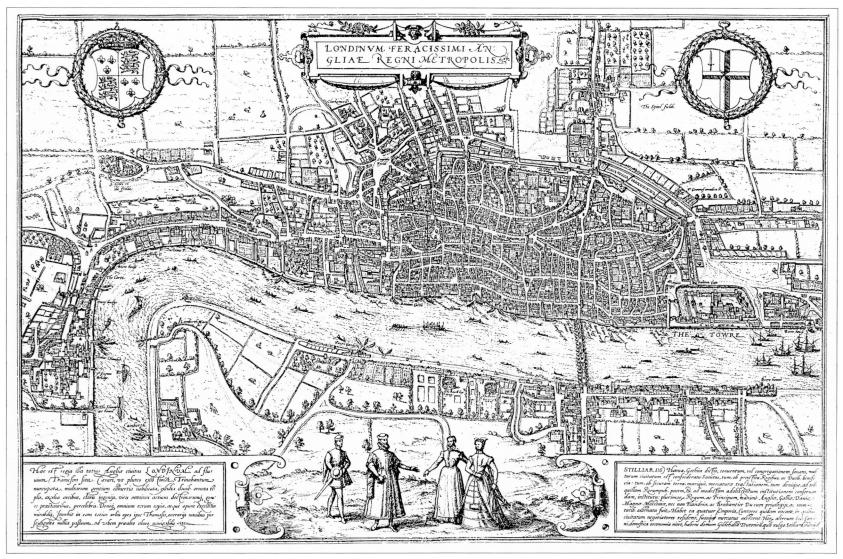

Map from 1572: Braun and Hogenberg

To so many people, a different place ...

Down by the Docks, scraping fiddles go in the public houses all day long, and shrill, above ... the din, rises the screeching of innumerable parrots brought from foreign parts.

Charles Dickens *circa* 1820

If the discommodities of the City offend you, yet may the country about your parish of Stepney afford you the like delights to those ... wherein now you keep.

Sir Thomas More 1478 - 1535

They went jostling, laughing and jeering into the forefront of the battle ... and they fought the fire, and they fought panic and disease and sleeplessness, and they used burning incendiary bombs as hand torches by which to do the rescue work — and presently the Luftwaffe reeled back.

The Mayor 1939-1940

The humours of the place are rough and coarse — as the performances in the penny gaffs and public house sing-songs testify; but there is everywhere a readiness to laugh.

Gustave Doré 1872

PREFACE

Traditionally, people have moved away from the East End. If ever I move too far away, to some Suffolk pink-wash house wrapped in wisterias, perhaps, so that I am no longer within easy reach of its dear old streets, I shall need a companion such as this book.

London's East End: Life and Traditions is meant mainly for those who have left, or whose ancestors left the East End. I hope it will bring back the sooty fish-and-chip smell to those who once knew it. For the rest, to whom the names Whitechapel and Wapping are just echoes of their family's past, albeit as familiar as the words Mum and Dad, I shall try to paint a picture.

There is a poignancy in searching for the history of an area where the past has been all but obliterated. Slum clearance and the Blitz and generations of developers have wiped the East End nearly clean of its heritage. A few signposts are left: street names, a churchyard here and there, things in museums, documents tucked away in archives.

> When Walter Besant wrote his book on East London he prefaced it thus:
>
> There are no monuments to recall the past; its history is mostly a blank — that blank which is the history of woods and meadows, arable and pasture land, over which the centuries pass, making no more mark than the breezes of yesterday have made on the waves and waters of the ocean.

Its history is not a blank. There are no picturesque half-timbered houses or venerable antiquities — after all this is the working end of town — but the story of London's eastern flank is nearly as rich as that of its fine neighbour, the City, and much more so than that of the western and northern suburbs.

INTRODUCTION

The story of the East End did not start with the Victorian slum which grew, like an ugly boil, on the side of London. Nor is its earlier history the empty tale of winds whipping across empty marshland or decade upon decade of tilling. Most people seem to think, in so far as they think about it at all, that before industrialization there was nothing but green villages on the City's eastern side. In the middle years of the last century, it is said, these villages were swallowed up, scarred by railways and polluted by factories. Row upon relentless row of brick boxes sprang up, where men and women slept and ate in the brief time that they were allowed free from their working shifts. Tenement buildings rose, and with them all the forbidding public buildings associated with Victorian urbanization, work houses, police stations, hospitals, prisons and great dark, warning churches which glower still, reminders of death and sin.

In fifty years the East End went from maypoles to manufacture, from rustic idyll to Jack the Ripper land.

It was not quite so.

Since medieval times the east side of the City has been London's backyard, with workshops and shipyards, bakeries and mills, breweries and distilleries interspersed with allotments and market gardens. In the early years of the fourteenth century a commission was set up to look into the smell caused because the smelters of Wapping, East Smithfield and Southwark were using sea coal instead of charcoal. Lime kilns gave Limehouse its name at least six hundred years ago, and probably earlier. In the Hearth Tax records from the time of Samuel Pepys half the residents of east London were classified as 'poor'.

The City walls enclosed the wealth of London. While the polite overspill of palaces and mansions extended westwards along the Strand to Westminster, outside Aldgate and Bishopsgate and the postern gate by the Tower, lived and worked the 'rag tag' folk as Shakespeare called them, the 'limbs of Limehouse and their brothers the Tribulation of Tower Hill'.

When Ben Jonson's vice Iniquity, in *The Devil is an Ass* set off to find the parts of town where he felt most at home, he flew off east:

Let us survey the suburbs, and make forth our sallies
Down Petticoat Lane, and up the Smock-Alleys,
To Shoreditch, Whitechapel and to Saint Kather'n's

That is not to say there were not pleasant leafy villages in the east. Stepney, Bow, Bethnal Green and Mile End were, not so long ago, salubrious 'commuter' belts, where merchants and politicians had fine houses. In 1610 the windows of Stepney church glowed with the jewelled colours of thirteen coats of arms.

But the inner suburbs — East Smithfield and St Katharine's, just east of the Tower, Whitechapel, outside Aldgate, Spitalfields and Shoreditch, north of the Bishop's Gate — these have had what might be thought of as East End characteristics for at least four hundred years.

Accordingly, there is 'living memory' in these pages but it is not just a recollection of the 'good old bad old days', of cosier times when neighbours were neighbours, of street markets and steam trains, of opium dens and the murder of prostitutes, of dock strikes and starving children. This book takes us back to the time when the East End echoed to the rumble of farm carts and the clatter of watermills, when Wapping was all windmills and Bow market gardens, when the lush pastures on the Isle of Dogs fed the finest beef cattle in England. We will return to medieval days when pilgrims stopped at Ratcliff Cross on their way to Waltham Abbey and the streets were thronged with monks and nuns and the air full of the sound of Whitechapel bells and the lowing of cattle. We shall look at the Roman watch tower which guarded the Thames from its vantage point on the south side of the Highway, about half a mile east of the Tower of London, and even cast an eye over the desolate flood plain which spread out on the City's eastern flank when Gog and Magog ruled over the lake city, Llyndin.

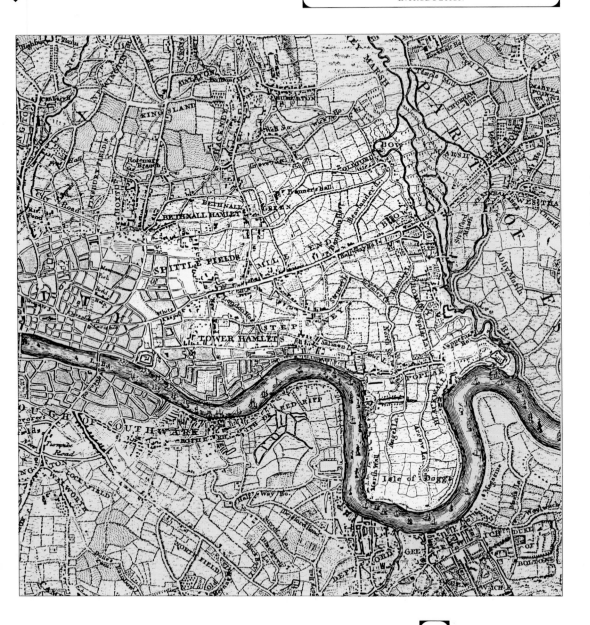

The area defined

The East End, for the purposes of this book, is the three-square-mile triangle of land bounded by the river Lea on the east and the City of London on the west. It corresponds roughly to the jurisdiction of the old manor of Stepney, which was separated from Hackney in 1652.

By 1700 there were seven parishes (Stepney, Whitechapel, Shoreditch, Aldgate, Bow, Bromley and Holy Trinity, Minories) in this area. Aldgate was, of course, a City parish but has always shared the characteristics of the 'inner East End' so will be included. The vast farflung parish of Stepney was made up of eight hamlets: Mile End Old Town and New Town, Limehouse, Ratcliff, Spitalfields, Wapping/Stepney, Poplar and Bethnal Green.

The triangle now all comes within the metropolitan borough of Tower Hamlets except Shoreditch, which belongs to Hackney. The 'lost villages' do not correspond exactly to any neighbourhood or other division.

THE EARLY DAYS

Celtic twilight to the Middle Ages

We know the Romans went swimming in the river: the prize treasures from a dig at Shadwell signal tower were two leather bikinis.

The Saxon Cross in St Dunstans is a relic of the Saxon East End.
The figures of Christ on the cross, the Virgin Mary and St John have been worn smooth by the passage of time.

The Highway is one of the oldest thoroughfares in London. It runs from half a mile east of the Tower to what was once Ratcliff Cross and is now the entrance of an underpass to the Isle of Dogs, cutting Wapping off from Stepney and Whitechapel. These days the only reminders of the past, apart from two restored warehouses, are old St Paul of Shadwell and old St George-in-the-East. They stand, one to the north and one to the south of the wide fast road, alongside the motley debris of function and improvement: garages and workshops, hoardings and boarded-up building sites, the odd pub, council blocks yellowing at the edges. Rising out of the petrol fumes, dwarfing St Paul and St George, towers a new red-brick terraced monster containing empty pricey *pieds a terre*.

The two churches are youngsters compared to the road itself, being some two hundred years in age, as opposed to two thousand. The road is said to have started life as an Iron Age trackway, following the firm ridge of land which ran through the marsh parallel to the bank of the Thames. It connected Llyndin, the lake fort, to the gravel spur which jutted out into the river at Ratcliff, making it a good landing place.

Unlike many roads round here, the Highway has retained, or at least recovered, part of its old name, Ratcliff Highway. It has had a rumbustuous history, hurtling down the centuries past sailors' cottages, chandlers' shops, brothels, sugar and starch works, gunpowder factories, alehouses and doss houses, churches and chapels. Within living memory, you could even hear the roar of tigers and the squawking of parrots here, coming from Jamrachs which traded in the rare and strange beasts that seamen brought home. Eighty years ago a lion could be purchased for sixty pounds.

On the south side of the road where Wapping Lane, once Old Gravel Lane, makes off for the river, stands Sovereign Court, an imposing new office building in the classical style. It was erected in the expansive late

1970s as part of the 'City moves East' redevelopment of Docklands and is now desperately bedecked with banners and signs inviting business to take up occupation. Its porticoed and pillared self effrontery, not unlike that of some brash Roman villa, is on the site of a Roman watch tower.

Roman origins

If you could block out the 'mighty roar of London's traffic', as they used to say on the BBC's *In Town Tonight*, this might be the ideal spot to begin a tale of the old East End.

Conjure up an early morning 1,700 years ago with the mist rising over a great sedgey marsh. Listen to the bugle calling across the wastes of the East End, the crunch of feet and the sharp-called orders, as the garrison is put through its paces. Sea gulls wheel and their cry cuts the damp air which hangs over the salty meadows, washed by the tide.

When the Romans came in 42 AD and built Londinium, 'the twin-hilled City of the South ...girt about by fen and marsh', they probably took over an Ancient British settlement on the high ground between the Thames, the Walbrook and the Fleet. There is no real evidence that Lyndin existed before. The only Celtic name surviving locally is that of Lyndin itself but the Romans were in the way of using the conquered tongue when they named their colonial cities.

If there was a pre-Roman settlement it would have been a collection of huts in a great windswept marsh. The river was many times wider that it is now, the tidal flood plain stretching up to Pudding Lane and down as far south as Clapham. At that time Bermondsey, Chelsea, Battersea and Westminster (Thorney Island) were islands.

The southern half of Tower Hamlets would have been too wet for habitation but there may have been huts in Whitechapel, Bethnal Green and Bow. And, the

Within living memory, Jamrachs, dealers in wild animals, was set on the Highway — one of the oldest roads in London, said to have begun as an Iron-Age track.

Highway may have been there, linking the hill fort with the landing place. The earliest sign of life in this neck of the woods are some tools found in Hackney Brook, dating from sometime between 5000 and 3000 BC.

Legend has it that London was founded in the year 1008 BC and, as legends have a disturbing way of turning out to have some foundation of truth, it is worth repeating. Geoffrey of Monmouth, a medieval 'journalist' monk, is said to have invented the tale to give London classical status. One Brutus, a descendant of Aeneas, founded 'New Troy' on Ludgate Hill and Cornhill, following a great battle between Corineus and Gogmagog, a British chieftain. The two combatants, later called the giants Gog and Magog, were adopted as the City's mascots and paraded in effigy on state occasions — for instance when Henry V returned from Agincourt and when Bloody Mary made her triumphal entry into London at Whitechapel. Until recently the pair still came out every quarter of an hour to strike the clock of St Dunstan in the West in Fleet Street.

But let us return to more substantial history. The Italian invaders built a wall of Kentish rag, fifteen feet high and enclosed the area of 330 acres which is still called the City. Six gates led out on to the main roads; on the eastern side at Aldgate and Bishopsgate and where the Tower of London now stands.

They squeezed the river into a straight jacket, embanking it on the northern side with terraces held in place by wooden revetments faced with masonry. They erected a fine basilica where Leadenhall market now is and an amphitheatre where the Guildhall stands. About forty thousand inhabitants lived within the walls. What happened outside is not so clear.

Whether or not they drained or embanked to the east is not known but there were two — possibly three — roads leading out of the town to the east. Along the river bank was the Highway (the Pretorian Way), going past the signal tower to the port of Ratcliff. A

The City of London was supposedly founded as New Troy when the mythical Corneus (here depicted in Roman military style) led Trojan invaders against Gogmagog of Ancient Britain.

The mythical giant Gogmagog who stood for the Ancient Britains against Trojan invaders lead by Roman Corineus, another giant is depicted in the Guildhall armed with bows and arrows and a globe of spikes.

road turned off the Lincoln Road (Shoreditch High Street), and followed roughly the direction of Bethnal Green Road and Roman Road, crossing the Lea at the Old Ford. The third is the Colchester Road, the Whitechapel/Mile End Road, which left the City at Aldgate and crossed the Lea at the straight ford (Stratford). There is reason to suppose that there was some 'ribbon development'.

It was thought, not very long ago — from the evidence of burial urns, coffins and bones — that the Roman East End was one vast graveyard, 'an immense field of the dead', that Whitechapel Road was a 'street of tombs', like the one in Pompeii. It was customary to have burial grounds outside cities, with tomb stones lining the roads, as a *memento mori* for travellers.

In 1576 they found a cemetery in Spitalfields, just where Christchurch stands today. John Stow, the historian, was fascinated by the glass vessels, some of which still had oil in them. The following century the remains of a woman with a figure of Cupid on her breast was found where Cable Street meets Brodlove Lane. A green marble tablet was dug up in 1787 in Goodman's Fields; it commemorates an 'incomparable husband', Flavius Agricola of the 6th Legion which came over with Hadrian and stayed until the end of the occupation.

In the nineteenth century finds were made in Red Lion Street in Whitechapel, the north-east corner of Shadwell churchyard and a stone cistern containing the remains of two children was unearthed in Wellclose Square.

Signs of life in the Roman East End appeared this century. In 1977 the watch tower on the Highway was discovered and in the following year third-century hobnail boots and oyster shells turned up in a building site at Goodman's Fields. More was going on in the East End than funerals.

From the slender evidence, then, it seems that there were people living in the inner eastern suburbs, in

A timber bridge spanned the river
across to the Roman walled city of
Londinium built on two small hills.
In the foreground is Southwark. The
imposing basilica in the centre was
reputed to be the largest building
in Britain.

Whitechapel and Shadwell and in Spitalfields and Shoreditch to the north. How many there were and what they did we cannot tell. Probably there were farmers and market gardeners supplying the city. Corn was most likely ground in mills here and bread made and taken in through Aldgate as it was for many hundreds of years thereafter.

Discoveries at the Shadwell signal tower site hint at what life was like for the soldiers stationed there. The tower was built in the third century, presumably to regulate river traffic and receive signals from the forts along the 'Saxon shore'. Bells may have rung out or beacons been lit to warn the citizens of the approach of pirate bands.

The soldiers lived well. Seventy per cent of the animal bones recovered were ox; the men evidently ate a good deal of beef, as well as mutton, chicken and goose. Oyster shells abound, scattered around like crisp packets. They ate off decorated East Gaulish plates; some eighty items of mess pottery were found. We know they went swimming in the river; the prize treasures from the dig were two leather bikinis.

Historians of feminist East London like to picture the fierce Queen of the Iceni here, in her chariot at the head of her forces, crashing through the leas at Old Ford and along Roman Road. In AD 61, when Roman London was still a new town, Boudicca rode in from her capital, Colchester, and burnt the city to the ground in revenge for the rape of her daughters and the invaders' disregard of her husbands' will.

For the most part, we can only speculate and wait for the Saxons to come and give the eastern suburbs their name and identity.

In the fifth century the legions were withdrawn and the fine four-hundred-year-old city, battered and care-worn from continual attacks by German pirates who rowed silently up the river to raid, loot and stay, fell into decay. Grass grew over the Highway, the Bethnal Green Road and the Mile End Road. Where the Italian

Celts went is anybody's guess. I dare say the farmers of Whitechapel went on tilling while the ruins smoked and swineherds continued to drive their pigs, rooting for acorns in the woods at Bethnal Green. Fishermen might still be seen in small craft among the swans' nests and clumps of irises in the marshes of Wapping and the Isle of Dogs.

The Saxon's landings and origins of many place names

London was re-occupied by the Saxons, the first settlers making their home in Lundenwic round about St Clement Danes and then moving into the old Roman city and making it their own.

The street name Knighten reflects the time when a guild of thirteen knights were put in control of a rough area on the outskirts of the city in the tenth century.

Sometime in the three hundred years following the collapse of Roman rule the German tribesmen took over the East End; Stibba came to Stepney, Bleda to Bethnal Green and Weappa to Wapping. The country was re-Christianized and a small wooden church appeared on the City's eastern flank in the village which Stibba had given his name, founded in the mid-tenth century by Dunstan, Lord of Stepney Manor, saint, bishop, archbishop and powerful politician. The Church began its six-hundred-year rule in east London. The East Enders came out from the City and in from the country; the Church supplied the houses and marked out most of the streets.

Knighten Street, a newly named Docklands' creation off Wapping High Street, is a reminder of the guild of knights who were put in charge of the rough patch just outside the City on the east in St Dunstan's day. The 'suburb' which had grown up between Aldgate and the river had been left 'desolate and foresaken by the inhabitants' because the Bishop had imposed 'too much servitude'. Presumably a police force was required to watch over this haunt of robbers around the Minories and Leman Street. The eastern boundary of the guild's patch was Nightingale Lane (once Knichten Guild Lane), now Thomas More Street, which curves round the wall enclosing St Katherine's marina. In those days a stream ran along the line of the road and went into the Thames.

The knights' 'contract' was a strange fairy-tale affair. The thirteen of them had to engage in three successive combats, one above ground, one below and one in the water. They also were required to take on all comers on an appointed day in East Smithfield, 'running with spears'.

By the time William the Conqueror's commissioners surveyed east London in 1086, Stepney combined with Hackney was established as the chief manor under the lordship of the Bishop of London; his vast estate ran from Millwall to Muswell Hill. Of the

In AD 296 Constanius Chlorus, who had crushed rebellion in Britain and rescued Roman London from destruction, had this medallion struck in Gaul — it is one of the earliest pictures of London.

isolated farm in the meadows by a broken bridge. One of the Bishop's tenants was a William de Ver and a namesake of his held land in the island in the fourteenth century. On the basis of this it is thought that the island was walled by the time of the Conquest and used as pasture.

Of all the familiar and famous East End place names, the only ones which appear in Domesday are Stepney, and Hoxton and Haggerston further north. Over the next few hundred years the others emerge from a medieval twilight — Shadwell, Limehouse, Ratcliff, Wapping, Whitechapel, Bethnal Green, Bow, Bromley, Poplar, Shoreditch. Some started as hamlets and grew into suburbs; some started as City overspill and gradually acquired their own identity. Eventually all came together and merged into the 'bottomless pit of decaying life' which Beatrice Webb described less than a hundred years ago.

Chaucer's time

Bishop's ten subtenants, only two were English; the rest were Norman magnates, some of whom had taken over the farms that had been held by canons of St Paul's before the Conquest.

Robert son of Roscelin had estates in Bromley. Edmund, son of Algot had a new mill in Old Ford. The famed bakers of Bow were perhaps already at work. There are five other mills mentioned but there is no way of knowing where they were. In Stepney and Hackney there were a total of 183 peasant households, comprising perhaps nine hundred souls. There was arable, pasture and meadow land and pannage for eight hundred pigs.

The strange manor names mean little to us now — Huskarls and Helles, Cobhams and Ewell or Rylehouse, Rumbolds; Aschewys in Mile End and Garlek House in Brook Street, Poplar. Only Pomfret or Pontefract in the Isle of Dogs, suggests a picture — an

Before walking round the villages, let us proceed with Geoffrey Chaucer, out of Aldgate and 'survey the suburbs' as they might have seemed to him when he lived in lodgings over the gate, about three hundred years after the Conqueror's survey.

On 10 May 1374 the poet took the lease of rooms with a cellar beneath in the massive twin-towered gatehouse which stood astride the road twenty-five feet east of Jewry Street on the south side and between Duke's Place and Houndsditch on the north. The gate had about a seventy-five foot frontage and the roadway between was twenty feet in width. There was a wicket gate at the side to let pedestrians through.

A 'little loge' stood outside Aldgate, only twelve by seven feet; it was let out for a shilling a year to a 'caretaker' who was responsible for keeping the road under the gate in good repair. There was a weigh house with a large open shed at the bottom where corn was weighed

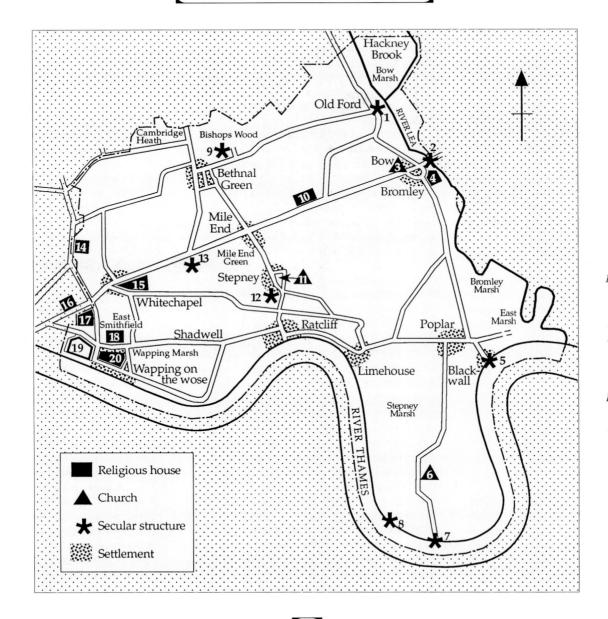

Chaucer's Aldgate in the late Middle Ages.

1 King John's Palace
2 Bow Bridge
3 St Mary's Bow
4 St Leonard's Priory
5 Potter's Ferry
6 Chapel of St Mary
7 Greenwich ferry
8 Deptford ferry
9 Bishops Hall
10 Mile End Leper Hospital
11 St Dunstan's, Stepney
12 Great Place
13 Mile End Manor House
14 Priory of St Mary Spital
15 St Mary Matfelon
16 Priory of Holy Trinity
17 Abbey of St Clare
18 Abbey of St Mary Graces
19 Tower of London
20 St Kathanne's Hospital

■ Religious house
▲ Church
✳ Secular structure
⣿ Settlement

at the Great Beam before it was milled. Just to the north was a free-standing tower.

While Chaucer was in residence there were threats of invasion from the French; ordinances of 1377 provided for the fortification of the gate with portcullises and 'barbykanes'.

When the first bell of the day tolled out from St Thomas Acon, the great gates were swung open and the business of the day began. Carts started arriving from the east. Tuppence a week had to be paid on every iron-bound cart carrying victuals or the blood and entrails of slaughtered beasts; dung carts paid a penny and those loaded with grain paid a halfpenny. Herds of cattle were driven through, going from the East End pastures to Smithfield. Pigs were a familiar sight — there were two Hog Lanes round here in Chaucer's day; they were later named Royal Mint Street and Middlesex Street.

Against the background of the constant tintinabulation of bells from St Botolph, the church by the gate, and Holy Trinity Priory, the lowing of cattle, the creak and rattle of carts and the clip of hooves, were the shouts of street vendors selling 'costard apples', rabbit and venison pie, roast pork, pheasant, bittern, hens, 'strawberries ripe', eels, pepper and saffron, mackerel, 'hot peascods', cherries.

Blacksmiths cry 'coal, coal and blow their bellows:
'Huff! Puff!' says one, 'Huff! Puff!' the other.
They spit and they sprawl and they tell many stories.
No man for such water-burners can get a night's rest.

The smells were farmyard but this was no village. The area east of Aldgate, as far as Aldgate East underground station and a bit beyond, and stretching down to the Tower and up to the Bishop's gate, was already a relatively populous suburb. The workers, who later characterized this part of London, were already in residence here. The records mention fishmongers and

butchers, potters, bakers, chandlers, gold-beaters and goldsmiths, fell-mongers, vintners, saddlers and cord-wainers, brewers and hatters, spurriers, cooks and janitors, clerks, 'medecines' and chaplains. The Most commonly occuring are bell founders and there are references to the related trades of buckle, pail and metal-pot manufacture.

A hundred years before, there were enough people living here for a chapel of ease to be built for them less than a mile from St Botolph's. The chapel was white-washed and gave its name to the hamlet around: Whitechapel. By Chaucer's day it had acquired the status of a parish church.

What the exact numbers of these East Enders were is impossible to say; the Chantry certificate of 1548, give some idea of the relative size of the different suburbs 170 years after Chaucer but before the great early modern influx of country folk which changed the character of the area. Whitechapel had 2,500 communicants and six priests; Stepney 1,360 communicants and one priest; Shoreditch had 800 communicants and three priests.

Already this was beginning to be London's backyard; Chaucer's father owned twenty-four shops in Whitechapel, although there were fine houses and farms too. Further out, most of the East End villages were large and flourishing, as one would expect from their proximity to the markets of the City. Bow had its own chapel by 1311 and Shoreditch had its own church from the twelfth century. The wealthy had mansions out at Bethnal Green and Stepney and there was even a royal palace in Poplar.

Looking east, along the notoriously muddy road to Mile End and Bow, the poet would have seen stalls, shops and houses with signs swinging from them, pitched roofs, not closely snug together, long gardens and fields stretching out beyond. To the north the moat, from which Houndsditch gets its name, ran alongside the high City walls.

Since Domesday the church had taken an even firmer hold on the eastern suburbs. The Lord of Stepney Manor, the Bishop of London, still ruled over all — or nearly all — and monastic establishments abounded. The streets must have been full of priests, monks and nuns.

Old father baldpate
Say the bells at Aldgate

The old version of *Oranges and Lemons* refers to the tonsures of the black Augustinian monks of Holy Trinity. This was an enormous and ancient foundation a stone's throw from the gate. It was inside the City walls, it is true, so no part of our East End but it owned St Botolph's and a deal of property in Aldgate and White-chapel and was therefore an important presence in the area.

Not far away, in the Minories, which took its name from the establishment, were the Sorores Minores, Franciscan nuns brought over in 1293 by Blanche, Queen of Navarre. Further down towards the river, where St Katharine's marina is now, was the Royal Hospital of St Katharine's. On the other side of East Smithfield was the new Cistercian Abbey of St Mary Graces and in Bromley the Benedictine Convent of St Leonard. Chaucer probably knew that well and modelled his Madame Eglantine in *The Canterbury Tales* on the prioress there, who spoke the French of 'Stratford atte Bow'. North of Bishopsgate were three religious houses in close proximity — Bethlehem, the mad house, St Mary Spital, which gave Spitalfields its name, and, off Shoreditch High Street, the nuns of Holywell had prayed for over a hundred years.

As the curfew sounds and the doors of the Ale gate clang shut, Chaucer's Aldgate slips back into the past and this tour of the villages begins with a ride cross country to the East End's heart, Stepney and the parish church of St Dunstan.

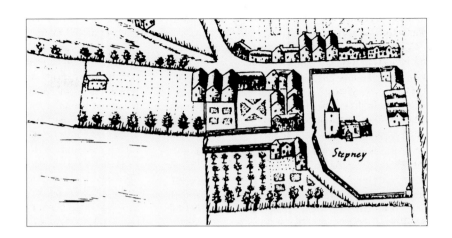

STEPNEY

The church and village at the heart of it all

A small wooden church stood among the cottages; snipe and curlew wheeled up from the wastes of the marsh to the east and stag ran in the woodlands up at Bethnal Green.

Stepney at the time of Samuel Pepys; a plan drawn in 1681.

It is hard to imagine today that Stepney was once a village ruled by the Lord of the Manor with cottages and gardens generally associated with rural areas rather than London suburbs.

Children of today's nicely bred newcomers, returning to regentrify and plant geraniums in the window boxes of their artisans' dwellings, ride ponies in Stepney today. There is even a farm to lend an unfamiliar country air.

In spite of the backcloth of gas works and high rise, there is enough greenery around to let the imagination wander back a thousand years to the time of the stone rood. A small wooden church stood among the cottages; snipe and curlew wheeled up from the wastes of the marsh to the east and stag ran in the woodlands up at Bethnal Green. When Stibba the Saxon and his band landed at Ratcliff they may have originally settled quite near the river bank, hence Stibba's Hithe or landing place (Stybbanhythe in a charter of *circa* 1000 AD, Stibenhede in the Domesday Book and Stebenee by 1198). Some people think they rowed up a navigable channel, later called the Black Ditch, and built their village where St Dunstan's stands now.

For several hundred years after its foundation St Dunstan's was the only church outside the City's two eastern gates. It must have been the only village of any size, if you discount the true suburbs which were growing up immediately outside the walls; the white chapel outside Aldgate was built in the thirteenth century and the flour-milling centre at Bow acquired a chapel of its own in 1311. By the time *Oranges and Lemons* was sung, Stepney was a flourishing place of market gardeners and silk manufacturers; the latter is witnessed by the long association of the Mercer's Company with the area. According to the rhyme, the bells of poor Shoreditch (Fleet Ditch in the original) promised to pay up *'When I grow rich'* Stepney's bells were able to sneer with superiority *'When will that be?'*.

Medieval Stepney was a working village, inhabited by a mixture of rich and poor, farming folk and millers, silk weavers and throwsters, coopers and brewers, gentlemen and merchants. A Parliament met there in 1299 at the house of the Lord Mayor, Henry le Waleys.

Stepney church in the 18th century

To find the church...

Cross over the Mile End Road (one of London's dirtiest and most lorry-laden arteries) by Stepney Green underground station, and find Whitehorse Lane. Walk along by its post-war concrete and rusting chrome for a few minutes and you will come upon the church, standing there, surprisingly, among trees.

*Overall distant view of
Stepney parish*

*High-rise buildings of the
1980s invade the skyline
of terraced chimney pots.*

On a wild wet blustering September evening in 1993 a new rector was instituted at the parish church of St Dunstan and All Saints, Stepney. The old church was bursting at its seams, nearly as full as it used to be three hundred years ago when five galleries were erected to accommodate the first large influx of immigrants. The bells, made in the Whitechapel foundry, pealed out into the damp air as clouds of clergy were blown and buffeted across the grass, their surplices billowing like sails as they processed in pairs from the night into the Church of the High Seas with its brand new red ensign hoisted on the church tower. Known as the sailors' church because of all the seafarer's around, St Dunstan's is the only building of any antiquity in the East End with Saxon figures just visible above the altar. 'St Dunstans,' said the Bishop of Stepney, was, 'glowing in the love of all its thousand-year history.' Certainly, it must have the strongest claim to be the heart of the East End.

A rural retreat

By the opening years of the sixteenth century the village and the country round, of which Victoria Park is the only reminder now, was a favourite spot for wealthy citizens to build rural retreats. In 1503 Henry VII's queen made a note in her account book for payments made for attendance on the Duchess of Suffolk at her house in 'Stebenhath'. The Marquis of Worcester had a mansion just to the east of the church, roughly where the adventure playground is now. Its great red brick gatehouse was still standing long after the house had gone and provided accommodation for clergy well into the next century.

Those exalted residences have left behind some relic to assist History the Romance in a recollection of fine brocades and silks sweeping along gravel paths by box hedges, of picking cherries and sniffing old roses — in Stepney. Just to the south of the church is the Colet Arms, and to the north Dame Colet House, both celebrating Stepney's most famous vicar, the humanist divine and Dean of St Paul's, John Colet. His father, Sir Henry, twice Lord Mayor, lived in a mansion which

Inns and a school have been named after John Colet, Stepney's most famous vicar and a friend of Sir Thomas More.

stood just to the west of St Dunstan's; Great Place and his tomb is in the church (1510). Even in the East End's 'stockbroker belt', life was perilous. Sir Henry's pious wife, Dame Christian, bore him some twenty-two children of whom only John survived.

John Colet made Great Place a safe house for the friends of the Reformation. Sir Thomas More would visit, sailing down river from his house in Chelsea and landing at Ratcliff Stairs. Impressed with the beauty of his friend's home, he wrote:

> If the discommodities of the City offend you, yet may
> the country round about your parish of Stepney,
> afford you the like delights to those which that
> affords you wherein you now keep.

Erasmus may have been a visitor there; he was a good friend both of Colet and of Richard Pace, another vicar of Stepney. Pace was, for a time, Henry VIII's secretary. After eight years at St Dunstan's he fell out with Cardinal Wolsey and was put in the Tower where he went mad.

St Dunstan's parish magazine is called *The Kindle*, a reminder, unwitting, one assumes, of those dramatic days in Stepney church. In 1540 the vicar, William Jerome, was burnt alive for preaching an annabaptist sermon at St Paul's Cross and calling MPs, 'Butterflies, fools and knaves'.

There are even royal connections. Beneath the east window there used to be a large black marble slab:

> *Here lyeth Henry Steward, Lord Darle*
> *of the age of three-quarters of a year.*

The baby was the brother of Lord Darnley who married Mary Queen of Scots. Sir Thomas Spert, the founder of Trinity House has a tomb in the church. Ben Jonson Road, formerly Bull Lane and once Cow Lane, takes us back to a December day in 1594 when Lucy

Harrington married Edward, Earl of Bedford in St Dunstan's. She was Ben Jonson's patroness and also John Donne's.

The *nouveau riches* mixed with the nobility. St Dunstan's vestry was a meeting of Elizabethan sea dogs, gentry and 'captains of industry'. In 1597 John Gardiner served. He owned the famous Ratcliff sugar house, which must have been one of the first of its kind, processing the cane newly bought from the West Indies. It was just north of Cable Street probably where the Martinau Estate now is. Lord Morley was on the vestry. He lived on Mile End Green and contributed twenty light horse and thirty muskets to the Armada defence force. It was he who received the famous 'Mounteagle letter' from his father-in-law, which revealed the Gunpowder Plot.

The seafaring end of town

So much for the fine and famous. Most of the ghosts here are of ordinary working people; it was in Shakespeare's day that Stepney started to gather them to itself in large numbers, not, as one might imagine, in Charles Dickens' time. The parish register records the burial of a servant of Sir Walter Raleigh's in 1596 and of a dumb fortune-teller from the Highway in 1628.

By 1600 the population of Stepney and its hamlets was something in the region of thirty thousand. From the 1580s onwards economic recession and changes in farming methods brought thousands of country people into London, with the eastern suburbs and Stepney's maritime hamlets taking the heaviest load. This was now truly becoming the 'seafaring end of town' and many of the newcomers took their chance on board ship. There were fortunes to be made in the New World from tobacco and sugar and the streets of Ratcliff were paved with Spanish gold. The country East Enders were employed by shipwrights, ropemakers, anchor smiths and carpenters. They became

watermen and lightermen, worked in the sugar and glass factories, cleared out the ditches which crisscrossed the marsh and went out to Poplar and Bow to help with the harvest. The 'rag trade' employed a good number. The 'heavy footed country folk' which the poet Middleton noticed wearing away the floors in St Paul's cathedral, were pouring into St Dunstan's now, trudging over from the riverside and down from Artillery Lane and Bethnal Green.

In May 1607, for instance, it was mainly sailors and their wives, most of them from Wapping and Limehouse, who brought their precious bundles in for baptism. There was a joiner, a player, a vintner from Mile End, a baker, a rope-maker, a silk weaver from 'Tenters' and one from Collier Lane, a bricklayer and two shipwrights. In the overcrowded and insanitary suburbs couples were lucky if their child survived to become a toddler and they might be back again within a few months, following behind a tiny coffin. It was hard burying work — small wonder the sexton, Francis Whiteacres, neglected the bells in (1601) and lost his temper with a churchwarden, telling him to 'shake his eares among dogges'. Galleries were put up to make room for the vast congregation and Stepney Church became famous for multiple christenings and weddings. In April 1623 fifty-two babies were baptized. Wapping acquired its own chapel in 1617, which eased the load for the overworked clerics.

Between 1590 and 1630 the population trebled, swelling to about forty-eight thousand. Government restrictions prevented new housing developments, or tried to, and many of the old mansions were converted into lodging houses. A sailor's widow ran one in Whitehorse Road; she took in girls who worked in the silk and lace industries. The earliest surviving Stepney parish register has on its first page an order of the Court of Star Chamber dated 1598 committing two 'Rachmans' to the Fleet. They had built tenements in Hog Lane (Middlesex Street) and Shoreditch and crammed in a large number of 'divers persons of very poor and base condition'.

In Shakespeare's day, as in the dark slum days three hundred years later, the Poor Law was over-burdened and there was much talk of 'idle beggars' and people 'fiddling the social security'. One alarmist, writing in the early 1600s, reckoned that there were as many as two thousand on poor relief in the suburbs and out-parishes. Such was the problem that warning books were published which described all the different categories of shysters, like 'Abraham Men', who pretended to be lunatics and 'seekers for glimmer of fire', who claimed their houses had been burnt down.

The seventeenth century

Between the Armada and the Civil War Stepney became a very different sort of place from the one whose 'delights' Sir Thomas More had relished. Still there were open fields, orchards and fine houses but there were many more labouring men and women about and the concentration of them around mean courtyards, in shacks and lodging houses, provided a fertile seed bed for political agitation and a focus of religious discontent, especially when times were hard. The East Enders had the reputation of being well to the 'left' (Puritan) in church matters and in politics (Parliamentarian). In the lanes-turned-alleys and the crumbled half-timbered 'bed sit' conversions, grew up the *sans culottes* of the English Revolution.

St Dunstan's was a grim place in the early seventeenth century, and the years leading up to the Civil War, as the humanist tradition of Colet was overlaid by the starkness of the Puritans. The glowing theatrical fun of the old ways, with candles and saints and embroidered copes, was replaced by long stern sermons and black clothes. Women who became pregnant or took their knitting to church might find themselves hauled up before the Archdeacon over at

The old mansion in Stepney known as King John's Palace.

Newgate church. In 1595 the organ was removed from Stepney church and they did not get it back for ninety-three years. The sexton, William Culham, a 'disorderly' chap, found himself in trouble in 1647 because he ran an alehouse in the village, The Rose. Not only that, he was a 'scoffer against the godly'.

There were a good number of 'godly' around; one of the attractions of Puritan London was the spectacular performances given by the 'Morning and Evening Stars' of Stepney. They were Dr Matthew Mead, who lectured in the morning, and William Greenhill, who was the evening lecturer, thundering out from *Ezekiel* to the open-mouthed gathering of rope makers, sailors, weavers and shipwrights.

Under Cromwell's Puritan rule Mead was the minister at the new chapel in Shadwell and Greenhill took over at St Dunstan's. Before that he had been pastor of Stepney Meeting, an Independent chapel, the first of its kind. Originally the sailors, silk weavers and others trooped up to his rather splendid 'flat' over the Marquis of Worcester's gate house. The first entry in its register, dated 15 October 1644, is the baptism of a baby born to Captain John Robinson from Shoreditch, setting the tone for what was, to begin with, a very seafaring gathering. Rachel, a child of the famous Pett family of ship builders was baptized there in 1655. In 1674 the Meeting acquired its own chapel in Bull Lane (now Ben Jonson Road) and the Estates of Holland donated pillars to hold up the roof.

Walk west from the church along Stepney Way today and discover Stepney Meeting — the oldest congregational church in the world. It moved from Bull Lane in 1844, was bombed and then rebuilt in 1955, a pale irregularly-angled building, which stands among a holiday-camp-like wilderness of sand-coloured housing estates, brightened by bollards and litter bins painted the purple of Stepney Neighbourhood. These days, as well as services, they have tea dances for the old folk from the Rest-a-While Centre,

bowling and karate. The local Citizen's Advice Bureau meets here too, and the poster announcing its sessions are put up in Bengali. There is a notice on the board outside; 'This church welcomes all people'. Mead and Greenhill would approve; both agitated for church unity — no bishops or prayer books mind, but love and truth. Greenhill's message will do for now:

Buy the truth and sell it not — do not Judaize, do not Gentilize, do not Romanize, but Christianize.

When he died he left ten pounds to the poor of Stepney 'with regard for their church membership'. At Mead's funeral in 1691 the minister said:

His Judgement in reference to matters of Church Order, was for Union and Communion of all visible Christians. It may be, in time, forgotten that ever such a man as Mr Mead, was Minister in Stepney.

The Restoration and onwards

Underneath the west window of St Dunstan's is a plain stone tablet to: 'Honist Abraham Zouch of Wappin Rope maker', who died in 1643 and his widow who remarried and then died on Restoration Day. Perhaps the excitement of the 'street party' was too much for her. On 29 May 1660 the 'Black Boy', Charles II, was restored to the throne amid scenes of jubilation. The East End 'fountains ran with wine' as did the rest but what the East Enders, many of them Protestant dissenters, thought about the turn of events is not on record.

Young people were still coming in from the shires; by the 1680s one third of the capital's population lived outside the eastern gates. The Mercers put up almshouses in Stepney village — you can still see them, rebuilt but in the same place, with carefully tended gardens and a plaque to Dame Mico, the founder.

Stepney church still had its gentry — Dame

Thomasina Dethick, widow of the Garter King of Arms was buried there in July 1663 — but now the pews and galleries were filled up with sailors and servant girls, artisans and weavers:

Here lies the body of Daniel Saul
Spitalfield's weaver and that's all.

The plague bell tolled out with terrifying regularity in the hot overcrowded alleys of late summer. In the devastating year of 1665 nearly nine thousand bodies were buried in St Dunstan's churchyard.

Atishoo, atishoo,
We all fall down.

So for the poor East Enders Good King Charles's Days were far from golden. These were threatening, dark years; what with the cart-loads of bodies rumbling up and down Whitehorse Lane, rumours of a Dutch invasion and the swingeing new taxes to be paid, the Hearth Tax and the Poll Tax. In spite of the King's personal preference for toleration in religious affairs, fierce laws were brought in to quash 'conventicling'; those who continued to attend chapel rather than church, as many did hereabouts, ran the risk of fine or imprisonment. Stepney was a hot bed of discontent and there was talk of local involvement in plots against the government.

The Bull Lane Chapel flourished, attracting the largest nonconformist congregation in London. Dr Mead, who was the pastor after Greenhill's death, introduced a May Day sermon to spoil what bit of fun the apprentice boys and girls had — no more rollicking on Mile End Green or up in the woods at Bethnal Green. The May Day Sermon was an annual event until a few years ago.

Life was not all dreary and desperate, although it might appear so to us, looking back at our ancestors through tax lists and burial registers. If any of the Restoration Stepneyites had left us a nostalgic account of their childhood in the 1670s, maybe it would seem as cosy and safe and fun as any picture conjured up by reminiscences of slum life in the 1930s.

Some residents lived to a ripe old age, like the unsuitably named Mistress Goodlad who produced twenty daughters and made it to the ripe old age of ninety-nine. As in current memoirs of the East End, there were 'characters' around to have a laugh about. If you had been there in 1680 you might have seen the skeletal Roger Crab with his strange pale-green skin. He 'had his skull cloved to the brain' when fighting in the Parliamentary Army and subsequently 'got religion', went vegetarian and lived on water, bran broth, turnip leaves and grass chopped together which cost him three farthings a week.

Then there was 'Honour and Glory Griffiths' a captain who attracted William III's attention by rescuing a fishing boat from a French frigate. He was always writing to the Admiralty and acquired his nickname because all his letters were addressed to 'their Honours and Glories at the Admiralty'.

In the next century Stepney churchyard was quite the place to go for a Sunday afternoon stroll to find the 'characters' buried there and inspect the inventive inscriptions on their tombs — an early hint of the later famed Cockney wit. 'The people of that parish', wrote Sir Richard Steele in *The Spectator* for October 1712, 'have a particular genius for an epitaph'. Dr Johnson, writing some decades later, agreed:

> This afternoon I went to visit a gentlemen of my aquaintance in Mile End, and passing through Stepney Churchyard, I could not forbear entertaining myself with the inscriptions on the tombs.

By 1700 the population of the parish had grown to something in the region of fifty-thousand — that

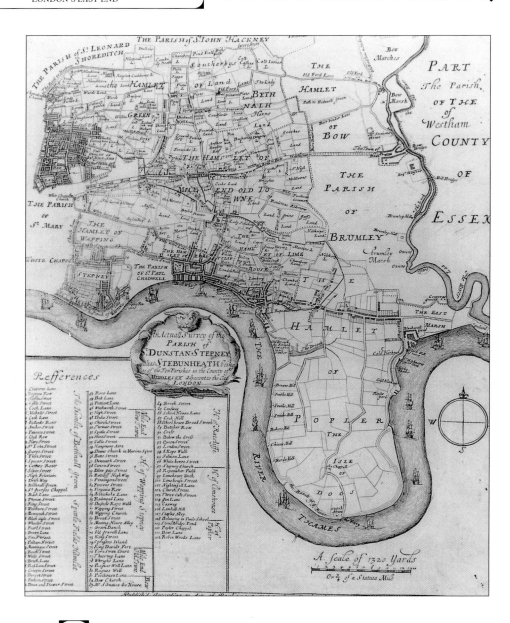

*Joel Gascoyne's map of St
Stepney in 1703*

*Sea cadets still gather for
an annual service in 1955
in a church whose history
has always been associated
with seafaring traditions.*

included Spitalfields, Mile End Old Town, Bow, Poplar, Limehouse, Ratcliff, Bethnal Green and the 'new town' up at Mile End. There were said to be about nine-thousand houses. The clergy at St Dunstan's were not able to bear the load; even in those godless eighteenth-century days 'rites of passage' had to be dealt with. Shadwell, the seventeenth-century new town, acquired its own church in 1669, Wapping chapel had been given parish status in 1694. Now the other hamlets started breaking free: Bow became a parish church in 1719, St Georges in the East was built on the Highway in 1727, Christchurch, Spitalfields in 1729, St Anne's, Limehouse in 1730, St Matthew, Bethnal Green in 1743.

The eighteenth century was the heyday of the 'Church of the High Seas'. A stroll around St Dunstan's, inside and out, will introduce the visitor to mariner upon mariner, jolly jack tars, many of them, but more are captains and masters. Do not think that Stepney had yet lost its residential status; a rare survival of fine houses on Stepney Green, five minutes walk from the church, are a reminder of these days when the congregation at St Dunstan's, free of the rabble from the more 'down-market' hamlets, was led by many gentlemen in the seafaring line.

Great Place, the Colet house, still dominated the village but now it was the Spring Garden Coffee House. Had you taken a turn down Whitehorse Lane some wintry evening in the 1790s, you would have walked into a scene from a Christmas card. Opposite the church was the old half-timbered mansion, warped and crazy in shape from two hundred years of wear, the flicker from its many candlelit windows spilling out on to the snow. In the snug bars, naval officers, splendid in gold braid, drank coffee with shipwrights and East India Company magnates in tricorn hats and drew on clay pipes. There might have been some ordinary seamen, sporting spotted kerchiefs and swapping yarns. Perhaps the boatswain of *The Acorn*, Robert

Oldfield, was there; he is now, but six foot under. His tombstone stands up against St Dunstan's west door, a step away from the coffee house. It is blackened with soot, mossed and dribbled over with bird droppings but the lettering on it is quite legible. He died on Boxing Day, 1816:

From toils and troubles on the Main
Death kindly set me free.

These were stirring times in Stepney, with the 'bloody monster' of the French Revolutionary armies threatening the lives of local lads. On Sunday 5 August 1798 Thomas Thirwall, chaplain of the Corps of Volunteers of the Hamlet of Mile End Old Town preached at St Dunstan's:

The pages of history never presented a period in which the fate of kingdoms and empires hung on so slender a thread as the present ....

A nation is risen up amongst us, whom Providence seems to have destined, no less the scourge of her enemies, than the destruction of herself ....

This nation, whose crimes and impieties have seldom beeen equalled, and never surpassed, by the most barbarous and uncivilised ...whose political jealousies and jarring interests nothing could have healed and reconciled, but the sense of one common danger'.

The Mile Enders sat spellbound in their pews:

Curb the fury of this bloody monster .... Your country's freedom sounds the trumpet, and beseeches you, in the name of the throne, the altar, and your families, to stand at the breach between them and an horde of Savages'.

Stepney manor depicted in a mid-Victorian East End album.

Did the volunteers notice the old marble Startute tomb as they filed out?

This life is a warfare
Come Lord Jesus come quickly

Before leaving the village and going up to the manor house, it is interesting to reflect on what Stepney became just a few generations after Thomas Thirwall's sermon. The number of country East Enders who came in, changing the character of the place over three hundred years, are as a trickle compared to the swarms which invaded then led by the Irish in the 1840s. By the late nineteenth century St Dunstan had no less than ninty-seven daughter churches but it was said that the only gentlemen to be found in the whole East End were clergymen — it had become 'Not a wery nice neighbourhood'.

Stepney: The Manor

Since Domesday, and before, the Lords of Stepney manor, who ruled over most of Tower Hamlets and Hackney, were the bishops of London.

The founder of the church, Saint Dunstan, was the chief landlord in the tenth century, as his successors were for six hundred years. Over the west door of the church is a carved spandrel depicting the saint tweaking the Devil's nose with a pair of tongs. Saint Dunstan was Abbot of Glastonbury, Bishop of London and Worcester and the Archbishop of Canterbury, a powerful prelate who practically ruled England. An ancient legend tells how he was in his metal workshop (he believed in pious creative labour) when the Devil appeared to tempt him, perhaps in the form of a woman. The tongs featured in the armorial bearings of Stepney.

Wentworth Street in the 1950s.
The street was named after the
Wentworth family — once lords
of the manor in Stepney.

Children of the Green Coat Charity School — founded by the Vitners' Company — dressed in 18th-century costume to celebrate Vintners' Day.

Providence Place, Stepney in about 1909

Soup kitchen in St Dunstan's

St Dunstan's Stepney: an outing in the 1950s.

Stepney cabbies.

The darts team at The Mercer's Arms.

'The cut': the local name for the Iron Bridge which joins Ben Jonson Road and Rhodeswell Road May 1959.

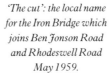

Perhaps he, like his successors, lived in Bethnal Green. They hunted from the house there and in the first half of the fourteenth century there were tournaments. The last Bishop to spend any time in Stepney was Braybrooke who died in 1404. He has an unlikely monument — an old people's home in Stepney Way — Braybrooke House. I wonder if any of the residents there know that he was famous for persecuting Lollards, trying to stop cobblers working on Sunday and failing to put into force laws against prostitutes!

The route from the village and the church to the manor is still discernible; it is about two miles. Go along Whitehorse Lane, cross the Mile End Road and go up Globe Road. Cross Roman Road and continue up Old Ford Road. You will now be in a tree-lined avenue called Approach Road. Looking up Approach Road, Bonner Gate, one of the entrances to Victoria Park, can be seen at the far end. The manor house was just to the right of the gate, where the Chest Hospital is now.

Bonner, who gave his name to the gate and to the manor house, Bonner's Hall, was Bishop of London in the bad old days of Bloody Mary and was responsible for sending many a local Protestant to a human bonfire in Smithfield. If you linger here you may meet his ghost. Better that you don't. He rides still, they say, now and again, in a coach drawn by four black horses, and if you see him, you will very soon be dead.

After Bonner's death, the new Bishop surrended the manor to Edward VI. The Wentworths bought it and were the Lords of Stepney for some two hundred years.

The Wentworth lords were an unfortunate family. One of them, the Earl of Cleveland, a Cavalier, lost most of his money financing Charles I in the Civil War. His heir died of plague, leaving a widow, Lady Philadelphia, to cope with the burden of debt left by her father-in-law. She did so by selling off land for property development along the Mile End Road.

Lady Philadelphia was a forceful woman and presided at the meetings of the manor court herself.

The account of the proceedings is kept in leather-bound volumes in the Greater London Record Office.

Her only child, Lady Henrietta Maria, is a much more romantic character. Aged seventeen, at a Court masque she met the dashing Duke of Monmouth, Charles II's illegitimate son, who had been married off to an heiress when he was only fourteen. By all accounts, they fell in love. Fifteen years later, the handsome Duke led his ill-starred rebellion against his uncle, James II and was condemned to death. One wonders how many of the Wentworth's Stepney tenants were there on Tower Hill when the Lady of the Manor's royal lover calmly laid his head on the block, declaring her to be 'the choice of his ripened years' and 'a lady of virtue and honour'. After nine months she died of a broken heart.

Tales of long-dead lords and ladies of Stepney Manor might seem too far away and irrelevant to today's East End to be worth repeating. But, within the lifetime of our senior citizens, East End houses, many of them, were still under the control of the manor court. In the twenties it used to meet in The Rising Sun; a group of six or seven elderly men, mostly interested in the dinner which had become an important part of the session. The last entry, before the Deputy Steward, William H Hebblewhite closed the great, rusty court book with a final thud just before Christmas 1925, records the surrender and admission of a Jewish woman (of Railway Arch Works off Commercial Road) to her deceased's father's house in Ratcliff Highway. Using the same words as had been used since Lady Philadelphia's day, she was to ...

Have seisin ... by a yearly rent of 2d services, suit of court and customs thereof heretofore due .... for a fine of Ten shillings.

The very first surviving entry on the court roll for Stepney Manor is in a similar vein, six hundred years before. On the Thursday before the Feast of St Simon and St Jude in 1318, John the Wheelwright's lands were surrendered to the Lord. It is written on a faded leather-bound parchment mebrane eighteen inches long. One wonders what the Wentworth lords and ladies would think of the only obvious memorial to their long stay in Stepney. Lady Philadelphia and the others are remembered solely in a street name — Wentworth Street, where the Sunday market, Petticoat Lane, scatters its rubbish and sells cheap bright clothes and Indian souvenirs to tourists.

East End clergy
at St Dunstan's.

ALONG THE ROAD TO THE EAST

Aldgate and Whitechapel

Even in Chaucer's day this was already 'London's backyard'

An engraving of Aldgate: The High Street in the 19th century.

It was from here that Mr Pickwick set off in a coach bound for Ipswich.

On the site of the Great Eastern's coal yard, not far from the London Hospital, are the Whitechapel car auctions. It is quite a sight on a selling night. Dealers and young men in anoraks, out for a bargain, crowd into a covered yard, lit by flares. The cars roar and thunder in, stop and rev their engines, and roar out again, scarcely allowing inspection time — one would have thought. With an undetectable nod or wink the purchases are made; fags are stamped out and off the cars go.

Aldgate and Whitechapel grew from the great thoroughfare to the east which led from the old gate out to the ford over the Lea and on to Colchester and Ipswich. It has always been a place of coming and going, presided over by Saint Botolph, the patron saint of travellers, to whom Aldgate church is dedicated. It is accustomed to cars, lorries, trains, Hackney carriages, stage coaches, hay wagons and carriers' carts. Petrol fumes overwhelm it now; it was sooty railway smoke in our grandparents' day and before that the Whitechapel Road was famous for the mud churned up by the continuous parade of horse-drawn traffic.

St Botolph's, Aldgate, was a thin strip of a parish, comprising a quarter of a square mile, stretching up alongside the city ditch towards Bishopsgate and down the Minories to the Tower. Whitechapel lies to the east and, in the past, took in part of the riverside. Unlike Stepney village, these two grew up as true 'suburbs', owing their being entirely to their fine neighbour. They are urban deep down, having started life as a Roman shanty town outside the walls and ribbon development along the road to Colchester. There was no village green; there is no heart and there never was one. There was a gate and the road; humanity gathered along the highway and spread towards Shoreditch and down towards the river. As the docks developed the parishes were scored with more routes, bearing wagon loads of spices and sugar, timber and tea, coffee, pipes of canary and all the spoils of a vast trading empire.

The Pickwickians in transit.

*Four London churches
have been named after the
British Saint Botolph.
This one at Aldgate was
founded during William
the Conqueror's reign but
its present structure dates
from about 1744.*

From the days of Pepys, and perhaps before, wagons gathered three times a week for the hay market at Whitechapel. You can see them still, painted on tiles in the public library. Daniel Defoe, who grew up in the area, said that in his youth Brick Lane was a 'deep dirty road' frequented chiefly by carts fetching loads of bricks 'that way into Whitechapel'.

On the coach route

By 1750 most of the arterial roads to London had been improved by turnpikes and the coach routes had the capacity of many thousand passenger miles a week. The streets were thronged with smiths, ostlers, farriers, wheelwrights and innkeepers.

Up at Whitechapel Bars (posts put across the road half a mile from the city gate are commemorated these days in a shopping centre called Aldgate Barrs) was the Hackney carriage stand. Cabs were relatively much more expensive than they are now; in 1820 it cost a shilling to travel a mile. To go from the Bars to Wapping (St John's Church) or Bethnal Green (St Matthews Church) incurred a charge of eighteen pence in the 1820s.

New Road, which runs down from the London Hospital to the river, was built in the opening years of the nineteenth century to carry traffic back and forth from the London Dock. Soon after came the great Commercial Road to service the East and West India Docks and later Commercial Street which cleared away the rookeries as it swept up through Spitalfields.

When Dickens' Pickwickians set out for Ipswich they climbed up on to the box of the stage coach at The Bull Inn, bending their heads to avoid knocking them on the archway as the horses turned in the cobbled yard and drew their creaking swaying burden out into Aldgate High Street. The Bull was one of four large inns and coffee houses combined which stood just outside the city gate, near where the bus station and the

Aldgate underground stand today. The Three Nuns, a reminder of the days when the Abbey of the Poor Clares was in the Minories, had stood to the east of the church since the days of Good Queen Bess. In the 1840s you could take a coach from there to Halstead and Braintree. There was still a pub there called after the nuns in the 1960s.

A little further east was The Bull at number 25 and, an old neighbour, The Blue Boar at number 31. The Saracen's Head on the south side of the road and The Bull were the two main 'coach terminals'. In 1822 stage coaches left twice daily for Ipswich and East Anglia, at 8.45 am and 6.45 pm.

As if coloured by the restlessness of the road, people came and went, rarely putting down roots; families did not often stay for more than a few generations. Throughout the last four hundred years Whitechapel has been a transit camp.

Remnants of the past

At first glance there seems to be nothing left of the old days and precious little to remind the new Indian immigrants that they are heirs to a long tradition. St Botolph is still there, as he has been since Saxon times, standing guard now over a sweep of fast road instead of the city gate. The present church is not of any great age, having been built in 1744 by George Dance, the elder, in a classical style, facing the wrong way round, lying north south instead of east west. In the porch is a stone tablet which lists the names of the incumbents, known since 1108. The first is Norman, Prior of Holy Trinity. When the Knighten Guild surrendered the soke of the port to Holy Trinity the priors became the rectors at Aldgate. According to an old legend, one of the twelfth-century priors spent all his income on vestments and there was no money left to buy food for the monks. Thomas Becket's mother, amongst others, vowed to provide a loaf every Sunday.

The gate itself, which some say was christened aeldgate in Saxon times — it was ruinous and dilapidated even then — was taken down for road widening in the 1760s. A Mr Mussel bought the remains and made a façade to his house in Bethnal Green with them.

No trace remains of Holy Trinity church which presided over a tiny parish off the Minories.

The Hoop and Grapes is the only remnant of the tall gabled houses and inns with galleried yards which lined the wide boulevard still in the 1890s. Some of the inn yard names survive, like Black Lion Yard and King's Arms Yard and there are a few cleaned-up survivors of the maze of courts and alleys which wove around behind them: such as Half Moon Passage and Frying Pan Alley.

These days brand new offices, shops and flats are pushing out eastwards into the dingy remains of Jack the Ripper land. They didn't bother to resurrect St Mary's Church after the bombing (it had been rebuilt in 1675, 1875 and 1882) and the only trace left of the white chapel's descendant is a scrubby patch of churchyard littered with crisp packets and cider bottles. 'Itchy Park' they call it, now because of its flea-ridden beggars.

The ancient bell foundry is still there, with its five-hundred-year-old ancestry and an elegant neo-classical façade, a stranger among the garages and leather wholesale shops in the Whitechapel Road. It has been on its present site since 1738, on the corner of Fieldgate Street, the old path to Stepney village. From as early as 1420 there was a bell foundry in Aldgate. Robert Mot had the foundry in 1570 and the present owners still use the sign of the three bells, as he did.

There are a few tombs in 'Itchy Park' and some monuments to eighteenth-century worthies in St Botolphs but, for the most part, all that is left to signify the past are the names: *The Minories*, where the Minoresses had their Abbey, *Houndsditch*, built over the City moat once filthy with dead dogs, *Goodman's Yard*,

the site of a Tudor dairy farm, *Crosswall*, *Tenter Street*, where the cloth workers used to peg out fabric to bleach and *Leman Street*, developed in the late seventeenth century by Sir William Leman.

London's backyard

This area has perhaps changed less in character than the rest of the East End. It is still full of foreigners and the same trade predominates — the manufacture and distribution of clothes. Whitechapel has been doing the same thing for many hundreds of years. The clothes stalls in Petticoat Lane, the racks of dresses which swing along the pavements on rails and the many wholesale garment shops are nothing new. In Shakespeare's day they pressed and stitched the brocades and silks worn by the court and city gentry, they starched ruffs and made hats. A hundred years ago the place was notorious for its tailors' sweat shops. These days cheap frocks and leather jackets are sold to shopkeepers and visitors and there are shop windows spangled with the brilliant colours of saris and golden ornaments from the east.

Even in Chaucer's day, this was already 'London's backyard', with enough inhabitants to warrant the thirteenth-century chapel built by the Matfelun family to be made into a parish in 1338. From the number of Aldgate and Whitechapel entries in the earliest surviving Correction Book from the Bishop of London's Court (1470-1473), it seems that the inhabitants were a rather loose-living brawling crew. There was a good deal of fornication among servants, prostitution and squabbling.

The very first entry concerns adultery in Aldgate. Rosa Smyth from the parish fell out with Agnes Frostie and called her 'harlot and bawdie'; Agnes Ordo of Whitechapel called Margaret Knock 'stronghore'.

An early authentic 'working class' voice from here is that of Isabella Newport, involved in a matrimonial

*Metal moulds at the Whitechapel bell foundry in Whitechapel
Road where traditional skills still perpetrate the medieval
craftsmanship of the foundry which cast the bells for
Westminster Abbey and recast Big Ben when the
original Stockton-on-Tees bell cracked before
going into operation in 1859.*

suit against her husband in 1492. She pushed him into Houndsditch and called him a 'bald, whoreson cuckold' and expressed the desire that 'sum goode fellowe…shall make hym to pysse above his gyrdlested [waist]' — a fifteenth-century equivalent, perhaps, to suggesting a good 'kick in the balls'?

In St Botolph today there are bearded beggars with newspaper for socks. The staff there devout themselves to the homeless and down and outs. Aldgate parish has had a poverty problem for four hundred years — just before the Christmas of 1583 they distributed to eighty paupers 'all the collection gathered at the communions and put into the poore box'. On New Year's Day in 1587 the curate, Mr Hayes, held three communions specifically for the purpose of raising money for the poor. 306 people turned up, consuming six gallons and a 'pottell of malmsy'. The tailors and button-makers, needlemakers and haberdashers, watermen, gunsmiths and brewers must have had a good slurp out of the chalice!

As in Stepney, the end of the sixteenth century was a time of mass immigration into the suburbs from the shires. Folk tended to come to the area where there was accommodation for them. Aldgate and Whitechapel were more built up than the rest of the area and the newcomers were squeezed in. St Botolph, says John Stow, was 'pestered with lofts and seats for them'. By 1600 there was something in the region of six thousand people crammed into Aldgate's quarter of a square mile and about a thousand less in the larger parish of Whitechapel.

In Shakespeare's day parts of the two parishes were well on the way to becoming slums, especially down in the liberty of East Smithfield, to the east of the Tower where the rag-tag folk congregated in the alleys off what is now Royal Mint Street: Swan Alley, Sparrows Court, Bell Alley, Rose Alley, and Pond Alley. The 'void ground' in between the 'thinly scattered tenements' on the south side of the High Street was built

Recasting the Great Bell for Big Ben's clock tower at the Houses of Parliament.

Sadak Schneiders and Son, wholesale clothiers and cap manufacturers of Durward Street, Whitechapel. This photograph was taken sometime during the First World War.

over and alleys pread out on both sides.

The stretch north of the main road (between Aldgate and Aldgate East tube stations) which in Henry VIII's time had been occupied by the long gardens of large houses, was covered with allotments. Harrydance, the parish clerk at Aldgate in the 1580s and 90s writes of the 'gardens near Hog Lane (Middlesex Street)'. There was still a good deal of open ground, as the maps show, but between the Reformation and the Civil War the 'East End' was truly born.

*A rag merchant's home
in Coulston Street
Whitechapel.*

Rich and poor alike

Before the country East Enders arrived, Hog Lane was lined with elms and there were stiles and bridges over streams. It was the lane up to St Mary's Hospital (the Spital of Spitalfields) and …

…citizens [went] therein to walk, shoot and otherwise recreate themselves.

Stow complains with an old man's nostalgia:

Now, there are houses all along the way, a continual building throughout, of garden-houses and small cottages; and the fields on either sides be turned into garden-plots, tenter yards, bowling alleys and such like.

*They've turned our local palais
Into a bowling alley
And fings ain't what they used to be*

By 1608 it has been rechristened Petticoat Lane, and Ben Jonson's vice Iniquity flew up there and along Smock Alley, a turning off it. The Boar's Head Tavern, a galleried inn like The George in Southwark, was in a court off the Lane to the east, at its southern end. Here East Londoners came to see plays performed before the two theatres in Shoreditch were built for that specific purpose.

It was not a slum as we know it — a dark world alien to the well-to-do where only do-gooders and clergymen dared go. Rich and poor mixed in the same parishes, with tenements and cottages in courts and alleys behind the larger more respectable establishments on the main streets. Watermen and labouring men lived in the 'new houses bilt by one Arthur More beinge in Mr Thomas Goodman, his grounds' off Rosemary Lane, while the Goodmans themselves lived in the Minories.

For Stow, who grew up before the 'heavy trot and iron stalk' of countrymen's hobnailed boots thumped and clattered up and down the streets, the neighbourhood had 'gone down'. But Gondomar, the Spanish ambassador, and the jeweller to the court of James I are both said to have lived in Petticoat Lane.

It was hard for the country East Enders, cut off from family support and a prey to the diseases of insanitary urban conditions. The infant mortality rate in St Botolph's parish in the 1590s was twenty per cent higher than in the Victorian slum time. In the plague year of 1603 the curate at St Botolph's buried one third of his flock. Along at St Mary Matfelon that August between twenty and thirty souls were committed to the Almighty daily. If the plague didn't get you, smallpox and syphilis might; life was precarious and often all too short.

On a bleak January afternoon in 1587 the great bell of St Botolph's was rung to announce the burying of Richard Pellett, a gentleman from Maldon who had been staying at The Crown in the High Street. As the parish clerk wrote in his diary …

For want of a trusse, the Bowells of the said
Richard Pellett ded issues owt of his
Bodye weareof the said
Richard ended his life.

A deal of squabbling went on in that world of strangers, as is evident from the rise in the number of slander suits, and witches rode. In November 1589 Anthony Cutler's wife, Alice, was indicted for bewitching a baker's wife until the said wife wasted away and died.

Working life

Most people were engaged in the 'rag trade', worked in the foundries, on the river or at building, baking and brewing. There were a number of silk weavers; one lodged at the sign of the Flower de Luce in Houndsditch in the 1590s, along with a 'player of Enterludes' and others.

Down by the river there were at least four breweries, The Hartshorn owned by Peter Miller, The Ship and one owned by Anthony Dowfield. One of the numerous Dutch settlers brewed near the Tower. In Houndsditch and the Minories there were gun makers and bell makers, clocks-smiths and locksmiths and a variety of workshops interspersed with garden plots and the ubiquitous bowling alleys. In the 1590s one of the smiths, aptly named Vulcan Skinner, fathered a bastard on a Dutch butcher's wife. About half-way along Houndsditch, on the east side, were the works where the Owen brothers had made armaments for Henry VIII's military enterprises. In *The Mary Rose* exhibition at Portsmouth is a bronze demi-cannon made by them in 1542. Up in Brick Lane they dug clay and fired bricks; its southern entry into Whitechapel was so muddy that it was called 'Dirty Lane'.

It must have been a fairly scruffy part of town with builders' rubbish, bags of lime, workshops and stalls and vegetable patches all around. As in later years, there were a number of large inns strung along the High Street; as you walked along the east from St Botolph you would have passed under the signs of The King's Head, a tavern owned by Mr George Clarke, just outside the gate, The Woolpack and The Crown, owned by Mr Philip Shipman. The Blue Board and The Three Nuns, which was associated with the Pickwickians, were already there. It was, of course, not only inns which sported painted sign boards — there would have been a whole forest of them, announcing shops and lodging houses and even large private dwellings.

Royal Mint Street, formerly Rosemary Lane, was a slum area even in Shakespeare's day. It later became the home of the notorious second-hand-clothes market 'Rag Fair'.

The area between Aldgate and the river was known as Goodman's Fields for several hundred years — Goodman's Yard is still there, labelled in glittering letters on a new office block. Before the Reformation Old Man Goodman rented a farm from the nuns in the Minories. During Elizabeth I's reign Goodman's son, Philip, a member of the Pewterer's Company, let the land out for grazing and then as allotments, making a packet thereby!

South of Goodman's Fields, in Rosemary Lane (Royal Mint Street) was the notorious 'Rag Fair' where 'old clothes and frippery were sold'. In later years Richard Brandon, who cut off Charles I's head lived there. It is said he was offered twenty shillings by a gentleman for the orange stuffed with cloves which he had from the King's pocket but refused the offer and later sold it for ten shillings in Rosemary Lane.

Ann Talbot

Before moving on, it is interesting to take a look into the lives of a small group of locals whom we know about from their appearance in the bishop's court.

In the 1620s there lived in Rosemary Lane an elderly foreign-born woman, a silk winder. Her son, Robert Talbot, married a wife of Dutch descent and after seven years they parted. At first Robert rented a room from a thread dyer and twister in Aldgate and then went back to his mother. The wife, Ann, went back to her father, first at his lodgings in Wapping Wall, then in East Smithfield and then in Petticoat Lane, took a lover called Mason and became pregnant. The child was undoubtedly Mason's. He often took it on his lap and evidently Ann would say 'That is yours' and 'That is like you'.

The adulterous wife was abandoned by her lover, he perhaps taking ship to get away. When she took her baby girl to be baptized at St Botolph's, according to Old Goodwife Marten — a shoemaker's wife from

Sounding the emergency fire alarm bell at the London Hospital, Whitechapel in October 1939.

A bacteriological laboratory at The London Hospital in 1933 — such ordered sanitary conditions were a far cry from earlier days. Founded in 1740 by a gathering of gentlemen at The Feathers Tavern in Cheapside, the London Infirmary moved from Moorfields to Prescott Street in 1741. In an area full of brothels and taverns, patients were ordered to go to church and pray in gratitude if they were cured or they were refused future treatment. There were no sinks or flushed water and 'soil' was dumped at night in the cesspool or street. Until the 1751 Gin Laws, many nurses were dismissed for being drunk; bed bugs were a constant problem. The new hospital was built in Whitechapel's green fields in 1757. Sir William Blizzard (Founder President of the Royal College of Surgeons) established the first medical school associated with a hospital in Whitechapel in 1785, complete with a laboratory, dissecting room and museum; Dr Barnardo was a student at Whitechapel in 1866.

Towcester who 'maintained herself by washing and scouring abroad' — Ann said the father was a 'sea farun man and was at the East'. Her friend, the launderess Dorcas Clingdove, tried to get her a job nursing 'with a gentlewoman in Kent'. When that came to nothing Ann evidently took her husband to court to try and extract maintenance.

These wives worked to keep themselves, as most ordinary East End women seem to have done. Families moved from lodging to lodging, not apparently staying put for more than a year or even a couple of months — moonlighting maybe.

It was a strangely public life by modern standards, too; the Brick Lane drover's wife who nursed Ann in her confinement, said she had seen Mason 'at tymes upon her'. Down at the seafaring end of town, all sorts of business was transacted in the inns and alehouses and it was usual for working men and women to take all their meals in victualling houses or pubs.

Parliament and plague

When the kingdom collapsed in Civil War, twenty years after Robert Mason ran away from his mistress and baby girl, the tailors and sailors of Whitechapel and Aldgate were, like their neighbours, supporters of Parliament. In 1642 they fortified London against the Royalist armies:

> ....the sailors raised a mound and made trenches where women of good fashion and children labour hard.

Whitechapel Mound stood 329 feet high, just to the west of the present London Hospital. In the eighteenth century coaches took tourists up there for a good view over the eastern suburbs. It was demolished when they built the New Road down to the London Docks at the beginning of the nineteenth century.

*The Great Plague Pit
in Aldgate.*

In the lifetime of Daniel Defoe (1660-1721), who was married in St Botolphs and the historian John Strype, a silk merchant's son from Petticoat Lane, the urbanization grew apace; Spitalfields became 'all town' says Defoe and 'in a very few year' he reckoned, Mile End would be 'entirely joined' to the City.

French weavers came into the north of the parishes and made Spitalfields their own. Sephardic Jews from Spain and Holland, brought back into the country by Cromwell, favoured the newly developed area south of the High Street, for a short time the most select of suburbs. Many of them were quite wealthy men and considerable benefactors in the parish. They rented fine three-storey houses in the new streets when these grew up around the twelve acres of open ground still known as Goodman's Fields — Leman Street, Mansell Street, Alie Street and Ayliffe Street.

The alleys down round Rag Fair and to the north of the High Street were still of a very different character. Brick Lane, according to Sir Christopher Wren who had tramped round the site on foot, was 'unpassable by Coach, adjoining to Durty lands of meane habitations'. He recommended paving. Brick houses with 'sufficient Conveighances for the water' were erected on both sides of the street and, amongst other things, 'two little sheds or places called Banquetting houses'.

The overcrowding was worse than it had been and when the Great Plague came in 1665 it wrought appalling havoc. As Defoe wrote:

They dug the great pit in the churchyard of our parish
of Aldgate. A terrible pit it was ... about forty feet in
length, and about fifteen or sixteen feet broad ...
about nine feet deep; but it was said they dug it near
twenty feet deep afterwards ... For though the
plague was long a-coming to our parish yet, when
it did come, there was no parish in or about
London where it raged with such violence as
in the two parishes of Aldgate and Whitechapel.

Homes and gardens

In the 1690s Whitechapel (excluding Wapping) had about three thousand houses. A detailed tax list for 1694 allows a good look at the place.

Although there were some quite wealthy people living in the newly built Wentworth Street, there was a dye house there and most of the Petticoat Lane area was poor. Catherine Wheel Alley, which ran parallel to the Lane (a truncated remnant survives) had eighty-six smallish houses while Bell Yard had sixty-nine cheap dwellings (three to five pounds annual rack rent). In Brick Lane and Montague Street there were, as Christopher Wren said, 'mean habitations', mainly two-pound houses.

In the block bounded by today's Old Montague Street, Princelet Street, Brick Lane and Greatorex Street was Leonard Gurle's 'Great Nursery'. Gurle took it over in the 1640s and it stayed in his family into the eighteenth century. Fruit was his specialism and he produced a hardy nectarine which he called 'Elruge' (his own name backwards).

It is strange to reflect that what later became the most notorious slum in the country was once famous for its flowering trees and shrubs, honeysuckle, jasmine and lilacs. Not far away, on the opposite side of the High Street, standing to the east of the church, the great Whitechapel windmill creaked and whirred where now the Habib Bank conducts its business.

Over on the south of the High Street was Red Lion Street, as the top of Leman Street used to be called in those days. There was an empty brewhouse and thirteen houses in the course of construction. In Peacock Court, where the haymarket was held, there lived, among the poor in a 'parcell of old houses', a couple of rich Roman Catholics.

The streets around Goodman's Fields were at the 'top end of the market' in Restoration Whitechapel. Building plots, which were still available in 1694 on the west side of Leman Street, were going at a shilling or 1s 6d per foot. In Goodman's Fields itself there were thirty substantial houses and fifty-six in Mansell Street. Many of the householders had considerable 'personal estate'.

Alie Street and Prescott Street (the first street in London to have numbered housing) were very desirable. In the latter lived seven sea captains, a knight, two doctors, and a couple of Spanish Jews. Most of the houses had an annual value of seventeen pounds, some considerably more.

The area was not entirely residential. In Lamb Alley on the south side of Goodman's Yard was Michael Rackett's glass and bottle factory which he had bought in 1678; his stock was valued at one thousand pounds. Whitechapel was famous for its glass beyond the confines of Great Britain and bottles and chemists' phials were exported to France.

There was also a factory in Salt Petre Bank to the west of Wellclose Square which belonged in 1689 to Philip Dallow, while another one nearby, in Whites Yard off Rosemary Lane, made window glass. There were two more glass factories in Ratcliff.

Sir William Leman, who gave his name to Leman Street and owned property in Alie Street and Mansell Street, owned tenters in Goodman's Yard where the textile workers pegged out their cloth.

Down at the bottom of the parish Rosemary Lane was a mixture of old houses and new. Cheap housing was in the course of construction in some of the courts and alleys, like Blue Anchor Yard with its five tenements, 'a parcel of unfinished houses' and about thirty small houses.

In the days of Pepys and Defoe, then, Whitechapel and Aldgate were populous and growing, inhabited by a mixture of the 'meaner' and the 'middling' sort, with a fair sprinkling of well-off Roman Catholics and Jews. Tailors, sailors and weavers made up the majority of the inhabitants.

Deaths from Plague in London

Year	Number of deaths
1603	30,578
1604	896
1605	444
1606	2,124
1607	2,352
1608	2,262
1609	4,240
1610	1,803
1611	627
1612	64
1625	41,313
1630	1,317
1636	10,400
1637	3,082
1638	363
1647	3,597

In the year 1665

Month	Number of deaths
June	590
July	4,117
August	16,229
September	26,219
October	14,373
November	3,454
December	886
Total in 7 months	65,868

During September over 1,000 corpses a day were being put into communal graves. Overall, in 18 months 68,576 deaths from plague in London were actually recorded but it is probable that the real number of victims was nearer 100,000.

The diaries of Samuel Pepys provide many snippets of information about life in the East End in the seventeenth century.

A fighting place

On January 12th 1698 there issued a royal edict that the local churchwardens should make a special collection for the poor especially the poor weavers. A petition from the Whitechapel prison at the time of Charles II, from a mariner called John Atkins and his mates, sets the seafaring tone:

For want of good observation, by bad steerage they are fallen into the great eddy of Whitechapel prison.

Whitechapel had its own prison and court house; for the government the area was something of a trouble spot, seething with sedition and dissent. In 1684 Stepney was accounted 'The most factious hamlet of the Tower Division' and in these two adjoining parishes the many nonconformist chapels attracted large congregations. In 1685 two Whitechapel brewers were arrested for treason.

A vibrant chattering, polyglot Soho sort of place it was. In the market, country East Enders, mariners, gardeners and Welsh dairymen jostled French weavers, Jewish merchants, Spanish pedlars, Dutch brewers and German sugar bakers. As if there weren't antagonisms enough spawned in that neighbourhood where few had roots, there were the simmering political and religious conflicts left over from the Civil War when the nation had stood divided. Protestant nonconformist dissent was strong in the East End, as was seen in Stepney, and many of the locals chose the plain worship in one of the many 'conventicles'. Even the two churches were at variance. Dr Welton, the High Church non-juror, led his congregation in opposition to the new regime after 1688, refusing to take the oath acknowledging royal supremacy. Then he put up as an altar piece a painting portraying the liberal White Kennet (then Bishop of Peterborough, once curate at St Botolphs) as Judas Iscariot. It was a fighting place.

The records of a slander suit allows us to peep behind the doors of one of the many lodging houses of Restoration Whitechapel.

Just along from 'Itchy Park', on the north side of the Whitechapel Road is a new office block, Black Lion Court. In the days when Samuel Pepys rode out along the High Road to take the air in his coach, Black Lion Court, which adjoined Leonard Gurle's nursery, was one of the poorest and roughest spots in the parish.

In one of the lodging houses there lived, typically, a motley crew of people from different parts of the country, and they jogged along in a fair amount of disharmony. Amongst others were a Welsh farmer and his wife, Anne Shelley who ran a 'cafe', a Yorkshire labourer and his wife, an old Cornish widow, and Margaret Ford, who may have been 'on the game'. The cafe owner, Anne Shelley, fell out with Margaret Ford, supposedly over so slight a matter as the old widow's night cap and a brawl ensued. Shelley was heard to scream down the staircase:

She [Ford] is a whore, and a common whore, and drunken whore, and is drunk everyday of the week!

Into the eighteenth century

Leaving the scolds at Black Lion Yard, it is time to move on to the next century, into the days of stage coaches and tricorn hats. Gentlemen still attended St Botolph and St Mary Matfelon, and it may be appropriate to view first some remnants from those times — the Maddox family tomb which dominates the remnant of Whitechapel churchyard, perhaps, or the bust of Sir John Cass, Sheriff and MP in St Botolphs, with curly wig and full lips. Sir John founded a school which still bears his name. In preparation for the dark days to come, our eighteenth century tour begins in earnest a little to the east of the windmill by 'Itchy Park', on the other side of the main road, where the only relics from two hundred years ago are ghosts. Here, in the 1790s, stood the workhouse.

On Sunday evenings the old schoolmaster officiates at prayers and sermon. There they are, a flock of white-capped heads — about three hundred grown-up paupers, mainly women, and perhaps ninety children. Dinner today was boiled mutton; it costs the parish two shillings a week to keep each pauper. How different it will all be in a hundred years' time.

'... endless swarms of ragged children, fill road and pavement. The Jewish butchers lounge — fat and content — in their doorways'
Gustave Doré.

O Lord our God, whose mercies are over all our works, we humbly beseech Thy fatherly goodness ... for the welfare of all them that dwell within this parish ... we intreat Thee for a blessing on those who bear rule within it, that they may conscientiously and tenderly discharge the trust reposed in them; providing for the fatherless and widows and maintaining peace and order among Thy people: accept, moreover, O Lord, our prayers for all them who at this time inhabit this house: may they eat their daily bread in quietness and with grateful hearts ... preserve them industrious, sober, honest, kindly affectionate to one another, orderly and virtuous: let no corrupt communication proceed out of their lips

This is the calm, ordered, smug eighteenth century, in Whitechapel and Aldgate. Off Catherine Wheel Alley was a court called 'The Land of Promise'. London is prosperous and busy and so are its eastern suburbs, making textiles, clothes, glass and bells, brewing beer, refining sugar, dealing in 'slops' (second-hand clothes) and servicing the naval and docking activities down by the riverside. Most of the poor work at silk winding and the 'infirm pick feathers'. Some are employed by Truman's brewery in Brick Lane. It is still a mixture of classes and gentlemen of 'fortune, sense, reputation and parts' sit on the vestry.

By the end of the century there is 'a vast increase of the number of Jews' in Goodman's Fields but most of them are well off and useful members of society. They have been gradually arriving over the years; in 1733 one Solomon Demaza had a smithy in Castle Street while the widow Demaza had a snuff house in Goulston Street (where Tubby Isaacs shell-fish stall now stands). The German sugar bakers have arrived; Christian Schutz has a sugar house in Wentworth Street and the German Lutheran church is founded in Little Alie Street in 1763. Churches are built for the Danish and Swedish sailors.

A view of the projected
London Hospital, Whitechapel
by William Bellers 1752.

*The Eastern Dispensary
in Leman Street, Goodman's Fields.*

In the 1790s when the artist John Constable was staying with his mother's relatives, the Watts, in Aldgate, Whitechapel parish (now free of Wapping and Spitalfields) held about thirty thousand souls in 2,500 houses. Market gardens and open ground still spread out on the east side of the parish and the windmill still ground corn.

There is some rioting among the weavers when the industry starts to become mechanized, and racketting down in 'sailor town' and around Rosemary Lane but, basically, everything is under control. The poor are quite nicely looked after, either at home or in the workhouse, although there is something of a problem with the influx of Scots and Irish who tend to 'live idle lives' and become 'chargeable upon the parish'.

For the old there are almshouses, such as Meggs' along the road towards Mile End, established in 1658; for the young there are schools, like those founded by Sir John Cass and Sir Ralph Davenant. There is even a hospital now, starting life in Prescott Street in 1741, looked after by beadles in blue frock coats with red buttonholes and scarlet waistcoats. Mercury injections which make your teeth fall out are given for syphilis. 'The London' moved to its present site later on in the century.

Whitechapel parish still has a number of chapels but they are no longer centres of sedition: three baptist chapels, in Church Lane, Little Alie Street and Little Prescott Street, an Independent chapel in Alie Street, a German Lutheran chapel in Little Alie Street, a Danish chapel in Wellclose Square and a Sabbatarian meeting house in Mill Yard. A number of Quakers live in the two parishes. They attend the Devonshire House meeting in Bishopsgate.

Law and order

In the eighteenth century a watch house is manned nightly and Whitechapel has sixteen headboroughs and a constable to keep things in order. The poor are overseen by four officials and there is a prison for small debtors. Church rate, poor rate, watch, lamp and scavenger rates are duly collected, without too much trouble, as is the Land Tax.

The only consistent irritant to the tax gatherers is the Quaker fraternity, mostly wealthy successful men of business whose convictions prevent them from paying tithes, church rate and poor rate. As pacifists they will have nothing to do with the militia. They are regularly raided and have goods distrained but, of course, do not put up a fight.

In 1763 Thomas Collier of Catherine Wheel Alley lost seven coloured sheepskins in lieu of church rate. Samuel Hetherington of Petticoat Lane had a copper saucepan and a cover worth eight shillings removed. The JPs took a whole lot of womens' slippers from William Roper and a mahogany pillar claw table. John Sherwin of Wentworth Street, a baker, had his day's baking removed.

Eighteenth-century Whitechapel is quite a theatrical place. Goodman's Fields had come down in the world somewhat since the days of Pepys, although there are still naval officers around. Among the mulberry trees and tenter grounds for the textile workers are places of entertainment — some more dubious than others. There is The New Wells, Odell's Playhouse in Alie Street and The Turk's Head Bagnio in Ayliff Street. Garrick made his name playing Richard III in the Ayliffe Street Theatre and, until quite recently, there was a pub in Leman Street named after him to remind the passer-by. It has recently been done up and acquired some Dickensian associations — more appealing to potential customers no doubt.

A good deal of thieving goes on — but no-one is really sure whether it is worse than it used to be or whether 'they' are clamping down more than before. To steal a couple of silver spoons or a linen table cloth, and be caught passing them in Rag Fair, will mean

being hauled up at the Old Bailey in a trice. *The Daily Post* for 22 September 1736 reported that an innkeeper was robbed by a highwayman at Acton and one William Rine was caught in Rag Fair selling the innkeeper's whip and wearing his clothes! The unlucky are strung up for all to see in Tyburn or sent off to Botany Bay. When the authorities want to make a point they do the hangings locally, in Sun Tavern Fields. Pirates run 'protection rackets' down at Wapping and are hanged at Execution Dock but that is a world of its own.

In what a self-satisfied manner did the customers rub their hands in The Three Nuns when news of the unthinkable Revolution in France broke on the hot night of 18th July 1789. More interest was voiced in the tavern about the outcome of a boxing match involving the champion, a local Jewish lad called Daniel Mendoza. When he retired, having 'made a mint', he bought a pub of his own in Whitechapel. *Plus ça changes.*

Inhabitants of Whitechapel

Let us take one last look at a few inhabitants who have left pieces of information about themselves to remind us of the Whitechapel of the whirring windmill near the ducking pond before gentlemen of fortune and parts left the area for ever.

Dominating 'Itchy Park' is the imposing tomb of the Maddox family. On its north-facing side is, amongst others, the name of Richard Maddox esquire. His will can be seen in the Public Record Office; it is an important fat document, tied at the top with a green ribbon and an impressive seal.

Richard was a wealthy bachelor. He lived in St James's Place, just inside Aldgate, and was a follower of Whitfield. He had East India Company stock, two houses in St Katharine's rented out to brewers, three houses in Shoreditch and tenements in Golden Lane. Among his possessions were a gold repeating watch, a

silver harlequin, gold 'shirt sleeve buttons', a 'plain gun', a 'silver mounted gun', pistols, a brass blunderbuss, a bible bound in blue morocco, four volumes of *The Universal Voyages and Travels* and a barrel organ.

Also in the Public Record Office is an account of some of the 'idle' Irish immigrants who were beginning to settle down at the south end of the parish in the Rag Fair area. No gold watches or leather-bound books for them. The records relate to the dispute over the money left by a young woman who lived in Blue Anchor Yard and died there in the year they stormed the Bastille.

At the west end of Cable Street, on the south side, there is a pleasantly casual arrangement of new flats with trees and grass. This is Blue Anchor Yard, first developed in the 1690s, a large court of cheap housing and tenements. A hundred years later it must have been a fairly dilapidated place.

In August 1783 James Fallon, a Dublin tailor, and his two sisters came to London from Ireland with a friend called James Hoy, a hairdresser who had known James 'since he was in petticoats'. They took lodgings at The Black Horse and Crown in Victualling House Yard, (where Royal Mint Court is now) and within three months Fallon had taken up with a rich publican's daughter called Mary Deacon who lodged at Bell Dock in Wapping. On 13 November the Fallons — with the hairdresser, another tailor with whom James had worked in Dublin, and a man called Malone — made off up to Shoreditch church in a Hackney carriage with Mary Deacon. There Fallon married Mary, or so it is claimed, and they set up home in Blue Anchor yard. How long they were together we do not know but at some stage he went as a 'captain's tailor' aboard a sloop of war called *The Hound* and was in the West Indies for three years.

In 1789 Mary died, leaving some cash, and Fallon's sister, Bridget Delaney, who 'goes about the Town selling Handerchiefs and muslins and Glass and China', set about trying to get hold of the money — her

A huddle of infants, children and dishevelled folk on Wentworth Street in Whitechapel.

Jack the Ripper

All six murders believed to have been committed by Jack the Ripper took place within one square mile of Whitechapel in three months of 1888. Each victim was a prostitute, had her throat slashed and her body mutilated by somebody with evident knowledge of human anatomy. Taunting notes were sent to the police by someone claiming to be the murderer, one of which enclosed half a human kidney.

7 August - Martha Turner, aged 35 - in George Yard Buildings, stabbed repeatedly
31 August - Mary Ann Nicholls, aged 42 - on pavement of Buck's Row
8 September - Annie Chapman - found in backyard off Hanbury Street
30 September - Elizabeth Stride - in the backyard of a working men's club, Berner Street, with her throat slashed but her body not yet mutilated
and a second victim - Catherine Eddowes, aged 43 - in Mitre Square
9 November - Marie Kelly, aged 24 - at her lodgings with her body dismembered and strewn around the room; charred clothing found in fireplace

brother was in prison for robbery at the time.

It was all very suspicious. Some said that Fallon had been married to one Polly Duffy by a 'Roman priest' and the witnesses, in true Irish fashion, protested too much when they were warned of the dangers of perjury. James Hoy 'apprehends that the punishment ...in this world is the pillory and hard sufferance in the next'. Bridget Delaney said she realized that if she lied she would be 'very severely punished both in this and the next world'. The minister who performed the marriage was conveniently dead and the entry in St Leonard's parish register had been tampered with.

The windmill, sailors and silk winders, The Boar's Head, witches and Leonard Gurle's nectarines are long lost; Whitechapel, for most, is Jewish sweat shops and murders wrapped in foggy gloom, a land of unhappy foreigners, making shift until they can earn enough to move on. But before dismissing its past, remember milk still came hot from the cow in Whitechapel in 1900, as John Stow drank it in 1535, and hay wagons were seen at Aldgate within living memory.

EAST OF THE TOWER

St Katharine's and East Smithfield

Here comes a candle to light you to bed
Here comes a chopper to chop off your head

Outside Tower Hill tube station stands William the Conqueror's castle — a small square fortress with lead-capped turrets, hedged about now with a sprawl of later buildings. In the Middle Ages the whitewashed keep dominated the riverside to the east of the City. It was a palace, 'the direct and most secure' prison and, as far as the locals were concerned, perhaps most interesting as a zoo. They must have gaped at the polar bear who arrived from Norway in 1252, as he swam about fishing in the Thames and at the elephant who came from the King of France a few years later. The royal menagerie of exotic beasts remained here until 1834 when the animals were taken off to the new Zoological Gardens in Regent's Park and the Lion Tower which had housed them was demolished. The king's castle is the key to the growth and nature of life hereabouts.

In the days before the Victorian slum this was the East End's 'city of terrible night', the blackest, most despairing part. A seething suburb grew up around a place of punishment and royal revenge, of damp rat-infested dungeons, thick walls enclosing the screams of the tortured. Traitors were brought in by boat, through the massive iron and oaken gates to the rhythmic tramp and stamp of the guards and the roaring of the royal lions. The young princess Elizabeth, sent here by her sister, in 1554 sat down in the mud and refused to go in: 'I am no traitor!'

These days the Tower has a lingering Ministry of Works post-war feel about it, which renders as harmless curiosities the rack which pulled Guy Fawkes into excruciating confession, the thumb screws, the iron manacles and the human cage called the Scavenger's Daughter. Even the wooden block itself and the axe seem innocuous in the busy tourist season, part of ice-creams and hot dogs and a hurried glimpse of the glittering wonder of the crown jewels. 'Move along there, please, give everyone a chance to see the exhibits!'

Executions, plague and pillory

From Edward IV's time there were public executions on Tower Hill — hangings and decapitations. A scaffold would be erected, built high enough to give onlookers a good view and draped in black crepe. Crowds gathered; a muffled drum roll hushed out its unearthly sound as local sailors and tailors and their women jostled with the guards in the chill of early morning to watch the masked executioner, the priest and the victim act out the dreadful play.

Here comes a candle to light you to bed
Here comes a chopper to chop off your head

The Three Lords pub in the Minories is a reminder of the last of these events when, in the presence of a vast throng, Jacobite Lords Balermino, Kilmarnock and Lovat were despatched. Meanwhile, in a field a mile to the east, pirates were strung up on high ground 'so that they may be seen far into the river Thames,' says Stow.

Death was all around. When the Black Death wiped out half of London's fifty thousand inhabitants between 1348 and 1350, hundreds of corpses, still in their clothes, were slung into two great pits which were dug in the place where Royal Mint Court now stands, facing the entry to Tower Bridge. The remains of 760 human skeletons were found during excavation.

Near to the plague pits was a pillory for the punishment of minor offenders. There were a good number of them around here. The oldest document held by Tower Hamlets Local History Library is the lease of a property in an aptly-named Pillory Lane, East Smithfield, dated 1574. In medieval and early modern times the Tower's hinterland throbbed with low life; it grew up as the service area for the castle, a traditional way for medieval towns and suburbs to develop. Houses and workshops, breweries and alehouses, farms and garden plots gathered around inside the walls and two great monastic houses serviced the needy and kept order.

Already, in medieval times, this was a true East End, stuffed with gambling dens and brothels and alive with foreign immigrants, with do-gooders struggling to clean up the place and help the needy.

A poster from sometime in the 1820s or 1830s advertising the Tower menagerie.

Butcher's Row and the old Fountain in the Minories depicted in the late 18th century.

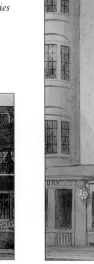

The changing face of the Thames by the Tower — as shown in this detail from about 1540 when sailing ships were there in abundance . . .

. . . and in a more recent aerial view of Tower Bridge area.

The building of
St Katharine's Dock.

Among the Dutch gamblers and pirates' molls, worked the white monks from the Cistercian Abbey of St Mary Graces (the 'Abbey of Tower Hill') and the brothers and sisters of St Katharine's Hospital, wrapped in long black cloaks embroidered with Catherine wheels.

Today it is a nothing sort of place; all roads whirling round office blocks and banks of traffic roaring with agitation at traffic lights. It has been cleaned up beyond recognition and the old names have been lost: Eastminster (recalling the Abbey of Tower Hill) was erased by recent road widening; Nightingale Lane, marking the Knighten Guild's boundary, was rechristened Thomas More Street in the 1930s for no good reason. St Katharine's Marina has, at least, kept the name of the ancient hospital.

Relics of the past

The Tower and a few archaeological remains are all that are left to remind us of the past. Just by the tube station is a good solid remnant, a rare surviving block of city wall. Walk through the subway east from the station to find the ruins of the medieval postern gate which in Chaucer's day was the pedestrian exit from the city into the Abbot of Tower Hill's patch. It was once famous for its cheese shop.

A little further east, past Tower Bridge, running parallel to the river bank is the road called East Smithfield. Formerly a patch of open ground, it later gave its name to this whole area east of Tower Hill. As you approach its western end, traffic apart, the vista is not so very different from six-hundred years ago. On the left are the tall gates and high walls of the old Royal Mint, now superior apartments; the right-hand side of the road is lined with massive buildings, broken by the elephant-guarded entrance to St Katharine's Marina. In the fourteenth century the road was similarly flanked, with the gatehouse of the Cistercian abbey on the Mint site and the church and buildings of St Katharine's Hospital on the river side.

Founded in 1350 by Edward III, St Mary Graces was a luxurious monastery, Eastminster, and a rival to Westminster. At the Dissolution it was the third largest Cistercian abbey in the country. Some relics of it are kept by the Museum of London — including German drinking vessels, jugs and pots, and some fine bright blue-and-yellow stove tiles. On the eastern side of the red-roofed monastery building was the 'pineapple garden', a grove of conifers, where now The Mint pub stands. There was also a dove house and a cattle yard.

The Abbot was the Lord of the Manor of East Smithfield and so monks in white habits were to be seen busy about Tower Hill, collecting the rents. The Abbey also acquired the manor of Poplar and the brothers would have trudged across the marsh 'towards the Lyme house', on their way to the pastures and orchards, the rabbit warrens and the richly stocked fishponds of Stepney Marsh (the Isle of Dogs). In 1500 the tenants there paid fourpence a year for unmowed marsh and eightpence for pasture.

The Royal Mint was moved out of the Tower and into the building on Little Tower Hill at the beginning of the 19th century. Nowadays the Mint has been moved even further away — to Llantrisant in South Wales.

Crime, St Katharine's Hospital, pubs and mills

The Abbot of Tower Hill's territory in the immediate vicinity of the monastery was a dirty unruly part though not quite so bad as the Southwark Stews. In 1380 Peter James, the warden of the Fraternity of St Anthony's Foundation, in the 'Abbey Church next to the Tower', ran off with all the ornaments and jewels which belonged to the fraternity. One of the witnesses in the case was William Grene, Constable of Southwark, whose evidence was discredited when it was discovered he kept a brothel for both sexes.

Surviving rolls of the Abbot's Tower Hill court give some indication of the problems. In the 1450s the main business seems to have been controlling prostitution, gambling and gaming. Already there were quite a few seafaring men around, though many more were yet to come. They played dice and roulette. In 1453 Henry Buskyn was fined ten shillings for keeping a gambling wheel. In 1438 a sawyer called Gerard was fined for keeping a prostitute called Katerina; she and he were both 'common dice players'. The most popular game was was *cloyish*, a game like croquet which the Dutch had introduced. It evidently caused a great deal of trouble and was forbidden by a whole series of fifteenth- and sixteenth-century statutes. A wooden bowl was hit with a chisel-shaped implement through a hoop and bets were cast.

Joan and John Lovell were fined for making dung hills in the street. They also kept a brothel for at least eighteen years, turning up regularly at the Abbey Court to be fined and then carrying on just as before. Many of these houses of ill repute were kept by foreigners, Flemings, Italian and French who, from the rude names they were called, seem to have been as unpopular as immigrants always are. The locals spoke of 'Lombards and Galymen'.

The Royal Hospital of St Katharine, a stone's throw from the Abbey, ruled over the area now occupied by

Old house on Little Tower Hill. Heads of Roman emperors decorate this house built during the reign of Henry VIII. These may denote the discovery of Roman coins on the building site

the marina and the Tower Hotel. Today, set among the smart masts and tourist boutiques a strange space-age shrine can be found. They call it the coronarium. Here, as in a chantry chapel, prayers are still said for King Stephen and his wife Mathilda, who founded the hospital on the site of a vineyard in 1147, and for their sons Stephen and Eustace who died as babies.

Maids in white aprons
Say the bells of St Katharine's

This verse from the old version of *Oranges and Lemons* almost certainly refers to the much-loved and famous hospital which had the special patronage of the Queens of England, consort, regnant and dowager.

Under the terms of its 1273 charter, three brothers and three sisters, with a master in charge, cared for twenty-four poor people, of whom six were 'poor scholars' who helped out with the services. The inmates were, for the most part, female, elderly and infirm or 'fallen women' from the locality. They wore grey tunics with hoods and perhaps 'white aprons' and lived in almshouses which adjoined the sisters' house. Lunatics and the sick were sometimes taken in. As befits an institution which had Queenly patronage, the sisters of the chapter, who were often retired ladies-in-waiting, were accorded equality with the men.

Each year St Katharine's income was boosted by the tolls taken from the stall holders at a grand fair on Tower Hill. Toys, souvenirs, sweets and gingerbread in the shape of Catherine wheels were sold; tradesmen and entertainers came from all over London and its hinterland, attracting crowds as great as did the public executions. East London's fair was regarded as a major rival to Bartholomew Fair — the famous three-day marathon in Smithfield — and the City made various attempts to have it stopped.

November 16 was a good day for the poor here. One thousand halfpennies were distributed among them;

one coin each for a thousand individuals following instructions given by Queen Eleanor of Provence, to mark the anniversary of the death of her husband, Henry III.

St Katharine's does not seem to have been a quiet pious place, or, if it was, it had periods of rollicking and racketing. In 1257 there were complaints of drunkenness and quarrelling among the brothers. When Queen Philippa, Edward III's wife, issued ordinances for the governing of her hospital in 1352, she specified that black should be worn by the members of the Chapter:

They shall not wear any green or red or striped stuff, which might lead to dissoluteness. A Brother shall not converse alone with any sister of the house or with any other woman within the Hospital in any place where suspicion against them or scandal may be aroused.

The hospital and its church serviced a rough area and reflected that; it was a home for 'vagabonds and prostitutes'. In 1492 the Bishop's Court heard a case which involved a notorious prositute, one Margaret Morgan alias Smyth who had been committed to St Katharine's. Under Henry VI's charter of 1442, the hospital became 'exempt from all secular and ecclesiastical jurisdiction', rapidly attracting foreigners (mostly Flemish and Dutch) who needed to practice their trades unhindered by the restrictions of the City guilds. When Kentish rebels marched into London in 1470 they came to …

the Subarbys of the Cite and other places as Seynt Kateryns and Radclyf, they Robbed and dispoyled dyvers Dowchemen and their bere houses.

East of the precinct was a hermitage, remembered still in the name of a bridge into the old London Dock and a new block of flats. One John Ingram was the

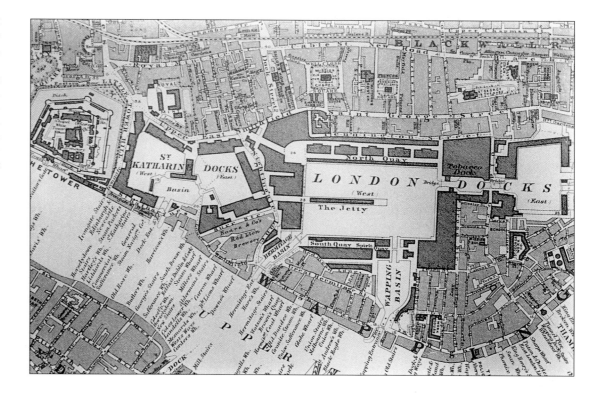

incumbent hermit in the late fourteenth century, living at the sign of The Swan's Nest. A number of pubs in the area have 'swan' in their names, a reminder of those long-forgotten days when banks of great white birds glided about in the reedy marshes which stretched out towards muddy Wapping in the Wose.

It was not all bawds and gamblers; there was work to be done. Fishermen and market gardeners rubbed shoulders with sailors, weavers and workers from the shipyards, breweries and mills. In the alleys off Rosemary Lane, with its house and windmill, lived wherrymen, lightermen and watermen. Next to the hermitage, down at the bottom of Nightingale Lane, were Crassh Mills, twin water mills, driven by the tidal river. The great wooden wheels had been clattering and crashing since the twelfth century, and probably before. Here, and in other mills over towards the Tower, corn was ground for the City. Reference is made to mills in St Katharine's original charter. When Sir Nicholas Loveyn, Lord of Bristol, Poplar and Penshurst Place, died in 1375 he left 'Les Molynes appellez Eastmilles' by the Tower to his 'very dear and well loved wife' and Crassh Mills to his sister for life and then to St Mary Graces.

Merry England

According to the antiquarian, Oldys, the Elizabethan poet, Edmund Spenser, was born in East Smithfield, the son of a cloth worker. A rare pictorial plan, dating from the 1590s, shows the southern part of the area as it was when Spenser wrote of 'merry London, my most kindly nurse' and 'the great tree' was a landmark there. A clutch of buildings congregate at the junction of East Smithfield and Swann Alley, probably just about where Cartwright Street now goes off to the north. Nightingale Lane wanders down to the twin flour mills dividing St Katharine's precinct from a sort of industrial park, open spaces, scored by dykes and drainage channels, dominated by a huge half-timbered brewery complex on the site of the hermitage. It could be mistaken by the modern eye for a coaching inn or post-modern supermarket. In 1520 a brewer bought the site (now a car park) and the hermitage became one of London's most celebrated breweries, The Swan's Nest; there was another one called The Black Swan, where The Mint pub stands in East Smithfield.

As in Stepney and Whitechapel, the sixteenth century was the first era of mass immigration into the East End from the shires. In 1586 John Wolfe published Spenser's *Shepherd's Calendar*, an appropriately pastoral piece for someone who had grown up among the 'country East Enders'.

Wolfe, who was of Dutch extraction, lived in East Smithfield towards the end of his life; his wife had a distillery there. Having become the most prolific and successful publisher in Elizabethan London, plying his trade at the sign of The Brazen Serpent in St Paul's churchyard, he embarked upon a speculative venture and invested in the building of a playhouse, as James Burbage (the father of Shakespeare's leading man) had done in Shoreditch. Shoreditch and East Smithfield were similar places; both were free of the restrictions of the City, 'working class' industrial parts with open ground which had been monastic property. It would be nice to think that it was money made in Mistress Wolfe's distillery which funded the enterprise; the year before work started on the theatre her husband had published *'A woman's worth defended against all the men in the world'*.

Far left
St Katharine's Hospital and the Brothers Houses in 1781.

Left
Charter of St Katharine's by the Tower.

Right
Wine barrels in London docks.

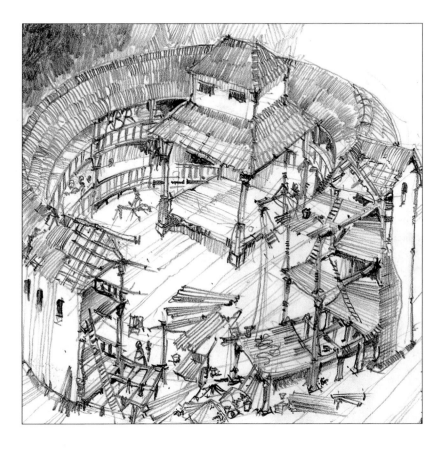

*Artist's impression of
Wolfe's half-built
playhouse in
Thomas More Street.*

Gresham's plea that it provided a valuable service to the area, was closed down, with the rest of the monasteries, in 1538. Most of the abbey land was bought by Sir Thomas Darcy who lived in the abbot's quarters. He pulled down the church and the chapter house but the rest of the buildings survived and by 1565 were used as a victualling yard for the navy and continued as such until the late eighteenth century. Houses and shops were built in East Smithfield by the Stepkyn/ Machleyn family, tenants of the abbey since the time of the murder of the little princes over at the Tower. The celebrated Lady Ivey, who owned a good deal of Wapping and claimed to own even more in Charles II's reign, was a Stepkyn.

The former abbot's court, under royal control at the Dissolution, was still having the same problems as one hundred years previously — but more of them. The new lay officials were busy trying to stop the dumping of rubbish in the streets, the 'harbouring' of suspicious persons and vagabonds and keeping down gambling and vice. Dutch brothel keepers were not just fined now — that had never worked very well — they were given a couple of weeks to get out, into somebody else's patch! 'Move along please!'

According to the records of the old abbot's court a bawd called Katerine conducted her business from the 'Reyle House' in the 1530s. Presumably 'Reyle' refers to the Royal Foundation of St Katharine's, which evidently had not changed much since medieval times. Enjoying the special protection of the Queen, the hospital miraculously escaped dissolution and, after Henry VIII's death, Katherine Parr's second husband was appointed master. One of his successors, under Elizabeth, was Dr Thomas Wilson who aroused a good deal of hostility by selling the fair rights to the City (for seven hundred marks) and closing the choir school, thought to be 'not much inferior to that of St Paul's'. His intention to sell off more privileges was scotched by a 'spirited petition'. The inhabitants declared:

The site Wolfe chose was Nightingale Lane, now Thomas More Street, just up from the tide mills and the brewery. It is marked today by the most spectacular of glittering glass piles, occupied by a Swedish bank. Building work started at the beginning of 1600 but the playhouse never opened. Theatres were dangerous places in Shakespeare's London; the regular bringing together and stimulating of large crowds tended to sedition and the spread of plague. From time to time

the jittery Privy Council would clamp down. On 1 April the Lieutenant of the Tower was ordered to take recognisances of John Wolfe, stationer of East Smithfield who, against the orders of Star Chamber, had started to build a playhouse in Nightingale Lane. Had he been allowed to complete it, who knows, perhaps this area would have had its very own Swan, Rose or Globe, east of the Tower instead of in Southwark.

The Abbey of St Mary Graces, in spite of Sir Richard

We have erected buylte and set up …
dyvers tenements and howses at our own charge.
Yea in so much we have made whole lanes and
stretes of the same tenements where before
was nothing but donghills, laystofs
[rubbish dumps] and void ground …
a great many of the inhabitants there
are seafaring men

By now the precinct was an overcrowded insalub-
rious town within a town, with about eight hundred
houses, mostly small, pushed into a patchwork of
courts and alleys, Pottlepot and Maidenhead alleys
among them. One wonders if Shakespeare had them in
mind when he made Falstaff speak of 'the pottlepot of
a maidenhead' (*King Henry IV, Part Two*). The acrid
smoke from tallow burning and the pollution caused
by the Royal Alum Works and Dutch breweries must
have made St Katharine's an unpleasant spot.

Immigration and 'scavellmen'

In Shakepeare's day this was perhaps the most concen-
trated immigrant area with the Dutch and Flemings,
who had been coming into this part of London in a
steady stream since the Middle Ages, predominating.
In 1567 the Duke D'Alva invaded the Netherlands and
100,000 were said to have fled in a few days. Many
came to London, mainly to St Katharine's, East Smithfield and Shoreditch. By 1583 there were 285 'aliens' in
the precinct and Ben Jonson's Vice Iniquity went to
'Drink with the Dutch there'. They were as unpopular
as the Jews were to be three hundred years later, and
for many of the same reasons. In 1586 there were riots
against the Flemish and the Dutch and in 1593 a bill
was introduced into the Commons directed against the
foreign retailers.

The records of a will dispute in the bishop's court in
1594 provide a 'close-up' of life among ordinary

*An 18th-century clothes
market: 'Rag Fair'
in East Smithfield.*

labouring folk from East of the Tower. The estate in question belonged to one of a gang of casual labourers who worked, amongst other things, as 'scavellmen' clearing out the ditches around Crassh Mills. They made a good living (most claim to have been worth some three to five pounds) by turn ditching, harvesting in season, 'binding of hay', practising the 'science of gardening' and working in the local sugar house. They ate out a good deal, taking breakfast of bacon or rolled lamb at The Rose or The Red Lion on Tower Hill. Sometimes women came in to dress the bachelors' victuals. Tom Davis, the party deceased in the probate case, lived in St Katharine's 'on the same wall' as a

sailor's wife who 'did for him'; she hadn't seen her husband for three years. Although he was only a labourer he was rich enough to consider going to take a cure 'at the bath'. Scavellmen had their own houses, presumably rented, each with a backyard and a 'necessary house'. The gang used to gather at The Mermaid alehouse, owned by a gunsmith called Morgan, to pass the time drinking while they waited for the tide to go out. They also played tables at the house run by an armourer in Aldgate.

Fifteen witnesses were called in the lawsuit, of whom only two were London born. Of the newcomers we know that four came from Shropshire, two were

Welsh, one Irish, two from the west country and one from Leicester. Most were middle aged and had come to London in their twenties or thirties. Five of them were women, all of whom worked — running cafes or as servants or 'dailies'.

All in all, it seems to have been a rather communal life, much of it lived in pubs and cafes, with a good deal of chatting on doorsteps and 'over the garden wall'. There was plenty of work around and the standard of living was relatively high. It was a hotchpotch of people from all over Britain with a fair number from abroad; strangers, many of them, to London and to each other. Tempers were quick and quarrelling and brawling

St Katharine's Dock

went on, with anger and resentment expressed against the Scots, Irish, Welsh, Dutch or Flemings by turn.

As the immigrant numbers swelled into the seventeenth century the area became increasingly rough; the slums around Rosemary Lane spawned the celebrated second-hand clothes market, 'Rag Fair'. In the days when an item of clothing might cost a year's wages, the poor could afford to dress only in cast-offs. The man who is said to have cut off Charles I's head lived in Rosemary Lane. On Friday 24 July 1629 there had been a great stir when that same king, having chased a stag all the way up from Wanstead, finally killed it in Nightingale Lane. A crowd gathered to watch and trampled down a vegetable garden. The fact that so apparently insignificant a tale was handed down is perhaps some indication of the feelings of the locals about the monarchy.

As the years passed, East of the Tower became more and more caught up in the 'seafaring end of town' and all it meant. Pickpockets and prostitutes were ready to fleece those who ventured down near the maypole in East Smithfield and many a case involving the riverside fraternity went before the sessions in Clerkenwell.

In 1784 St Katharine's was still an immigrant area, its inhabitants included 328 Dutch, 69 French (mainly hatters), 8 Danes, 5 Poles, 2 Spaniards, 1 Italian and 12 Scots. The old abbey site was the naval victualling yard until the end of the century when it became a tobacco warehouse; in 1808 the Royal Mint was erected there.

London docklands

The most significant changes in the area came with the opening of the London Dock in 1805 and the dramatic developments in St Katharine's nineteen years later. In 1824 a bill was put before Parliament which proposed the demolition of the precinct — houses, schools, workshops, pubs, church, graveyards and all — and the construction of a wet dock in its place.

There was an outcry from the inhabitants:

> The Docks will turn me out of a comfortable house where the rent is moderate.

> The Docks will ruin my trade.

> I was born in the Precinct, and my means of support wholly depend upon the neighbourhood.

> My ancestors and relatives have resided in the precinct 140 years, 31 buried in the two Burial Grounds and 2 in the Church.

As the eloquent petition presented to Parliament ran:

> Where is the Mother or Widow but would recoil with horror at the idea of the bones of her children, husband and relatives being dug up with the soil, exposed to the view of, and trampled under foot by every person passing that way?

But so it was; the St Katharine's Dock Company forged ahead. 11,300 lease holders and lodgers were to be thrown out without compensation. Ten pounds was allowed for the reburying of bodies; if relatives wanted the gravestone preserved, they had to pay for the privilege. On 30th October 1825 a crowd packed the old church of St Katharine for the final service and to grab what souvenirs they could.

The next day demolition began. 1,250 houses were pulled down. 'Dark Entry', 'Cat's Hole' and other courts and alleys crowded with insanitary timber-framed dwellings went and in their place was a vast basin of water leading into two docks of four acres each. Around them rose Thomas Telford's magnificent yellow brick warehouses, six stories high, supported by black iron columns.

The first bit of 'slum clearance' saw the hospital off to Regent's Park where the master and chapter were accommodated in a luxury to which they were not accustomed. The royal lions followed soon after. With the coming of the docks East of the Tower became a land of dark warehouses, of hustle and bustle with the smell of spice and tar lingering in the air. Mr Quilp from *The Old Curiosity Shop* lived on Tower Hill in these times. He collected rents from:

> …whole colonies of filthy streets and alleys by the waterside, advanced money to the seamen and petty officers of merchant vessels, had a share in the ventures of divers mates of East Indiamen, smoked his smuggled cigars

As the great ships slid in and out of enclosed docks East of the Tower was approaching its darkest hour — but that is another story.

The Royal Foundation of St Katharine's still exists, a mile to the east of its original home, at the end of the Highway. These days it is a gentle oasis of prayer and devotion, still receiving special attention from the Queens who become its patrons. Today's brothers and sisters occupy an eighteenth-century mansion, folded among rose gardens and firmly shut off from the old East End and new Docklands by high walls. Once it was the home of a West India merchant called Whiting.

A vast parking lot covers the land occupied by the Hermitage Brewery in Spenser's day. Arranged around two of its sides are fringes of newly scattered sand-coloured houses and maisonettes, very small and rather fairy-tale if you go there in the twilight and see them sparkling with blue flashes of burglar lights. The scavellmen and the stevedores have gone; there is no more spice in the air; the 'Tribulation of Tower Hill' are Japanese, with cameras. The '*maids in white aprons*' have given way to smart sailing types whose luxury yachts laze about in St Katharine's Marina, only occasionally nosing out into the empty river.

SHOREDITCH

In company with Shakespeare

'When I grow rich' say the bells of Shoreditch

Thus went the old rhyme — with irony. Poor dreary soulless Shoreditch never did grow rich. Today it is a tawdry noisy place, torn apart by lorry-laden arterial roads and scarred with all the sooty paraphenalia of the Great Eastern Railway. Small factories and shops selling mobile phones and leather goods announce themselves with brash colour, set in the tall grimy brick of Edwardian commercial buildings. Only the decent white eighteenth-century church, with stocks in the churchyard and its 'clerk's house' are there to suggest that it was not always so.

Even its name is ugly, the ditch of some old Saxon called Scerof or Scorre. They used to say that it was named after a royal drab, Jane Shore, Edward IV's mistress but this scrap of romance — according to the topographer, Cunningham — was a 'vulgar error', perpetuated by a ballad in Percy's *Reliques*:

> *Thus weary of my life at length*
> *I yielded up my vital strength*
> *Within a ditch of loathsome scent*
> *Where carrion dogs did much frequent:*
> *The which now since my dying day,*
> *Is Shoreditch call'd, as writers saye;*
> *Which is a witness of my sinne,*
> *For being concubine to a King*

The earliest reference to the name predates Jane Shore and her misdeeds by three hundred years.

But Shoreditch did have a good time — the most spectacularly good time of all the Eastern suburbs, and it is that following glory which merits exploring, never mind all the rest of its miserable drab existence.

A busy suburb

The village grew from ribbon development where the two Roman roads, Kingsland Road and Old Street, crossed — about a mile north east of the Bishopsgate out of the city. Like East Smithfield and Aldgate and Whitechapel, it lost its rural character in the sixteenth century and became a populous manufacturing suburb, acquiring a reputation akin to its lawless southern neighbour, the Liberty of Norton Folgate. The poet Middleton said Spitalfields and Shoreditch were 'the only Cole-harbour and sanctuary for wenches and soldiers'. Silk weavers and tinkers, brewers and prostitutes — all crowded in with the coming of the country East Enders; old mansions were converted into lodging houses and barns into bed-sitters. There were breweries and slaughter houses, smithies and gunpowder factories and a multitude of weavers' shops.

Monasteries, priories and nuns

In spite of its workaday character, there is magic in Shoreditch. The village was placed between sacred wells and flanked between two ancient monasteries. Holy Well is remembered in Holywell Lane, a scruffy alley running west off the High Street. The other well, St Agnes the Clear, or ' Dame Annesh Cleare' as Ben Jonson called her, was prized for her fine sparkling water. Once water carts would gather up in Old Street, just where the junction with Pittfield Street is now.

The two monasteries were the Benedictine Priory of St John the Baptist, Holywell and the Priory and Hospital of St Mary, Spital — from which Spitalfields derived its name. When John Cowper, vicar of Shoreditch, died in 1525 he asked to be buried in the quire of his church and 'torches to burn about my body in the day of my burying'; two of the torches were to be left burning in the church and one was to go to Holywell and the other to the Spital.

The buildings of Holywell Priory covered the eight acres bounded by Bateman's Row, Holywell Lane, the High Street and Curtain Road, the latter named after the high curtain walls which protected the Benedictine

nuns from the outside world. The area is still quiet and enclosed, cut off from the traffic noise; a strange atmosphere pervades the dark ways through high brick buildings.

A massive stone gateway on the High Street, then called 'Halliwell', led into a large area surrounded by

Left hand page
The old church of
St Leonard in Shoreditch

Shoreditch in 1642 from
Eyre's Views of the
Fortifications of London

convent buildings, a Norman church, a chantry chapel built in 1524 by Sir Thomas Lovel, the Prioress's garden with a dovecote, an orchard of one acre, an ancient house called the old Duffehouse, a farm, a malt house and a large barn called the 'Otebarn' to the east of the garden.

When Thomas Cromwell closed it down in October 1539 there were fourteen nuns in residence. The Prioress, Sybil Newdegate, the daughter of a sergeant at law, retired on a pension of forty pounds a year; Elene Claver the subprioress received £6 13s 4d; the pensions awarded to the ordinary nuns were between two and three pounds. One wonders how they felt, packing up their few belongings and leaving the haven with its doves and its orchard, walking out of the gate for the last time into the harsh reality of living as lone women on a modest income.

The buildings were almost immediately despoiled

and land sold off to developers. In 1692 a lease to William Bateman (of Bateman's Row?) described the property still in the old terms: 'Lady's Garden', 'Dovehouse Garden' and 'Convent Garden'. The stone gateway leading into the Priory from the High Street was left; it stood there until 1785. As its Victorian historian wrote:

> Thousands are daily passing over the scene of
> the good nuns' privacy, without so much as
> a thought of the prayers and labours that
> glorified it and made it blessed.

The hospital

St Mary Spital stood on the east side of Bishopsgate, outside Shoreditch parish, to the south. As the vicar of Shoreditch had his funeral torch left burning there, it is perhaps appropriate to consider the hospital here, rather than in the chapter on the weavers who invaded the site in the seventeenth century and made Spitalfields a French colony.

The priory and hospital were founded in the early thirteenth century; in 1303 there were twelve canons, five lay brothers and seven sisters. It was essentially a lying-in hospital which kept the children of mothers who had died in childbirth until they were seven years old. Elderly and crippled people were also looked after and a 'hotel service' was provided for pilgrims.

By the late fourteenth century the hospital was caring mainly for widows and orphans and subsequently poor men were also taken in. At the time of the Dissolution it was a hospital, almost in the modern sense, with eighty beds. Like now, there was distress and outrage when the four great London hospitals were threatened with closure: Sir Thomas Gresham petitioned Henry VIII that the Spital, St Bartholomew's, St Thomas's and St Mary Grace's should be saved and given over to the city to administer.

*18th-century view of
Shoreditch and
St Leonards.*

The Spital was not saved although with all their flair for publicity the Tudors kept the annual Spital sermon, a three-day marathon held on the Monday, Tuesday and Wednesday after Easter at Spital Cross. The Mayor and Corporation paraded in their splendour and the poor children from Edward VI's newly founded charity school, Christ's Hospital, were wheeled out, all clean, neat and pretty, a show to rend the heart and make the gathered bystanders appreciate the Protestant reforms and the abolition of those luxurious old monks and 'hoity toity' nuns.

On the third of April 1553, Henry Machyn saw, and noted in his diary:

> Alle ye chylderyn, boyth men and vomen chylderyn,
> alle in blue cotes, and …blue frokes.

The hospital buildings were partly demolished and partly made into tasteful conversions, according to Stow, 'for receipt and lodging of worshipful people'. After the Reformation fine carriages might have been seen sweeping in through the two stone gatehouses at the end of Spital Square and Folgate Street. The Spital precinct became a secluded and superior residential estate, occupied by foreign merchants and a number of wealthy Roman Catholics.

Sir Edmund Huddlestone and Father Garnet were among the residents, perhaps for sentimental reasons, perhaps for safety. Meanwhile something much more exciting was happening on the old nunnery land up at Holywell....

The playhouse

Shoreditch's strange magic may derive from the holy wells or from the legacy of the gentle nuns who farmed there, but probably it comes from a legacy of a very different kind. Stand in Great Eastern Street, the main route taking traffic north, just by the traffic lights at the junction with Curtain Road and Starwash car wash, ('ask for our famous £8 special — fast while you wait') and travel back in time a little more than four hundred years. You would then have been standing on a patch of open ground. On the Shoreditch village side, where once the nuns had tilled and prayed, is a tall polygonal structure, like a castle with external stair-

case towers. In the afternoons, except in plague times, a flag flutters from the crenellated turret topping the tiled roof. This is the 'great howse called The Theatre', built in 1576 by James Burbage, the father of Shakespeare's leading man, Richard. It was the first playhouse on English soil and, as will be seen, the physical antecedent of the Globe.

Two hundred yards to the south, now cut off from The Theatre by Great Eastern Street, there was a similar edifice, 'The Curtain', a game house which opened a year after the Burbage enterprise. The seventeenth-century gossip, John Aubrey, got it wrong as he often did, referring to it as the:

> Green Curtain, a kind of Nursey or obscure playhouse somewhere in the suburbs ... [where Ben Jonson] acted and wrote, but both ill.

Stages had no curtains in those days and its name was taken from the the curtain walls of the nunnery.

Shakespeare and company

Between 1585 and 1592 James Burbage shared the management and used The Curtain as an extension to The Theatre; Shakespeare's company regularly played at both houses before they went to Southwark. More 'down market' entertainment was presented at The Curtain — jigs, sword fights and wrestling as well as straight drama. In 1598 *Romeo and Juliet* had its debut at The Curtain. Stand on the corner of Hewlett Street and Curtain Road — and imagine a pretty boy on the platform of a 'wooden O' calling out, for the first time, to a spellbound crowd of apprentices and their girls 'Romeo, Romeo, wherefore art thou Romeo?'

Nobody seems to have taken a great deal of notice of Shoreditch's most illustrious connections. Admittedly there is a slim pamphlet called *Shakespeare came to Shoreditch* but nothing much beside. Sometime between 1585 and 1593 the bard came to London and it is not known where he lodged until 1597 when he turns up as a tax defaulter, living a little way inside the Bishop's Gate in the tiny parish of St Helen. It was a convenient place to live, handy for the Cross Keys in Gracechurch Street, where his company are known to have performed in 1594, and within reasonable walking distance (for sixteenth-century man) of The Theatre and The Curtain.

Others of the company lived closer to the two playhouses in Shoreditch: Richard Burbage lived in the High Street, just near The Theatre, as did William Sly and Richard Cowley. Henry Condell was just up the road in Hoxton 'a good flight shot' north of the church. The theatrical fraternity congregated around here and it is far from fanciful to suppose that Shakespeare lodged in Shoreditch at some time.

Henry VIII's court jester, Will Somers, had been a local man; Francis Langley, the merchant who built The Swan theatre was married in the parish church and Christopher Beeston, the governor of the King's

The Globe theatre is commonly renowned as the Elizabethan home of Shakespeare's plays. However, it was at Shoreditch where Shakespeare's dramas had their first regular performances — Romeo and Juliet had its premier performance at The Curtain.

and Queen's Boys, was born locally. An actor called John Aynsworth was buried in the churchyard in 1581, as was George Wilkins, the poet and player in 1613. It was just down the road in Worship Street that Ben Jonson ran a fellow player, Gabriel Spencer, through with a sword. He escaped the hangman's noose through 'benefit of clergy'; that is to say, he proved himself literate by reciting the verse of a psalm.

They were a rough crew, classed as 'vagrants' in law; Shakespeare himself was bound over to keep the peace. James Burbage's brother-in-law was his business partner and on one occasion accused Burbage of rifling The Theatre's cash box. A terrible row ensued and the locals heard Burbage bellowing out from one of the windows of the playhouse, calling his sister a 'murderous whore'.

A Oakden and Sons, Hardware Factors, now occupy The Theatre site, on the corner of New Inn Yard and Curtain Road, and bear the brown plaque which is the only hint of former glories — no Hollywood-style hype here. The playhouse was six-hundred feet in diameter and stood just over twelve feet from the northern side of what is now New Inn Yard, among the remains of the Priory farm buildings, including an eighty-foot barn which James Burbage converted into seven tenements, 'bed sits' for letting out to the country East Enders and making a quick profit:

Ruynous and decayed ... [it was] soe weake as when a great wynd had come the tenantes for feare have bene fayne to get out of yte.

History the Romance must countenance the fact that it was an exploitive business man who in fact made the Shakespeare phenomenon possible; had The Theatre not been a successful venture, the Burbages intended to convert the playhouse building into flats. The Theatre was, in the event, very popular and flourished for over twenty years.

A 16th-century map of Shoreditch: the cow at the top left marks the site of The Theatre. The Curtain was used as an extension to The Theatre and was the venue for general entertainment and sporting events as well as drama performances.

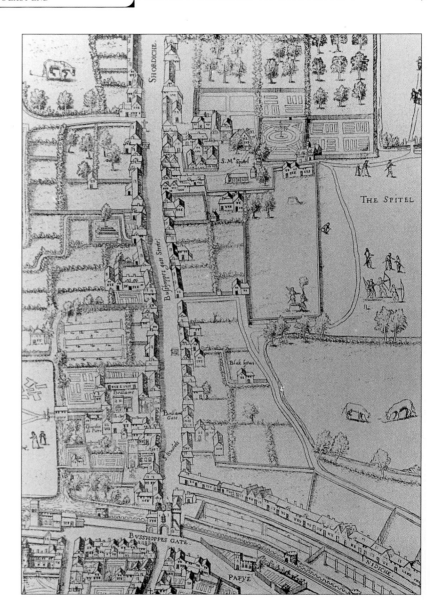

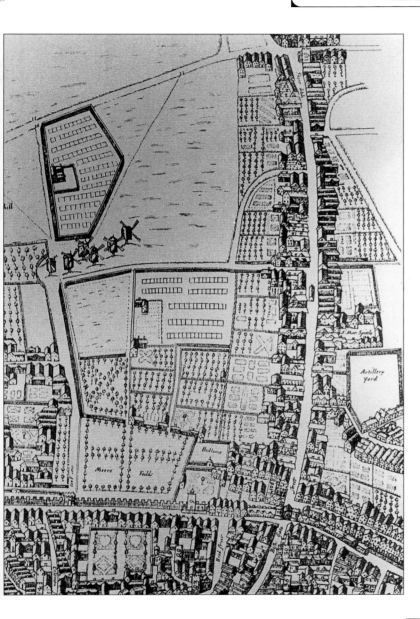

*Shoreditch High Street
in the 17th century.*

Theatre entertainment

Except during plague time — and when the government was having a panic attack about theatres fomenting sedition — the entertainment drew good audiences. Tailors and tinkers, cordwainers, apprentices, sailors, old men and young men, girls and boys poured in; they paid a penny to stand in the pit, tuppence for a seat in the galleries and threepence for a seat with a cushion.

Sunday was the most popular day, as one might expect. Not only was it a holiday, it was also the day that everyone was used to associating with theatrical entertainment. With the taking down of roods in churches and the snuffing out of lights at the Reformation, came the banishment of the comforting galaxy of saints; God the Father, Son and Holy Ghost were allowed in the grim prayer halls but the rest of the cast were banished. There were no more theatrical performances in church; the miracle plays stopped and the Robin Hood costumes were sold off.

Human thirst for escapism into other peoples' lives was, henceforth, to be satisfied by the drama — and professional companies sprang up, performing first in inns, like The Red Lion in Whitechapel, and then in purpose-built theatres. The sacred spot in Shoreditch, the site of the holy well and the priory, became a place of rumbustuous entertainment.

Just before Christmas 1598, following a series of legal disputes with the ground landlord of The Theatre, the Burbage brothers (their father was now dead), with fourteen others, dismantled The Theatre, packed on it on to carts and rumbled it down across London Bridge to Southwark. There, using the timbers and the tiles from Shoreditch they built The Globe whose light blazed out all over the world and down through four hundred years, leaving dingy old Shoreditch and the playhouse at the holy well forgotten in its shadow.

WAPPING, SHADWELL, RATCLIFF AND LIMEHOUSE

Once the river was the lifeblood of east London. Listen, as the hero of *Our Mutual Friend* did, to its sounds on a dark, blustery Victorian night:

The turning of steam paddles … the clinking of iron chains … the cracking of blocks … the measured working of oars … the occasional violent barking of some passing dog on ship board'.

Dickens's Uncommercial Traveller drums out 'Down by the Docks' to the rhythm of his boots as he strides manfully eastwards to Shadwell Basin.

Down by the Docks they 'board seamen' at the eating houses, the public houses, the slop houses, the coffee shops, the tally shops, all kinds of shops mentionable and unmentionable … Down by the Docks, the seamen roam in mid-street and mid-day, their pockets inside out and their heads no better. Down by the Docks, the daughters of wave-ruling Britainnia also rove, clad in silken attire, with uncovered tresses streaming in the breeze … Down by the Docks, you may buy polonies, saveloys and sausage preparations various … Down by the Docks the children of Israel creep into any gloomy cribs and entries they can hire, and hang slops there — pewter, watches, sou'wester hats — 'firtht rate articleth, Thjack'. Down by the Docks, scraping fiddles go in the public houses all day long, and shrill, above their din and all the din, rises the screeching of innumerable parrots brought from foreign parts.

The riverside hamlets

Down by the docks the seamen roam … their pockets inside out and their heads no better

An elevated view of the New Dock in Wapping in the early 1800s. Today the oldest riverside hamlet, Ratcliff, the ancient port of the East End, and Shadwell, the seventeenth-century 'new town', have been eased out by Wapping but Limehouse still retains some separate identity.

That was the riverside of Dickens's youth, of the 1820s when he went to visit his godfather, Christopher Huffam. The young boy, escaping from the miseries of his home life in Camden Town saw and heard all the maritime chatter as he walked east, through Wapping, Shadwell and Ratcliff to Limehouse. The riverside hamlets had, by now, grown together into one continuous sprawl.

Wapping

A Wapping execution was one of the sights of Tudor London: the victims were trundled along the 'filthy strait passage' in carts from Newgate and the locals came out to cheer or boo.

A 'whoppa', meaning something large of its kind, derives, some say, from the word Wapping — such was the frequency of bodies, swollen and bloated with sewery water, murder victims and suicides, being dragged out of the river and the docks. 'Mr Baker's Trap' was the name given by Dickens in *The Mystery of Edwin Drood* to a dock bridge in Old Gravel Lane, a common suicide spot. Today, between the giant warehouses turned apartments and blocks of flats built in imitation of warehouses that line the Wapping waterside, are occasional glimpses of the beaches where once the 'whoppers' were stranded. The approaches to the river are down steep stairs which originally led down from the top of the embankment walls to protect low-lying Wapping in the Wose from incursion by the tidal river.

In Tudor times Wappingers called upon to give their address would say they lived at such and such a wall. 'Wapping Wall', the street which leads to Shadwell, has retained its old name, and, further west, you can still go down Wapping Old Stairs. Their slimy descent to a patch of beach is approached along a dark passage by The Town of Ramsgate, standing near the Pier Head, once the entrance to the London Docks. Like many riverside inns, the pub is named after the coastal vessel which used to dock here, bringing in grain, dairy produce, fish and other commodities vital to the capital's survival. The Ramsgate, sidling on to the High Street, with its narrow bar and rickety balcony hanging over the river, is one of the rare relics of Wapping's seafaring days.

This stretch of riverside is the show-piece of the new East End, with old and new blended and ornamented — a strange emptiness, cobbles, lamps and neatness lend it the air of a stage set. Pier-head houses stand solid in their Regency elegance around a lawn and trees. Next is The Town of Ramsgate and opposite, the remains of the church and a fine school building. Go there on an April day when the spring sunshine makes St John's gold dome glow above a sea of white cherry blossom along by the old dock walls. Tourist guides announce, 'Just here Nelson bought his first naval uniform'. Not so long ago this pretty historical set piece was a dark rough land of docks and dockers. Before that it was London's 'sailortown' and once it was just a watery waste.

Reclaimed from the marshes

When Waeppa, the Anglo Saxon tribesman who gave his name to the area, first arrived with his band of refugees they probably settled on the only firm ground around, the gravel ridge on the eastern side of Wapping. The small settlement of fishermen's houses and farm workers' cottages probably lay between Garnet Street and Wapping Lane, once called New Gravel Lane and Old Gravel Lane. In the early thirteenth century there were two mills by the riverside in Wapping leased by one Terricus de Alegate from the Dean and Chapter of St Paul's. All the corn for the common bakehouse at St Paul's was ground there then.

Various attempts made at reclamation of the marshland began with a bishop of London and Lord of the Manor who drained a hundred acres in 'ancient time'. Flooding was a continual problem; just after Christmas 1323 a 'might flood, proceeding from the tempestuousness of the sea' breached the river wall, probably where Wapping Wall is now.

The oldest pub in London?

The 'College of Acon' — the monastery of St Thomas of Acon, based in Cheapside — was in possession of the mills by now and also owned a brewery by the Compass Ditch, near where the famous riverside pub The Prospect of Whitby now stands. It must have been some establishment as it was sold for an astronomical one thousand pounds at the Reformation. The Prospect's claim to be the oldest London pub may be dubious but the site certainly has an association with beer which goes back some seven hundred years.

Medieval Wapping

The medieval hamlet of Wapping was a cluster of houses on its eastern side, round the mills and the beer house, looking out on to a patchwork of ditches, dykes and pasture. When the tides were angry it was just a sheet of marsh, dotted with islands, like Prusoms Island which survived as a street until modern times. There must have been a patch of dry ground just to the east of Crassh Mills, where the hermitage stood.

In the time of Henry VIII a Dutch engineer called Cornelius Vanderdelft did a professional job and drained the 130 acres of marsh bounded by the Highway, Crassh Mills and the town of Ratcliff and the river. Wapping in the Wose was truly born and country East Enders moved in, to board ship and find employment in the myriad little workshops which sprang up to service the Tudor navy. By the end of the sixteenth century this was rollicking 'sailor town', peppered with wharves and warehouses, wooden cottages for sailors and alehouses run by 'Virginia widows', the wives of men who had taken their chance and gone off to seek their fortune in the New World. Still there was intermittent flooding and the government, although in general opposed to new building in and around London, encouraged the building of houses on the marsh walls, so that owners might be made responsible for the maintenance of these.

According to John Stow, Wapping High Street, running parallel to the riverbank almost to Ratcliff, a good mile from the Tower, became a 'filthy strait passage, with alleys of small tenements, or cottages ... inhabited by sailors' vituallers'.

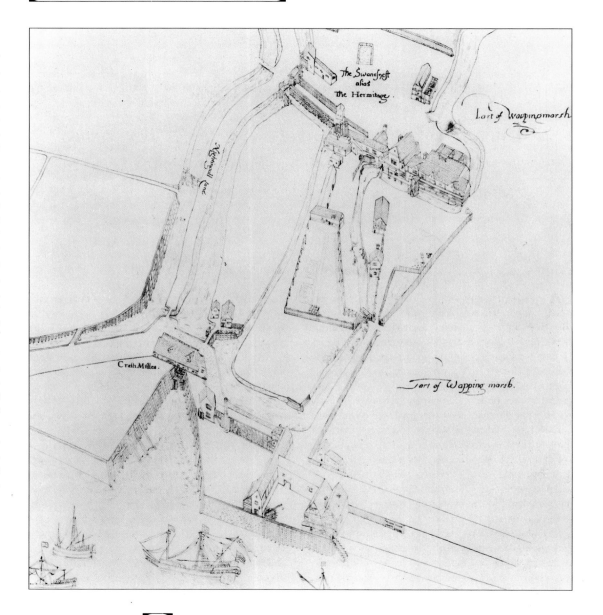

*Hermitage Brewery and
Crassh Mills area
in about 1590.*

A place of execution

John Stow seemed to think it was the removal east of the pirates' gallows which was the occasion of Wapping's development! In the fifteenth century sea robbers were usually hanged 'upon a gallows set upon a raised hill, for that purpose made, in the field beyond East Smithfield'. In the sixteenth century the scaffold was moved down river to what became known as Execution Dock. A Wapping execution was one of the sights of Tudor London; victims were trundled along the 'filthy strait passage' in carts from Newgate and the locals came out to cheer or boo, depending on their allegiance. Some pirates were, Kray-like, glamorous and powerful local 'heroes', running protection rackets, terrorizing and exciting the neighbourhood. When one such, Thomas Walton, was taken to his death in August 1583, he made a final dramatic gesture: he 'rent his Venetian breeches of crimson taffeta and distributed the same to his old acquaintances'.

Execution Dock was located somewhere in the region of the underground station. If you stand in the still narrow cobbled High Street today, especially in the half light at the beginning or the end of the day, it is not difficult to hear in the imagination the rumble of tumbril wheels and the clatter of hooves. When the parade reached the Dock the pirate was escorted to a local hostelry where, with much ado, a last ceremonial quart of ale was taken. The 'tag rag' Wappingers, mostly women and apprentices, in carnival mood, jostled, hot with anticipation, as he mounted the rough scaffold with a rope around his neck. When the body had stopped twitching the executioner cut it down and chained it to a post where it was left for the Thames' tide to wash over it three times, as the High Court of Admiralty prescribed. The corpse was then taken out of the mud, tarred, chained up with the head set in metal harness to keep the skull in place when the flesh rotted away, and strung up on a 'display' gibbet as a warning for any seafaring man sailing up the river.

In later times the bodies ended up in St Botolph's churchyard — their names are in the burial register.

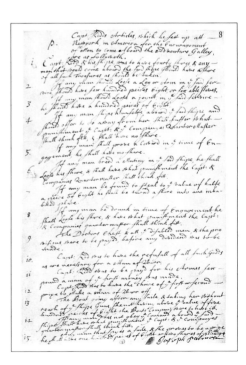

Documents relating to the execution of Captain Kydd.

Wapping Station in about 1910 — formerly the site of Execution Dock.

Wapping Station today.

One of the most celebrated of Wapping's happenings was the execution of the pirate Captain Kydd in 1701 — there is a pub in the High Street named after him these days.

The executions went on for several hundred years; people living in the closing years of the last century could remember a dead pirate hanging with a crow on his shoulder pecking away at his rotting flesh through the iron netting that enclosed his body.

When The Turk's Head in the High Street closed on 24 June 1936 the BBC were there to interview the landlord about the pub's licence to serve a condemned pirate with his last drink.

From pioneer camp to overcrowded suburb

Tudor Wapping was rather like a pioneer camp, a 'new town', a 'bed-sitter' land where young folk, more men than women, came to find work, especially seafaring and river work. There were seamen from Sweden and Holland and a contingent from Newcastle came down on the collier boats which brought the precious 'sea coal' to Wapping Dock. As in East Smithfield and Whitechapel it was a communal life, lived out in victualling houses and drinking establishments — and a dangerous one, in those plague-ridden alleys. Low-lying muddy Wapping had the reputation of being a particularly unhealthy spot.

From being a hamlet in a marsh Wapping turned into an overcrowded suburb in Elizabeth I's reign. By the turn of the century the inhabitants were petitioning for their own church; when they tramped the mile or so to Stepney church they were forced to leave their hearths unattended for several hours. It was hazardous to leave fires burning for so long in weatherboard cottages, or so the Wappingers claimed in their petition. At any rate, on 7 July 1617 the Bishop of London consecrated a church for them, on the site of the present ruin. It was dedicated to St John the Baptist, a chapel of ease to St Mary Whitechapel.

Prostitution

Early seventeenth-century Wapping was a rough place, rougher than it subsequently became, with a good number of prostitutes plying a very lucrative trade among the lodging house fraternity, especially the sailors. They can be discovered in the Bishop's Court suing one another 'for words' or 'affrays', as they were known. Had you been in Wapping Wall one August evening in 1627 you might have heard two bawds standing outside a brothel there and shrieking up to the madame of the house:

'You whore, was not a Fleming fetched out
of bed from thee or leapt out of a window,
when you dwelleth at the next dore unto
the Pope's Head!'
called one.

'You ...lay a Fleming for two shillings and an
Englishman for half a crown,'
shouted the other.

Dutch and Flemish refugees abounded in this part of town and were, as is made clear from the above exchange, regarded as the scum of the earth — coming here with their strange eating habits, 'taking our jobs and debauching our women!'

Elizabeth Barwicke kept a tavern in Wapping at this time. Many of the alehouses were kept by women. Often the wives of absent sailors set up a tap room in their cottage to make themselves a living. Elizabeth and her drinking companion Mary Wharton fell out and the survival of the records of the ensuing lawsuit allow us to listen in on a 350-year-old conversation in a riverside pub. Mary claimed that she went to law to clear her name; she was frightened that the church-wardens might have her up for being 'on the game' as the tavern keeper had on several occasions publicly levelled accusations of immorality against her friend. Some said that Elizabeth Barwicke was a trouble maker and the neighbours had ganged up against her, using Mary Wharton as a 'front woman'.

One day they were eating a pork dinner together in the tavern kitchen, as often they did, washing it down with claret; 'very lovingly' and 'pledging their hands often times', they were 'very merry in each other's company'. As happens with drinking companions the world over, once the alcohol really started to do its work, the comaraderie evaporated, the pupils of the Wapping bawds dilated and there was a dangerous edge to their voices.

'Dost thou know this room?'
slurred the landlady, leaning forward in
threatening fashion over the kitchen table
and narrowing her bloodshot eyes.

'I doe know it,'
replied the other.

'Well, if things in this roome would speake they would
tell straunge things of you!'
went on Mistress Barwicke.

Mary was alarmed at what might be revealed about her dealings in that very room with one Mr Pierson.

'Very slightly and carefully, good Mistress Barwicke',
she growled in low tones.
'Let these things alone and speake noe more of them!
For old and young will doe ...I will not swear for my
own mother with affraies!'

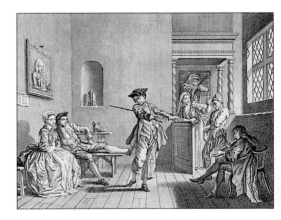

*Many alehouses were run by women,
often the wives of sailors away at sea.*

Riverfront scenes showing
The Prospect of Whitby
which some claim to be
London's oldest pub.

The position of The
Prospect of Whitby.

Riotous times in sailortown

Fifty years later Samuel Pepys, as Clerk of the Acts to the Navy, was a frequent visitor to 'sailortown'. He sometimes landed there late at night, coming back from the royal boat-yard at Woolwich, disembarking near The Town of Ramsgate as the moonlight glittered on the black water. He went down to Wapping to his 'carver's about his viol head', to entertain himself with a sailor's wife and to visit his friend Sir William Warren, a local property developer who owned a ship-yard and was a magistrate.

The area had become even more populous and vola-tile now than it was in Mistress Barwicke's day and Sir William Warren's was a demanding job. 'A pox confound the Lord Protector and all the Justices of the Peace', Robert Salter had called out in Wapping Wall just a few months before the King was restored — not that the monarchy was any more popular down there than 'Old Noll', or any other form of authority.

Alice Bent, a seaman's wife called Captain Valentine Jownes, Commander of the Wexford frigate, a 'rogue and horse turd' and scratched his face until it bled.

Mary Price led John Wythers on; she took him to Bugbyes Hole where she sold him to some seamen to be transported to Surinam.

The Prospect of Whitby stands next to the site of Pelican Stairs in Wapping Wall and may well have been called The Pelican in the 1660s. One John Forsherie lived just by the pub; on 5 May 1661 Sir William Warren took recognizances of him for his appearance in court to answer the complaint of Leonard Bezer:

...for inticeing and allureing his daughter-in-law Sarah Bezer to make marry a-shipp board, and when hee had, theire sold hir to be carried to Barbadoes being shee was with a child, heir to land, whereby hir husband, that is now at sea, may be much damnified by the loss of her.

The Prospect of Whitby's
victuallers' licence.

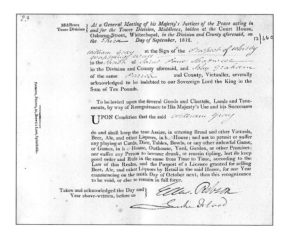

In 1667, when the Dutch came near to invading and Charles II's financial problems left his naval force unpaid, there were riots in Wapping. Pepys encountered gangs of sailors' wives:

> ...in the open streets and up and down,
> [crying]
> 'This comes of not paying our husbands'.

The Poll Tax

Later on in the same year, as if they were not burdened enough, the poor Wappingers, along with everyone else, were confronted with a swingeing Poll Tax, much worse than its modern counterpart. Pepys reckoned that it would be 'the hardest [tax] that ever came out'.

The returns of defaulters show just how much hardship there was in sailortown and how much resistance to paying the hated tax. Restoration Wapping had more poor residents, it seems, than the rest of the eastern suburbs.

In New Gravel Lane there were sixteen defaulters, five of them 'refractory'. In King Street, too, there were sixteen — of which eleven were 'poor' and some 'miserable poor'. In Babbs Lane Thomas Williams refused to open the door and in Love Lane (now King David Lane) Thomas Lisland 'shuts his doores and will not be spoken with'. In Prusom's Island the collectors found Oliver Whiteing gone to sea and his woman 'distracted'. In Meeting House Alley 'Baker and his wife lock the door'.

Of all the East End, Wapping was probably most 'to the left' in politics and religion in these troubled times; here lived the heirs to the *sans culottes* of the English Revolution. At least five 'conventicles' (as nonconformist chapels were known) drew the locals in for sermons and sedition. In the furore which stirred up folks against Roman Catholics at the time of the Popish Plot, Wappingers were at the forefront:

There are men of zeal that cannot sleep in their beds for dreaming of Irish Skrims and Smithfield Fagots.

Wealthy Wappingers

It would be a mistake to think that all the inhabitants were from the bottom ranks of society. Sailors, carpenters, smiths, ropemakers, workers from the three gunpowder factories, victuallers and alehouse keepers there were in abundance, living in the courts and alleys, like Three Foot Alley and Five Foot Alley, but all was not cheap lodging houses and mean hovels. Wapping was becoming more 'up-market'.

In Knockfergus, for instance (the east end of Cable Street) there was one very superior residence in the early 1690s, worth thirty pounds a year, with fields around it — the going rate round here was two pounds or three pounds for a small two-up-two-down and one pound for a 'bed sit'.

Alongside was a row of cheap dwellings erected by a developer called Streete. Virginia Street, which now leads off the Highway into Rupert Murdoch's empire, housed ten sea captains and Broad Street, nine. Warehouse and rope-walk owners, ship builders, brewers and distillers lived alongside their places of work.

Execution Dock was by no means just a waterside Tyburn — it was a great exchange with merchants' offices, warehouses and shops. John Kroger, for instance, operated from the 'East Walk Exchange' there, according to the 1677 'Yellow Pages'.

Probate inventories from this period allow a glimpse through the windows of some of the wealthy locals and suggest that those who followed fairly humble trades might still be quite comfortably off. A lighterman called Bartlett had much pewter and silver ware in his house as did Anthony Watts, an ordinary seaman who had a five-roomed house by the river. The developers who were investing in the area, like Sir William Warren, often made their homes there.

Robert Mutton, who died in 1669 was one such; he had houses, yards and wharves near Execution Dock and lived there himself. Francis Hooper, who died in 1692, had four sixty-pound houses in the Highway and eleven smaller thirty-pound houses in Wellclose Square. John Knight, gent, had a timber yard and a fine house; the lease was worth two hundred pounds (the equivalent of some £500,000 today).

Shipping magnates were the wealthiest Wappingers. Brian Harrison, described rather misleadingly as 'mariner', had part shares in a number of vessels and died in 1664 possessed of a personal estate of over three thousand pounds. Anthony Hare, who was engaged in the West Indies trade, had silk carpets in his servants' rooms, eleven pairs of sheets and a cedar chest of drawers, amongst other things. Henry Roach the shipwright lived in a three-storey house with eight rooms. He had silver plate which included a double salt cellar with three legs, shares in thirteen ships, a three-hundred pound lease on a house in the Tower Ditch and another dwelling worth £230 in New Gravel Lane.

John Knight, gent, had a timber yard.
In his bedchamber were found the following:

a little box with eighteen bands
six pairs of little cuffs
one little carder box
one coate
one hatt
two suites of clothes
one cloak
one loose coate
two halfe shirts
one red wastcoate
five paire of stockings
a ribben hatt band
garters

Judge Jefferies

Before leaving Pepys's Wapping take a last drink at The Town of Ramsgate. They will tell you there that this was the riverside inn where the notorious hanging Judge Jeffries, James II's Lord Chancellor, was captured, trying to escape during the bloodless coup of 1688 known as the Glorious Revolution. Jeffries was arguably the most hated man in the country, because of the merciless way he had punished the west country rebels who followed the Duke of Monmouth in his bid for the throne. When King James II was deposed Jeffries fled, disguising himself as a sailor and was recognized by a scrivener drinking in a Wapping 'cellar'. The scrivener caught his eye; Jeffries feigned a cough and turned to the wall — but it was too late and the Lord Mayor was called.

Jefferies was duly arrested and taken to the Tower where he is said to have drunk himself to death, unable, for many months, to eat anything except poached eggs.

It is a good story, but whether or not it happened in The Ramsgate is a moot point. Some say that he was taken in an alehouse called The Red Cow in Anchor and Hope Alley. Probably neither the local landlords nor the Japanese tourists will ever know the truth of it.

Wapping's heyday

From the Glorious Revolution until the time when the young Dickens marched 'Down by the Docks' was Wapping's heyday. When Britannia ruled the waves sailortown was 'a bit of Portsmouth old town nestling against London'. Picture it then, a jumble of anchor-smiths and sail-makers' workshops, cooperages, distilleries, and everywhere timber yards. Parades of solid sea-captains' residences, notably in Wellclose Square, intermingled with sailors' cottages and lodging houses, interlaced with drinking establishments of every variety. Gin and brandy were cheap

Judge Jefferies, the notorious 'hanging judge', was captured in Wapping when he tried to escape after the Glorious Revolution, disguised as a sailor.

and a report on the retailing of spirituous liquor in Tower Hamlets in 1735 says:

Unhappy mothers habituate themselves to these distilled liquors, whose children are born weakly and sickly, and often look shrivel'd and old.

Back and forth along the High Street went cartloads of merchandise brought from the West Indies and West Africa: molasses and rum, ivory, gold and red wood. Braided and tricorned captains of slave ships from the West Indies might be seen about the streets leading strings of 'blackamores' to be sold at The Black Boy and Trumpet at Wapping Old Stairs or The Dundee Arms perhaps.

Slavers docked at Wapping every spring. Sometimes the victims escaped and it was not uncommon to encounter a little black figure begging in Ship Alley or Broad Street. Leaning on the bars in taverns, swigging in tap rooms, having a 'ramble about' after months of confinement aboard ship were the sons of 'wave ruling Britannia' in their distinctive attire — trousers, not beeches, and short 'bum-freezer' jackets. A typical 'Jack Tar' was a little more than a schoolboy, swaggering around sailortown with loads of cash to spend, perhaps thirty pounds or forty pounds, while his brother, a plough boy earned a mere five pounds a year, all found. There were good pickings here for the local girls. 'Go down to Wapping and see life', Dr Johnson told Boswell.

Press gangs

The press gang officer, armed with a large expense account, would hire a room in one of the taverns, from where he conducted an investigation of the availability of seamen for his next trip. John Bull, with his notions of freedom, would not countenance the idea of conscription; the only way for the navy to recruit skilled

*Press gangs were busy in
Wapping making up the
deficit of trained seamen
to fight for King George.*

seamen for the on-going wars with France, was to go down to Wapping and kidnap the trained sailors and press them into the King's service.

The officer might learn that the crew of a privateer were going to be drinking at The Dundee Arms that night. By eleven-thirty they have all drunk themselves into a stupor, so off goes the gang and the sailors are carried off to fight for King George, whether they like it or not. Landlords did a good trade, being handsomely rewarded for tipping off the press gangs or delivering an unconscious bundle of drunken humanity aboard ship themselves.

The Bell alehouse at Execution Dock was, no doubt, one of the places visited by the press gang. It stood on the corner of Wapping High Street and Brewhouse Lane. From 1722 the landlord was one Samuel Batts, whose baby daughter Elizabeth was baptized in St John's in 1741. Batts supplied casual labour, such as coal heavers, to the masters of ships bringing cargoes into Wapping. Elizabeth was only three years old when her father died and her mother remarried, one John Blackburn. The couple ran The Bell together until 1750. It was a rough place where sailors and colliers drank and lodged.

On 22 September 1736 the *Daily Post* reported:

Yesterday morning a sailor, formerly master of a collier, who with two others of the same Fraternity lodg'd at the 'Bell Alehouse', the corner of Execution Dock, got privately out of bed and hang'd himself at the catch of the door. At dawn of Day his Chams [sic] wak'd and miss'd him, but, discovering him on his knees they imagined he was at his devotion.

Captain James Cook

One of the customers here, it seems, was the young James Cook from Whitby, serving on *The Three Brothers* which brought timber from Norway to Zachariah Cockfield's timber yard in Cinnamon Street.

The story goes that Cook, later the world's greatest explorer, met Elizabeth Batts when she was a child. She was sickly — little wonder if she grew up in the spit and sawdust of The Bell — and Cook vowed that he would marry her if she lived. And so he did.

There is a blue plaque on the red-brick terraced monster of the Highway, which marks the spot where James and Elizabeth Cook set up home after their marriage. After a couple of years, as they went up in the world, they moved up to a bigger house in Mile End.

Marriage documents of
Captain James Cook to
Elizabeth Batts, daughter
of the landlord of The Bell
alehouse in Wapping.
Cook had met her when she
was a sickly child and
promised to marry her
if she survived.

Famous men with Wapping connections

James Cook met Elizabeth Batts when she was
a young child living in a Wapping pub. They set
up their first home together on the Highway.
It was a Wapping man, the second lieutenant,
Zachariah Hicks, who first sighted Australia.

Six local men were on *The Endeavour* with
Captain Cook, including William Peckover, the
gunner from Gun Alley by Wapping Church and
Samuel Jones from Execution Dock.

The celebrated Captain Bligh of the mutiny on
The Bounty had lodgings in Wapping.

John Newton, the slave shipowner who wrote
Amazing Grace after his conversion to
Christianity, lived locally.

James Edmeston was born in Wapping; he wrote
a hymn that would echo through the years and
the churches of England right up until today:

Lead us heavenly father, lead us
O'er the world's tempestuous seas

*Wapping High Street,
looking west.*

This was truly the seafaring end of town but with the
coming of the docks at the very beginning of the
nineteenth century, the heart was torn out of old
Wapping. Houses and workshops were swept away by
the London Dock Company and while the population
of the rest of the East End, particularly Mile End Old
Town, grew alarmingly, the parishioners of St John,
who had numbered 5,889 in 1801, were reduced to
nearly half by 1811.

*Life was rough and ready
in the seafaring community
— with frequent brawls,
prostitution and the
constant threat of
the press gangs.*

Dockland

Irishmen, Scots and Welsh labourers were brought in to build the docks and the massive bonded warehouses which housed the stores of tobacco, rice, wine and brandy — for which the London Docks were granted a monopoly. Wapping remembered is high walls and the Dockers' tanner. Wapping now is remnants of that sea-born trade — Tobacco Dock, the shopping mall made out of a warehouse — the great commercial wharves converted into luxury flats, looking out on to an empty river. All that remains of sailortown are tourist mementoes in riverside pubs, a bookshop which bears that name in Tobacco Dock and some mossy tomb-stones. When you are next there just take a stroll around the churchyard, stranded on the High Street, and read what is still legible on the tombstones:

Miles Holmes, husbandman of this parish, died 1809

Thomas Shank, cooper of Wapping, died on Shakespeare's birthday in 1805

George Kent, victualler of 47, died 1809

Thomas Rolls, died 1817, plumber of this parish.

I doubt if there is a sailor to be found in Wapping now, or a cooper; certainly there are no husbandmen — victuallers and plumbers maybe. A survey of the new residents of Wapping made in 1992 revealed that half of them were 'professional and related' — judges, barristers, solicitors, accountants, valuers, financiers and the like. This, thought the London Dockland Development Corporation, was to be a new Chelsea, east of the Tower. Maybe ... but whatever its next mutation, Wapping will carry its colourful past, like a sailor's rolled kitbag, over into the future.

Shadwell

Once people flocked in to take the waters and
'many cures were performed by the use of it'

At the eastern end of The Highway stands St Paul's church, presiding over the parish of Shadwell. The original 'most disgraceful building of brick totally unworthy of description' was replaced in 1831. The parish is tiny, measuring, it is said, only '910 by 710 yards', a bite out of the side of Wapping's triangle.

The name *Schadewelle* is of Anglo Saxon origin and means a shallow well or spring. Maybe there was a settlement here in those distant times, on the gravel ridges which ran through the marsh. There was certainly habitation round here in Roman times, as we have seen. Maybe, for Waeppa's folk, it was just a place where they went for water. There were at least two copious springs, famous for their fine water. One used to issue through the base of the churchyard wall on the south side and the other was in Sun Tavern Fields. In 1745 one William Berry had a well sunk in Sun Tavern Place, where the Glamis Estate is now. Once people flocked in to take the waters and 'many cures were performed by the use of it'. Walking through today's dead dock debris and the monotony of unkempt low-grade dwellings, dotted with uneasy pockets of bright new brick and snarled about with thundering lorries, it is difficult to imagine that this was once a spa.

It is evident that by the mid-fourteenth century at least some of the marshy parts of Shadewellefeld had been drained as some of the locals were fined for not repairing the ditches. Most of the area was owned by the Dean and Chapter of St Paul's Cathedral and on or near the site of The Prospect of Whitby was the ancient brewery which belonged to St Thomas of Acon. Wapping Wall, the embankment which ran from Shadwell to Wapping, may have been built about the time when Vanderdelft drained Wapping in the Wose — or it may have been an older construction. A case in the Court of Exchequer in 1589 shows that one John Stepkin, grandfather of the litigant of the same name, built the 'wharf called Wapping Wall', probably 'on the frame of Carter's wharf' — presumably in the early years of the century.

In 1572 the river rose:

The force of the water was such as it breaks the wall in sundrey places and overflowed the wholle marches and drowned much cattell.

Following the breach, people were encouraged to build on the wall. Many did so, including a Mr William Page who, some twelve years after the flood, bought 110 feet of wall and laid foundations — only to find that he was breaking the law. The government, nervous of the swelling size of the capital city, had issued one of its many edicts against new building in and around London. Mr Page petitioned the Privy Council, asking to be allowed to finish the work. Whether or not this appeal succeeded is unclear.

A new town

Tudor Shadwell was a line of wharves along Wapping Wall and a scattering of cottages away from the riverside, with ditches and paths crossing pasture land. By Oliver Cromwell's day the face of this riverside hamlet had completely changed. Shadwell had become a densely populated 'housing estate' or 'new town'. Built all of a piece, it housed the newcomers who flocked in to work on the river and service the expanding navy. According to historian Strype, Shadwell became:

> ...one of the great nurseries of navigation and breeders of seamen in England, without which England would not be England.

Shadwell grew apace in the 1620s. By 1650 the seven acres that are now the Edward VII Memorial Park were closely packed with over seven hundred buildings. It would have resembled today's new estates to some extent but the houses were higgledy-piggledy by chance, not arranged with deliberate casualness. Down near the river — the more upmarket part — were the 'town houses', small three-storey dwellings with one room on each floor. The rest were two storey. Most were timber-framed; a few were brick. Unlike its modern counterpart, seventeenth-century Shadwell was a place of work and a self-contained town. It even had its own water supply by the 1680s; a four-hose engine used to raise water from the Thames which was then piped to conduits on the estate. Among the houses were warehouses, sheds, ropeyards, anchorsmiths, timber yards, brew houses and blacksmiths.

Another St Paul's

A chapel dedicated to St Paul was built on the Highway (now known as Upper Shadwell) because all these newcomers could not be expected to tramp up to

Inn signs at Shadwell — many of which reflected the occupations of the local residents

Existing Inns		
The Brewer's Arms	The Three Mariners	The Boatswain
The Noah's Ark	The Frying Pan	The Five Bells
The Whalebone	The Trumpeter on Horseback	The Lighter
The Swan with Two Necks	The Gate	The Two Sawyers
	The Gilded Helmet	The Anchor

Stepney church, where there was no room for them anyway! Matthew Mead (see page 27) was duly appointed minister and then in 1666 St Paul's was accorded the status of a parish church. Outside the church stood the whipping post. In 1669 'Poor Katherine Williams, silk worker' was one who suffered punishment there.

By 1681 provisions for the locals were being provided by a fully functioning market building and fifty-five shops; some of these were 'corner shops' and chandlers; others were workshops.

There were also forty-four drinking establishments; most were simple tap rooms. Some, however, were great 'Christmas card' inns — like The Queen's Head Tavern which the Widow Craven ran at 23 Ratcliff Highway, with its two bars and six drinking rooms. There must have been a veritable forest of sign boards swinging in Shadwell on a windy night, many of them announcing the other occupations followed by the residents. Between two thousand and four thousand souls were squeezed into St Paul's patch — watermen, boat builders, lightermen, ships' carpenters and riggers, anchorsmiths, brewers and ropemakers; one of them was a Zouch, son of the Abraham whose memorial tablet is in Stepney church. They were humble folk, for the most part, with only about thirty households of any financial status.

Thomas Neale Esquire, Master of the Mint, was the developer who created Shadwell. He bought the land from the Dean and Chapter of St Paul's and had 289 houses built. He was also responsible for the erection of the chapel, the market and the waterworks.

Did you know that ...?

The mother of Thomas Jefferson, President of the United States, came from Shadwell.

Sir Walter Raleigh set sail for Guyana from Limehouse in 1546.

The Vintners and Dyers Companies share the privilege of keeping swans on the Thames, and mark the bills with two or one nicks, respectively.

Most of the country's lifeboats were built in one shipyard in Limehouse between 1852 and 1890.

In the 19th century it was Limehouse, not Soho, that housed the Chinese community and here Oscar Wilde's Dorian Gray came for opium.

The concrete caissons for the D-Day Mulberry Harbours were built in the old East India Import Dock, pumped dry in 1943.

The scandal of Lady Ivey

In Thomas Neale's day the most colourful local character must have been Lady Ivey. Neale was involved in a series of celebrated lawsuits with her, contesting the ownership of a good deal of land in Shadwell.

Lady Ivey was born the daughter of John Stepkin (a descendant of the Stepkin who built Wapping Wall), a wealthy brewer and owner of the Hermitage, as well as other property in the area. Famed for her wit and beauty, she had a stormy marriage and her first brush with the courts was a Chancery suit between her husband and father over her marriage settlement.

Stepkin, a doting father, had settled everything on his daughter and son-in-law, leaving himself only his house in Wapping and six hundred pounds a year. When the marriage fell apart he attempted to retrieve some of this property. Sir Thomas Ivey, it was claimed:

… by his harsh and crewell usage did force his wief from him, shee being driven into that feare and Exegensie as to run barefoot from him at Eleven of the clock at night.

Leaving her home in Charterhouse Square, Lady Ivey ran to her father's house which was next door to The Swan's Nest brewery at the Hermitage. How the gossip must have flown around among the lady's tenants in the tap rooms of The Five Bells and The Lighter and outside St Pauls on a Sunday morning.

Famous connections

Shadwell flourished and grew in the eighteenth century, but still retained its nautical air. Neale's waterworks were enlarged, a charity school was founded in 1712 and there were three chapels — Presbyterian, Calvinist and Wesleyan; Wesley himself preached on several occasions in the church. The Quaker influence in the area was strong. On a board in St Paul's the list of charitable donations and legacies includes an impressive number of sea captains. Captain Cook lived at Upper Shadwell when he was first married and his eldest child was baptized in the church there.

Not far from the church is Shakespeare Walk, named after some local worthy. Here, in 1720, was born to the Randolph family a baby daughter who was christened Jane in the old church. Her father, Isham Randolph, was a seaman of some status, a colonial agent from Virginia. Probably when Jane was still a child, the family moved permanently to Virginia and settled on a farm there, calling the estate 'Shadwell', with some nostalgia, perhaps, for their London home.

When Jane grew up she married and had eight children. Widowed at thirty-seven, she had a struggle to keep the family going but succeeded against the odds — and her son, Thomas Jefferson, became President of the United States.

A change for the worse

While Shadwell's most famous grandson was reaching the heights of power in the New World, his mother's home town was beginning to change character. No longer the 'nursery of navigation', Shadwell became more industrialized. Increasingly, locals and Irish immigrants were employed in the coal trade, the chief employers being the Charrington family. In 1796 the East India Company's salt-petre warehouse was built at Free Trade Wharf. William Perkin, the inventor of synthetic dye, lived and worked in the parish.

In 1792 there were about thirteen thousand dwellings in Shadwell, most of them housing artisans, 'mechanicks' and watermen: 'Their homes and workshops will not bear description,' wrote the topographer, Malcolm. In 1800 the London Dock Company bought the waterworks for fifty thousand pounds. With the extension of the London docks into the Shadwell basin in the mid-nineteenth century, the population fell dramatically as rows and rows of houses were demolished to make way for the great sheet of water.

Along with its neighbouring hamlet, Shadwell — Neale's new town with its waterworks and its market, its spa and its naval officers — sank and merged into the darkness of the Victorian dockland.

Ratcliff

'The accumulated scum of humanity gathered here,
washed, as it were, from somewhere else.'
Charles Dickens

Ratcliff, the hamlet to the east of Shadwell, some two and a half miles in circumference, was once the port of Stepney and most probably the place where the first Anglo Saxons landed and settled — but today it is no more. Ratcliff has vanished. Its name survives only in Ratcliff Cross Street, a reminder of the days when the stone cross in the market place was the focal point of East End life.

Here, once upon a busy time, sailors' wives set up their stalls and gathered for the exchange of gossip. There was buying and selling, telling of travellers' tales, busking and banter. When Jane Seymour's brother — who had ruled the country on behalf of his young nephew, Edward VI — was executed on Tower Hill in 1551, they sang a ballad about him down at Ratcliff Cross.

In 1664 a charter was obtained for the market at Ratcliff. The site is marked now by the strangely ornamented entrance of the underpass to the Isle of Dogs which gapes with a hideous open mouth at the east end of the Highway, once called the Ratcliff Highway. One of the churchwardens at Stepney church is still known as the Ratcliff Warden.

School House Lane and The Orchard

To find some remnants of old Ratcliff, walk a little way westwards along the Highway until you reach Free Trade Wharf. On the opposite side of the Highway are School House Lane and The Orchard. For several hundred years there was, indeed, a school in School House Lane, which was originally endowed — along with almshouses in 1536 — by a member of the Grocers' Company called Nicholas Gibson, left in trust with the Coopers' Company. In 1898 a young journalist from *The Daily Graphic* remarked upon the 'unassuming Georgian façade' of the Coopers Almshouses. Sadly, not a single trace remains of the almshouses now and the Coopers School has long since been moved out to Upminster.

The Orchard is a narrow alley, overhung with buddleia — a remainder of the garden where Gibson's widow, Avice, had 2,800 roses planted in the days of Protector Somerset. She remarried and was a second time widowed and then lived as Dame Knyvett in a fine house near the school. The bedesmen and bedeswomen from the almshouses were employed to tend her magnificent garden. In 1549 the gardeners were paid ninepence a day, which were good wages, strawberry pickers received fourpence a day and sixpence a day was laid out for 'making clear of the alleys and bearing away of rubbish.' A bowling alley was paved in the garden, at a cost of three shillings. In 1578 the 'poor people' of the Aspitall' were paid two shillings to 'plucke up the pump in the yard'.

Sea captains and ships

Edward III had ships built at Ratcliff to fight the French; later, the building of the ships was done mainly in Deptford and they were brought to Ratcliff for fitting. Ratcliff's heyday was the sixteenth century when Elizabethan sea dogs like Sir Hugh Willoughby and Martin Frobisher set off from here on their voyages of discovery. The talk at Ratcliff Cross was not all of high deeds of gallantry, however. The locals were out to make their fortune on the Spanish Main and hard cash was infinitely more important than glory. In 1592 a Ratcliff mariner aged forty-six years went before the examiners of the High Court of

Admiralty and gave an account of an expedition led by another Ratcliff man, George Basset. With letters of reprisal against Spain granted for six months, the privateer set off in *The Anna Belinda* with a crew of twenty-five to raid enemy ships. Near St Mary Island they boarded an ancient vessel and robbed it of twenty thousand 'dogge fish' worth two hundred pounds. One wonders who counted the fish! Soon afterwards they somehow ascertained that a Spanish fleet was in the area and sailed off to the west of Flores to warn Sir Thomas Howard. To cut a long sailor's yarn short, Howard ordered the crew to board his vessel and the two hundred pounds of dogge fish was lost. They also had to take twenty-five sick and wounded home and were promised compensation but received none.

By 1600 the population was something in the region of four thousand and Stow observed that the hamlet had been 'increased in building eastwards' and, where once there had been a elm-lined avenue going out towards Limehouse, there was now ribbon development. In 1620 the famous shipwright, Phineas Pett, was building two pinnaces, *The Mercury* and *The Spy*

there. He complained of 'night stealing' and embezzlement. Ratcliff was fast becoming a rough and dangerous place.

Tax lists from 1664 show that most of the hamlet was owned by the Mercers' and Coopers' Company. By now the hundred-year-old sugar factory and the East India Company, whose shipyards were at Blackwall, were the most significant large-scale employers.

The great fire of 1682

The Quaker, Thomas Scattergood, wrote an account of the great fire of 1682, which devastated the area. As he was returning home from Gravesend he saw:

> …a very great smoke arise towards London, which we found to be a fire. It broke out in a boat builder's shop adjoining the East India Company's warehouse and salt petre works …it was supposed that between four and five hundred houses were destroyed. It came very nearly up to the Ratcliff Meeting House [in School House Lane].

King Charles and Nell Gwynne both gave money to help the inhabitants get back on their feet.

Glass

Parallel to the Orchard and Schoolhouse Lane runs a narrow way called Glasshouse Fields. Walk up here to discover a small red brick building with a pitched roof:

T. W. IDE "THE RATCLIFF GLASSHOUSE"

Glass has been made on this site for at least three hundred years. Certainly there was a green glass works somewhere in Ratcliff at the time of James I, owned by Sir Robert Maunsell. In 1691 Bowels Crown Glass factory opened on the Ide's site for the manufacture of window glass. Between here and the City, two lads carrying a large sheet of glass packed into wooden cases was once a regular sight.

Bottle glass was made in nearby King David Lane in two seventeenth-century factories; one of them, aptly named Nelson and Company, was begun by a group of retired sea captains.

Fire fighting equipment from the time of the Great Fire of London in 1666 — which occurred sixteen years prior to the great fire in Ratcliff.

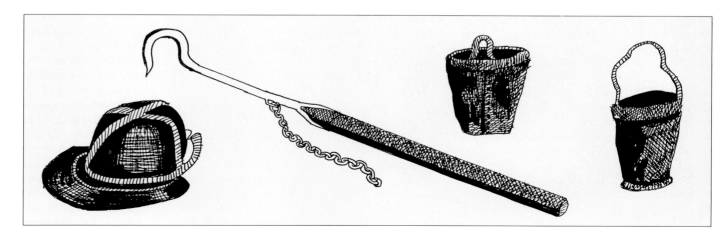

In 1794 a fire more terrible than that which had raged 112 years earlier consumed Ratcliff. Of its 1,150 houses, 455 were burnt down and 36 warehouses were destroyed; from School House Lane to Butcher Row not a single house was left standing.

Free Trade Wharf, which belonged to the East India Company, was rebuilt after the fire, and can still be seen, a solitary relic of the days when hangings were held in Sun Tavern Fields, to terrorize the populace of the lawless riverside.

The Ratcliff Highway Murders

Before the Jack the Ripper murders became the best known event in East End history, there were the Ratcliff Highway Murders.

A certain Mr Marr kept a lace warehouse at 29, Ratcliff Highway. On a December night in 1811 he sent his maid off to buy some oysters for supper whilst he shut up shop. The girl returned and rang the bell — again and again — but no-one answered. The constable was called and the door was finally broken open. Marr and his wife and baby and a shop boy were found dead — killed with a ripping chisel and maul. Twelve days later the landlord of The King's Arms, his wife and servant were discovered with fractured skulls and their throats cut. After forty false arrests, a man called Williams was arrested but hanged himself in prison. His body was paraded past the homes of his victims, raised high on a cart. The locals turned out in force to roar their rage, a stake was jabbed into his breast and the body was thrown into a pit dug at the corner of Cable Street and Cannon Street Road.

Between 1801 and 1861 the population of Ratcliff trebled, swollen by the arrival of poor Irish. In 1810 Commercial Road was built and cut the hamlet in half. The 'accumulated scum of humanity', wrote Dickens in *Our Mutual Friend*, 'gathered here, washed, as it were, from somewhere else'.

The Highway in 1900: a Sunday evening

Death and destruction

Fire

The narrow tortuous, overcrowded streets of London made it particularly vulnerable to fire and Ratcliff was not the only place to suffer repeated damage and destruction. The Roman trading centre beside the Thames was set alight by Boudicca and her tribesmen in AD 61. The original Saxon St Paul's Cathedral was destroyed in 961, restored — and burned again in 1087 while London Bridge was damaged in a widespread fire in 1135.

Rulings in the late twelfth century that the bottom sections of houses must be built with stone, not timber, and the that roofs should be tiled were largely ignored and fires still broke out repeatedly. Each ward had to provide its own fire-fighting equipment and long ladders were kept readily available outdoors during hot spells of weather.

In 1748 millions of pounds worth of damage was sutained in Ratcliff when a Dutch ketch transporting saltpetre burst into flames. The Custom House was wiped out in 1814 and the Royal Mint badly damaged in 1815. In 1841 the Grand Armoury at the Tower of London was destroyed and in June 1861 the entire southern waterfront of the Upper Pool caught alight in the Tooley Street fire which continued to smoulder until December. However, it was the Great Fire of 1666 and the 1940-41 Blitz which inflicted the greatest damage of all.

Victim of the Great Plague
collapses on a London street.

Plague

In Britain, 800,000 people died of the Black Death between 1347 and 1350. It reached London in September 1348 and was widespread by November, possibly killing over half the population. It recurred in 1665 as the bubonic form of the Great Plague. The onset of the symptoms were very sudden; high fever, swellings in the glands (called buboes — hence the name, bubonic), internal haemorrhages which caused bluish-black spots or purple patches (hence the term Black Death), a rose-coloured rash, agonizing thirst and delirium.

Many fled the city, including Charles II who took his court to Hampton Court, while watchmen stood guard over infected households who were locked inside behind their red-crossed doors for forty days. 40,000 dogs and 200,000 cats were destroyed by official exterminators paid tuppence for each body. This destruction of the cat population allowed the real culprits — the flea-carrying rats — to multiply.

The streets emptied, except for the swelling carcases of dogs, cats, horses and pigs, which burst in the unusually hot summer sun. 10,000 Londoners took up residence in boats moored on the Thames. Those who escaped to the countryside were likely to be stoned or pelted with manure.

Those quacks who survived thrived, selling potions of pepper, urine and salt. Posies of herbs and spices, as well as smoking tobacco, were seen as preventative measures, while doctors let blood with leeches and prescribed medicines made of powdered bones, blood, tree bark, toads and snakes.

Executions

Execution Dock, between Wapping New Stairs and King Edward's Stairs, was the riverside setting for the hanging of pirates (see pages 78-79) but the condemned perpetrators of other crimes could be put to death at the scene of the crime or taken by cart to proper places of execution such as at Tyburn or Smithfield. Stow describes seeing gallows set up on the pavement outside his house in Aldgate.

There were gallows at Tower Hill and on the marshes on both sides of the river. By the nineteenth century some two hundred offences carried the death penalty. Over three hundred people were put to death on Tower Hill, the last being Jacobite Lord Lovat, executed in 1747, at which time a spectators' stand collapsed and a dozen of the watchers were themselves killed.

Hangmen were hired by the City of London sheriffs. One hangman, Derrick (after whose gallows the derrick crane is named) was himself sentenced to death. He was reprieved by the Earl of Essex whom he later beheaded.

The new drop gallows was introduced at Newgate and in 1864 five pirates were hanged side by side. Burnings generally took place at Smithfield.

Public executions — of whatever form — always attracted large crowds and when a man selling pies fell over in a crowd of 40,000 in 1807, the ensuing chaos and panic left nearly one hundred spectators dead or dying. Many, including Dickens, objected to the horror of such public spectacles and from 1868 executions were confined behind prison walls.

St Anne's, Limehouse, is one of the tallest churches in England.

Limehouse

'Send me my nightgown, my bible and my lute.'

Plea to a wife in Limehouse
from Newgate Jail

Dickens, as has already been discovered, was more closely associated with the next place east, Limehouse. His godfather, Christopher Huffam, a rigger in William IV's navy, lived in a house in Church Row and worked in a yard in Narrow Street.

Church Row is still there, renamed Newell Street, looking much as it must have done in Dickens' day, a row of pretty, little, narrow stuccoed houses flanking the high mossy gate-posts which mark the entrance to the churchyard. Limehouse, unlike Ratcliff, still has a heart, and here it is — the great white Hawksmoor church, like a fortress with crenellated turrets. It stands back from the clamour of the Commercial Road in its park, rather like a startled horse, they say. Completed in 1724 and consecrated six years later, it is one of the tallest churches in the country and before it was dwarfed by the tower of Canary Wharf and the other glittery monsters of new Docklands, St Anne stood head and shoulders above everything around. It was one of fifty London churches planned under the Act of 1711, of which only seventeen were built, to be paid for by a coal tax on the Thames.

The churchyard is three acres full of trees and dominated by a strange conical pyramid of a tomb. In the spring there are pools of purple crocuses and forsythia bushes scatter gold among the headstones which have been uprooted and stacked up like rows of teeth. The long-dead inhabitants of Limestone — seamen and ship builders, lightermen, watermen, ship's surgeons and the rest — were removed from their resting place and pushed up together, three or four deep by the churchyard walls in 1887 by the Metropolitan Public Gardens Association.

Docks, pubs and limekilns

In Three Colts Lane, which runs down beside the church towards the river, is a reminder of Limehouse's docking days. The Five Bells and Bladebone: at 2.30 pm

The Grapes Inn, Limehouse, where characters from Dickens' Our Mutual Friend went to drink at 'the bar to soften the human breast'. Limehouse is also famous for its 'blues', its declaration and its shipping and marine associations.

Scenes of busy activity down at the docks by Gustave Doré. Above is Limehouse Dock, *left* Porters at Work *and on the far left* Warehouses by the Thames.

Handling a cargo of wool on South West India Dock in 1937.

five bells used to be rung in the docks to announce closing time. The pub is decked with lanterns outside, looking like a proper old inn, and inside is dark, with polished wood and ships in bottles.

By the Limehouse riverside runs Narrow Street, and strung along it, overlooking the Thames, are a row of fine eighteenth-century houses; Jerome K Jerome lived here in the 1860s and because of this rare survival of elegant, old 'river view' properties, Narrow Street was the first part of the East End to attract gentrification, long before there was any bright new Docklands. Among the houses is one of the most authentic feeling riverside pubs, The Grapes. Some say that The Six Jolly Fellowship Porters from *Our Mutual Friend*, was based on The Grapes with its 'bar to soften the human breast'.

Limehouse probably started life as a fishing settlement in the little cove at the angle of the Thames later called Limehouse Hole. The name first appears in 1367 as *le Lymhostes*, or limeoasts — kilns where chalk from Kent was burnt to make lime for London buildings. In 1397 one Peter atte Hacche owened two kilns. The original kilns may have stood where Lime Kiln Wharf is now.

The limbs of Limehouse

By Shakespeare's day the area was staring to change character; there is a reference in *Henry VIII* to mariners as the 'limbs of Limehouse'.

The sleepy fishing hamlet of Stepney parish, with a few cottages and smoking lime kilns, like its neighbours, was becoming a maritime suburb, a place of ship building and seafaring. Sir Walter Raleigh's half-brother, Sir Humphrey Gilber, lived there in the 1570s and it was from Limehouse in 1596 that Raleigh himself set sail for Guyana.

The first ship to be built and launched in Limehouse was *The Greyhound* which was built in 1586.

The 'limbs of Limehouse', like their fellows in the rest of Stepney parish, were a radical crew, politically — in their religious views. Edward Underhill, the Hot Gospeller of Limehouse, was put into Newgate jail in Bloody Mary's day for writing a ballad which attacked the Queen. He wrote from prison appealing to his wife in Limehouse for the necessary comforts: 'Send me my night gown, my Bible and my Lute.'

A countryfield sort of place

At the opening of the eighteenth century, as the 1703 Gascoyne map shows, Limehouse was still an open countyfield sort of place. There were just two streets — Limehouse, which ran along the river, and Three Colts Lane which led inland, up towards where the church now stands. There were rope walks, gardens and fields, and a shipyard or two.

Within thirty years the hamlet had grown enough to break away from Stepney and have its own church. The new parish absorbed part of Ratcliff and was bounded by Mile End New Town on the north and Poplar to the east.

When the houses in Narrow Street were built at the end of the eighteenth century there were only about nine hundred houses and one hundred and fifty acres of land not covered by building: there were ten market gardens and the rest was pasture given over to dairy farming. There were three ship-repair yards and one saw mill. A Mrs Turner ran a sail-cloth factory and a Mr Hall manufactured potash.

Limehouse Cut, a canal connecting the Lea at Bromley with the Thames, was opened in 1781. There were two charity schools for Limehouse children and the few charitable trusts kept the poor and indigent of the parish quite decently, with reasonable outrelief and places in almshouses.

How different it would all have become in a hundred years' time.

A walk around Limehouse

Limehouse is an interesting place to take a stroll: there are old churches, Georgian houses, riverside warehouse conversions and the remnants of Limehouse Chinatown.

Walking towards the Thames along Limehouse Causeway, you will pass Dunbar Wharf. A row of Georgian houses, including The Grapes and Booty's Wine Bar are found on Narrow Street. Limehouse Basin is on the right, and Hough's, a Victorian paper board mill, rises beyond.

Turn right now into Shoulder of Mutton Lane. Then turn right and left into Oak Lane. There are more Georgian houses in Newell Street on the left.

If you turn right into St Anne's Passage, you will be able to see Hawksmoor's beautiful St Anne's church.

At the top of the street and across Commercial Road, you will find what little remains of the old Limehouse Chinatown and can eat at The Good Friends restaurant in Salmon Lane which lies immediately ahead.

Turn right to see some old houses to the east. Continue into East India Dock Road, cross over to the north side and go up Saracen Street where there are more Chinese restaurants in Canton, Pekin and Nankin Streets.

1877: cargo of tea is unloaded by Chinese sailors in the East India Docks.

The Chinese Arrive

With the new century came the opening of the West India Docks in adjoining Poplar and the arrival of the massive Commercial Road, which opened as a wagon road for heavy traffic. Then, in the 1820s, the Regent's canal was carved out of the west side of Limehouse, curving its route around London on its way to the Midlands. Finally came the railway — the London to Blackwall Line.

The activities of the port of London brought the Chinese to Limehouse and, not so long ago, the streets were busy with small oriental figures, all in black with pigtails and little black hats. All that is left now to remind us of the steaming laundries and the opium dens which brought relief to the desperate, are the famous Chinese restaurants — The Old Friends and The New Friends.

Joseph Conrad

There used to be a pub where the West India Dock Road meets the East India Dock Road. It was called The Eastern Hotel, an old fashioned weatherboard place. In Joseph Conrad's *Chance* there is a description of the people which Conrad's sea captain saw when he was lodging there.

> The inhabitants of the end of town where
> life goes on unadorned by grace or
> spendour...passed us in their shabby
> garments, with sallow faces, haggard,
> anxious or weary, or simply without
> expression, in an unsmiling sombre stream
> not made up of lives but of mere
> unconsidered existences whose joys,
> struggles, thoughts, sorrows and their
> very hopes were miserable, glamourless,
> and of no account.

Rhyming Cockney slang

True Cockneys are born within the sound of Bow Bells, those that peal out from St Mary le Bow in Cheapside but Cockney rhyming slang and the sense of humour from which it is derived are both part of London's heritage, beyond the confines of that once-a-curfew bell.

The word Cockney actually comes from the Middle English word *cokeney* meaning a mishapen egg — a cock's egg — which in the seventeenth century had become a general bantering term applied to Londoners, their accent and their slang — of which some examples follow. It is a language that mutates and grows to accommodate new situations. While abbreviated forms (such as *apples* for *apples and pears* meaning 'stairs') are often used, thereby losing the rhyming element and making the meanings harder to fathom for the uninitiated, some of these terms have become commonplace.

Listen to the banter of the barrow boys in East End markets, the taxi-driver's quips, the sharp exchanges of wit by locals in their 'local' and perhaps you might gain an understanding of the pertinent rhymes and underlying humour.

Adam and Eve	believe
airs and graces	braces
alligator	later
almond rocks	socks
Andy Cain	rain
apple fritter	bitter (beer)
apples and pears	stairs
April showers	flowers
Aristotle	bottle
army and navy	gravy
Artful Dodger	lodger
Aunty Nellie	belly

baa lamb	tram
bacon and eggs	legs
ball of chalk	walk
Band of Hope	soap
bat and wicket	ticket
Bath bun	son/sun
Beecham's Pill	bill
bees and honey	money
bird lime	time
biscuits and cheese	knees

boat race	face
Bo-Peep	sleep
bottle and glass	arse
bottle of sauce	horse
bread and cheese	sneeze
bricks and mortar	daughter
Bristol Cities	titties
Brussel sprouts	scouts
bucket and pail	jail
bushel and peck	neck
butcher's hook	look
	'take a butcher's'

Cain and Abel	table
Cape of Good Hope	soap
Captain Cook	book
carving knife	wife
cash and carried	married
cat and mouse	house
china plate	mate
cobbler's awls	balls (testicles)
	'a load of cobblers'
coals and coke	broke

cock linnet	minute
cock sparrow	barrow
cocoa	say so
	'I should cocoa'
crust of bread	head
currant bun	sun
cut and carried	married

daft and barmy	army
daisy roots	boots
Darby Kelly	belly
Dickery Dock	clock
Dicky Dirt	shirt
Ding dong	song
dog and bone	phone
Donald Duck	luck
Duchess of Fife	wife
	'me ole Dutch'
dustbin lids	kids

early doors	drawers (pair of)
early hours	flowers
earwig	twig (understand)

eighteen pence	sense
elephant's trunk	drunk
Errol Flynn	chin
Fanny Craddock	haddock
feather and flip	kip (sleep)
field of wheat	street
fife and drum	bum
fine and dandy	brandy
fisherman's daughter	water
flowery dell	cell
fly-be-nights	tights
four by two	Jew
frog and toad	road

garden gate	magistrate
gates of Rome	home
gay and frisky	whisky
German bands	hands
Ginger beer	queer
Glasgow Rangers	strangers
God forbids	kids
greengages/Rock of Ages	wages
Gregory Peck	neck

ham and eggs	legs
Hampstead Heath	teeth
Hampton wick	prick (penis)
	'on me wick'
Hearts of Oak	broke
Holy friar	liar
Holy Ghost	toast
How d'you do	shoe
in the nude	food
insects and ants	pants
Irish jig	wig
iron tank	bank
Isle of Wight	right
I suppose	nose
Jack and Jill	hill /bill (cash)
Jack Jones	alone
	'on his jack'
Jack Tar	bar
Jack the Dandy	brandy
Jack the Ripper	kipper
jam jar	car
jam tart	heart
Jim Skinner	dinner
Jimmy Riddle	piddle
Joanna	piano
Johnnie Horner	corner
jumping jack	back
Kate and Sidney	steak and kidney
kingdom come	bum
King Lear	ear
Lah-di-dah	car /star
Lady Godiva	fiver

Lilian Gish	fish
linen draper	paper
lion's lair	chair
loaf of bread	head
	'use yer loaf'
lollipop	shop
longers and lingers	fingers
loop the loop	soup
Lucy Locket	pocket
macaroni	pony
Mary Rose	toes
Mickey Mouse	house (theatre)
mince pies	eyes
Molly Malone	phone
monkeys' tails	nails
Mother Hubbard	cupboard
mother of pearl	girl
mother's ruin	gin
Mozart and Liszt	pissed (drunk)
Mutt and Jeff	deaf
mutter and stutter	butter
nanny goat	boat /coat /tote
Ned Kelly	telly
near and far	bar /car
needle and pin	gin
Noah's Ark	park
north and south	mouth
Oedipus Rex	sex
oily rag	fag
old pot and pan	old man (husband)
Oliver Twist	fist
one and t'other	brother
on the floor	poor

orchestra stalls	balls
Oxford scholar	dollar
Oxo cube	tube (the Underground)
peas in the pot	hot
	'a bit peasy, ain't it?'
Peckham Rye	tie
pen and ink	stink
pig's ear	beer
pimple and blotch	Scotch (whisky)
pipe your eye	cry
pitch and toss	boss
plates and dishes	missus
plates of meat	feet
pleasure and pain	rain
potatoes in the mould	cold
	'a bit 'taters'
pots and dishes	wishes
Quaker oat	coat
rabbit and pork	talk
	'she don't 'arf rabbit on'
rats and mice	dice
read and write	fight
Robin Hood	good
Rosy Lee	tea
round the houses	trousers
rub-a-dub-dub	pub
salmon and trout	stout (beer)
saucepan lid	quid
sausage and mash	cash /crash
Scapa Flow	go (get out of here)
	'we'd better scapa'
Scotch pegs	eggs /legs
Sexton Blake	cake

skin amd blister	sister
sky rocket	pocket
sorry and sad	bad
stammer and stutter	butter
stand at ease	cheese
sticky toffee	coffee
stop thief	beef
tea leaf	thief
teapot lid	kid
tea, two and a bloater	motor
tiddly wink	drink
	'a bit tiddly'
tin tank	bank
tit for tat	hat
	'a new titfer'
tit willow	pillow
Tod Sloan	on own (alone)
	'on his tod'
Tom and Dick	sick
Tom Thumb	rum
Tommy Tucker	supper
trouble and strife	wife
trunks of trees	knees
turtle doves	gloves
Uncle Bert	shirt
Uncle Fred	bed
Uncle Ned	bed /head
Uncle Willy	silly
weeping willow	pillow
weasel and stoat	coat
whistle and flute	suit
you and me	tea

BETHNAL GREEN, SPITALFIELDS AND MILE END NEW TOWN

If it weren't for the weaving, what should we do?

A place of damask, velvet and silk brocade; of merchants, master weavers, retailers and dyers; as well as the poor and the working weavers

Had you taken a stroll round the area of Petticoat Lane in the days of tricorn hats and buckled shoes, when the Corps of Mile End Volunteers were preached into action against the 'Bloody Monster' of Revolutionary France by their chaplain in Stepney church, you would have heard then the clackety clack of looms on all sides. Sedan chairs, bearing patched and powdered ladies, would have carried their charges to visit their favourite weavers. There they would have ordered dress lengths of brocade or figured silk, while birds sang from their ornamental cages in many of the windows — for the Huguenot weavers were famous for their singing birds as well as for their weaving. Two hundred years ago this was a prosperous part of town which drew custom from all over the country.

Twelve to fifteen thousand looms were kept busy when the silk industry was at its peak here; and the work force was something in the region of thirty thousand. The three hamlets which were strung along the north of Whitechapel and Mile End Old Town — between Bishopsgate and Shoreditch High Street on the west and Globe Road on the east — had their heyday in the late seventeenth and eighteenth centuries. Spitalfields, a hamlet of Whitechapel, is best known as 'weaver town', while Mile End New Town, a hamlet of Stepney, was built especially to accommodate the weavers; it no longer exists, being divided between Spitalfields and Bethnal Green. Bethnal Green probably had more looms and certainly more inhabitants than its two neighbours and was the oldest of the three hamlets by about five hundred years.

Spitalfields in 1814 and as it is today

Bethnal Green

'I began visiting those of our Society who lived in Bethnal Green.
Many of these I found in such poverty as few
can conceive without seeing it.'

John Wesley 1777

The earliest reference to Bethnal Green is an eighth-century deed: Mathilda le Vayre of Stebonhethe made a grant of the courtyard next to her house in Blithehall in St Dunstan's parish. Some say the name Blithehall means Happy Nook, which would have struck the nineteenth-century inhabitants of this, by then most dire of slums, as most ironic. More than likely it means nothing of the sort but is derived from the Saxon name *Blida*.

The settlement was probably originally Roman, perhaps ribbon development along the road to the ford over the Lea, following the course of Bethnal Green Road and Roman Road. Certainly, when the Underground station was built in 1939 traces of a Roman road were discovered.

The medieval hamlet which grew on the site of Blida's farm was a sleepy sort of place with no direct route into the City. There may have been a great house or two, with cottages for the folk who serviced the nearby Bishop's manor house. The Green was the heart of the village which centred on the area where the museum and Victoria Park Square can now be found.

The Blind Beggar

Legend has it that in the thirteenth century Simon de Montford's son and heir, Henry, had a mansion here. Montford House, a red-brick block topped with a touch of crenellation, stands now on the north side of Victoria Park Square.

The story of de Montford, the Blind Beggar of Bethnal Green, was recounted in Tudor times and given great vogue by Percy's *Reliques of Ancient English Poetry* which was published in 1765. The story was evidently taken seriously enough to suggest that it may have had some foundation in truth.

Henry, believed to have fallen at the battle of Evesham in 1265, was — so the tale goes — found blinded and dressed as a beggar by a baron's daughter. She nursed him back to health. In time they were married and produced a beautiful daughter, 'pretty Besse' (Bessie). There is even, in fact, a Besse Street to commemorate her, running off Roman Road down by the London Buddhist Centre.

When Bessie grew up she was courted by four suitors at once — a knight, a gentleman of fortune, a London merchant and the son of a Romford innkeeper's daughter. All except the knight lost interest when they were told that they must seek the consent of her father, the poor blind beggar of Bethnal Green.

My father, shee said, is soone to be seene
The siely, blind beggare of Bednall-green,
That daylye sits begging for charitie,
He is the good father of pretty Besse.
His marks and his tokens are knowen very well;
He always is led with a dogg and a bell:
A seely old man, God Knoweth, is he,
Yet hee is the father of pretty Besse.

The knight duly went and asked the beggar's leave to marry his pretty daughter and Henry gave the couple a dowry of three thousand pounds and one hundred pounds for Bessie's wedding dress — an astronomical sum in the thirteenth century.

Elizabethan times

Elizabethan Bethnal Green was a fine place with at least three substantial properties. The Blind Beggar's old mansion was still there, or at least part of it. Nettleswell House was built in 1553. It can still be seen today, just next to the museum in Old Ford Road, although it does not much resemble its original form, having been much restored in 1705 and 1862. Meanwhile, John Kirby, a wealthy merchant, created for himself a flamboyant *nouveau-riche* residence in the

1570s; mocked (as such houses often were) by the locals, it acquired the nickname 'Kirby's Castle' but later was called Bednall House. The site, on the south side of Roman Road at the junction with Cambridge Heath Road, is now a vast complex of flats built in 1925. Remnants of a Tudor well were found in the garden of 18 Victoria Park Square.

Rubens, Ryder and Pepys

When Rubens was in England from 1629 to 1630 he stayed with Sir Balthazar Gerbier — using Gerbier's wife and children as models for some of his paintings. Gerbier had a house in Bethnal Green so here, undoubtedly, Rubens came to stay.

In 1649 Gerbier opened an academy by the Green; military discipline, architecture and elocution were taught there and the establishment was patronized by young men of fashion and learning.

Sir William Ryder, a friend of Samuel Pepys, lived on the very spot that the Montford mansion had occupied — or so Samuel Pepys believed. His diary entry for 26 June 1663 reads:

> By coach to Bednall-green to Sir W. Ryder's to dinner. A fine merry walk with the ladies alone after dinner in the garden; the greatest quantity of strawberries I ever saw, and good. This very house was built by the Blind Beggar of Bednall-green, so much talked of and sang in ballads; but they say it was only some of the outhouses of it.

The strange tale of Henry de Montfort seems to have caught on and by 1690 the badge of the Blind Beggar was used as a decoration for the beadle's staff. In the following century the Bethnal Green inn signs all showed the Blind Beggar and even the private mad house, which Kirby's Castle became in 1727, was called the Blind Beggar's House.

'There's a good deal of talkee yet to be done, sir,' a sensible drayman said to us … 'before they teach English workmen that there's sin and wickedness in a pint of honest beer.' Gustave Doré 1872.

The eighteenth century

Now the spacious genteel suburban village began a radical character change with a huge influx of weavers. Gentry still lived by the Green; one wealthy man had part of the stone arch of the old gate at Aldgate built on as the façade of his house in what is now Victoria Park Square. The French silk workers who had begun to arrive in Elizabeth's reign had established a flourishing industry which attracted weavers from all over the country. Bethnal Green initially took the overspill from Spitalfields and Mile End New Town and came to house as many, if not more, weavers. On a chill December morning in 1768 two of them, guilty of rioting and machine breaking, John Doyle (of Irish origins) and John Valline (of French) were executed at the crossroads by The Salmon and Ball pub.

The North side of Victoria Park Square was called Jews Walk. Some hundred or so years ago after the great Huguenot immigration Jews came to Bethnal Green from Spain, Portugal and the Netherlands. Similar to the fraternity in Goodman's Fields and unlike nineteenth-century East End Jews, they were not desperately poor folk scraping an income together from whatever source they could. By and large, they were successful merchants and traders although there were poor men among them — as is evident from Hogarth's cartoons of swarthy long-haired pedlars, sporting great wide-brimmed hats. One of the community was the celebrated boxer, Daniel Mendoza (see page 52). He took a house in Bethnal Green; a blue plaque marks the spot in Paradise Row.

There are still some remnants of the eighteenth century in these parts; numbers 17, 19 and 21 Old Ford Road, built by Anthony Natt in 1753, are still there as are the houses at 17 and 18 Victoria Park Square, built at the beginning of the century — though the latter have been much restored and have an Edwardian appearance. The weavers' church stands still, tucked

The chimney sweep who became the Mayor of Bethnal Green: The local paper reported in November 1931 'Councillor Tim Brooks . . . intends to clean chimneys during his mayoral year'.

The pomp and ceremony of religion offered a welcome contrast to the drabness and drudgery of everyday toil.

away in a green corner, but that was rebuilt in the mid-nineteenth century, when Bethnal Green was the one of the most overcrowded slum areas in the capital.

The change in that hundred years was perhaps more marked here than in any other of the East End villages. when St Matthews was first built its catchment area was populous and industrial but, of its seven hundred or so acres, 190 were still arable and there was 140 acres of market garden. When the mail coach stopped at the Cambridge Heath Turnpike and thundered off up Hackney Road to Cambridge, in no time at all it was passing open fields and woodland.

Before leaving this pleasant spot and turning the attention, fleetingly, to the dark days, take a look into the house of a local brewer, by means of his probate inventory, dated 1754. All his brewing equipment was in a 'shop' on the ground floor and in his stable was a 'lame gelding'. He lived upstairs, where the men compiling the inventory noted:

> an alarm clock in a walnut case
> an old velvet cap
> two wigs
> an old morning gown.

The list of debts owing to his estate gives some notion of the extent of the custom and the names of some of the the East End's eighteenth-century 'boozers'. Most money was owed to him from the Whitechapel glass house; other creditors were:

> a school master from Southwark
> Mr Keene — the organist of Whitechapel church
> the Chamberlain of the Fleet Prison
> a Spitalfields weaver or two.

Grim times

Between 1790 and 1795 there was a 'great increase' in the number of houses and the population had grown to an astonishing 74,988 by the turn of the century. An influx of Irish and English country folk brought the total to 129,680 in the following hundred years. Living conditions were appalling and infant mortality rose to unknown heights. The Gibraltar Row Cemetery, opened to accomodate the increasing number of corpses, was filled with tiny coffins. Water was supplied to the serried ranks of cramped, look-alike urban cottages 'thrice weekly and for two hours at a time and at low pressure'. The weaving cottage industry had all but collapsed by now and the inhabitants trooped off to the numerous factories which mushroomed up all around. Many of them worked in the furniture industry.

Help was at hand. An old wool store in Three Colts Lane became the Salvation Army's 'dingy cradle' and the Oxford House and St Margaret's House were opened as centres for the fortunate to help the less fortunate. In 1857 they built a museum to bring a beam of cultural light into the desperate bleakness. Everywhere they put up churches, great grim edifices; they were never filled.

Religion and asylum

For some religion was an escape and a comfort. The Oxford Movement brought back the gentle saints, candles, incense, lace, gilded vestments and all the glowing trappings of Anglo Catholicism banished from the East End long ago in the days when Nettleswell House was built. If you go to St Matthew's for the patronal festival on 21 September you can see it still. Dancing priests, bobbing swiftly in twinkling gold, their heads aslant, their faces in stained-glass-saint mode, lead a procession following a fan-shaped reliquary — a sort of ecclesiastical conga. It is a full house and a poor one. Mums with babies and toddlers and Dads, even, in cheap anoraks, all know their 'Hail Maries' and sit, spellbound, in a haze of swirling incense and tinkling bells. Better this than four enclosing walls in a tower block; better this than a dank back kitchen with babies dying and water coming slowly three times a week.

John Kirby's crumbling old mansion still housed lunatics on the Green. In 1841 the asylum had 587 occupants, of which forty-five were staff. The inmates included sailors, cabinet makers, an upholsterer, a druggist, a milkman, a lawyer, a tailor, a draper and a number of lunatics whose occupation was not known. Or so the census enumerator was informed. In 1843 they pulled it down and built anew; local lunatics were confined there until 1920 when the asylum was moved to Salisbury. During the First World War German shops were looted and their owners were put in the mad house on the Green.

The story continues ...

In the twenties and thirties there was some energetic slum clearance and new blocks of flats were put up, like that which occupies the site of Kirby's Castle. In the Second World War 2,233 houses were completely destroyed and at the end of the war the population had dropped to less than half its 1901 total. What with post-war rehousing in the new towns of Essex, by 1964 there were only 46,420 people living in Bethnal Green and these days there is even an air of gentrification creeping in.

The Blind Beggar is not forgotten. The Mayor of Tower Hamlets sports on his magnificent badge an enamel representation of Henry de Montfort and his daughter, Besse. In fact, the Blind Beggar became more famous in this century than he had ever been before when the pub named after him in the Mile End Road was scene of a notorious gang murder. In 1966 George Cornell of the Richardson gang was shot there by one of the Kray twins.

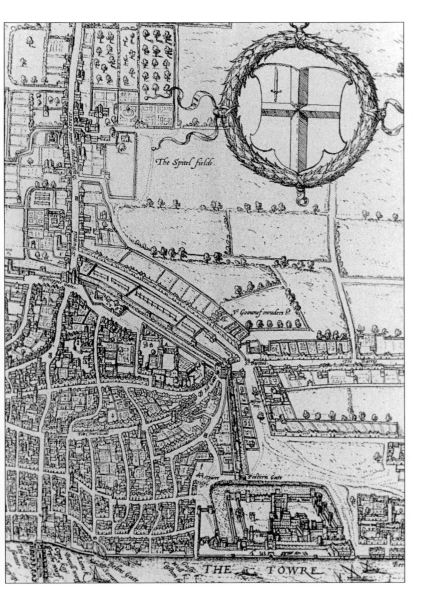

Map of the Spital fields that were set to the east of the medieval hospital and priory of St Mary Spital.

Spitalfields and Mile End New Town

In Henry VIII's day ... you would have been able to hear the thunderous blasts of canon from the fields, here where the gunners from the Tower practised their skills.

Spitalfields is probably the only part of the East End which has some nostalgic magic about it for the generality. Perhaps this is because elegant houses from the good silken days still survive in Fournier Street, Princelet Street and Wilkes Street — and some have been restored to their former splendour, a rarity for London's backyard. In Artillery Lane, still a narrow shop-filled passage with a good old feel about it, there are eighteenth-century shop fronts.

Perhaps it is because of the Huguenot immigrants who came here, some of whom were much richer than the usual refugees who have made the East End their home for hundreds of years. They came, many of them, with money and status and a trade.

Perhaps it is because the area still vibrates and chatters with colourful life, with its busy markets and Indian shops and its knots of strangely dressed people on street corners.

Medieval Spitalfields

To start at the beginning. Once upon a medieval time, as we have seen, there was the hospital of St Mary Spital, standing a little way outside the Bishop's gate, its lands stretching back over the area where the remnants of Spitalfields Market now are. In 1399 the environs were called 'Spittlepond'; its ancient name was 'Lolesworth'. There was open ground where teazles grew, where once had been a Roman cemetery.

The tiny Liberty of Norton Folgate, remembered in Folgate Street, adjoined the hospital and that was an unruly urban patch when Chaucer was around. For the rest of the area to the east of the great road, where these days on a Sunday Petticoat Lane market spangles the streets, there were fields. Middlesex Street was called Hog Lane then and pigs were driven up and down from Whitechapel.

Norton Folgate was an area of just 8.37 acres which, by some accident of history, had aquired autonomy. It was free of the parish, looked after its own poor and had its own manor court to deal with petty crime and local regulations. In the fifteenth century this area — like St Katharine's, free of the restrictions of City and parish — was attracting foreigners, some of them of an undesirable nature. Records of the manor court survive from the fifteenth century to bear witness to the Liberty's rough reputation.

*A bird fair
in the East End.*

*A deal is proffered at
Petticoat Lane market
in 1930.*

Keeping the courts busy

In June 1459, for instance, the court sat — presided over by William Brewster, Canon Residentiary of St Pauls Cathedral. John Herryson, barber, and his wife Alice were bound over to keep the peace for various acts of violence towards their neighbours. They had pelted Robert Patynson with stones, attacked Henry Cordewaner with daggers, drawn blood from William Gerard 'galoche maker', broken John Hanybone's windows (*fenestr et latyses*) and knifed Peter Standefast.

Like the Abbot of Tower Hill, over in East Smithfield, the officials of Norton Folgate had trouble trying to suppress the troublesome game of cloysh (see page 60) and the gambling which went with it. At the same session that the wild barber and his wife were bound over, one Herman Yonker, presumably one of the many local 'Dutchmen' (this term covered Germans and Flemings), was prosecuted for running a cloysh alley and allowing Sunday betting and 'affrays' in his yard. He and one Henry Galochmaker also sold beer illegally, as did a whole list of others.

In June 1466 one John Palmer was brought before the court for serving a false measure of beer 'vocat [called] a pynt'. He shouted out in a loud voice proclaiming his innocence. Today, opposite Liverpool Street station, it is possible to take a pint in Dirty Dick's, the famous old pub named after an eccentric nineteenth-century warehouseman, Richard Bentley — and there reflect on what happened just down the road some five hundred years before.

A stone's throw from Dirty Dick's are Artillery Lane and Artillery Passage. In Henry VIII's time, on a Tuesday afternoon you would have been able to hear the thunderous blasts of canon from the fields here where the gunners from the Tower practised their skills. When Shakespeare walked up Bishopsgate to the theatres in Shoreditch from his lodgings in St

William Hogarth's Prentices at their Looms *shows a typical 18th-century Spitalfields workshop with the silk weavers busy working the enormous looms.*

Helen's in the 1590s, he would have passed on his right the new Spitalfields development — the monastery conversion. Farther east there was no building yet, just the brick field from which Brick Lane acquired its name. Within a hundred years, however, the scene would be very different, rows of houses and workshops, full of foreigners, the French weavers for which the area became renowned.

Weaving silk

Silk weaving had reached a high standard in France, centred on Lyons and Tours. Most of the operatives were Protestants and when the turmoils of the Reformation made them exiles, great numbers of them came to England. However, it would be a mistake to think that there was no silk weaving in the East End before the seventeenth century. There was an indigenous industry in Whitechapel and Aldgate and the local parish register entries show that certainly by the end of the sixteenth century it was flourishing, stimulated, no doubt, by the influx of religious exiles following the Massacre of St Bartholomew in 1572 and the sack of Antwerp in 1585. The Aldgate parish records for the 1590s are more informative than those for the adjoining parishes of Whitechapel and Bishopsgate, and provide the occupations of many of the inhabitants.

Smallpox

On 29 December 1594 they buried Elidal Tolly, son of Edward, silk weaver of White Bear Alley in St Botolph's churchyard and the next day David Inglishe, silk twister of Jennings Rents. Both had died of smallpox. Next month a weaver from Pond Alley was laid to rest and the stillborn son of Thomas Pearce, silk weaver of Ship Alley off the Minories. In March, William Duke, 'stranger silk weaver' of White Bear Alley died and in April the baby daughter of Edward Graye, silk weaver

This engraving from 1749 shows the feeding of the silk worms with their diet of mulberry leaves.

of Shoreditch, and Agnes, the wife of Thomas Clarke, silk weaver of Mr Gaskins Rent at the — rather apt — sign of The Flower de Luce in Houndsditch.

Arrival of the Huguenots

The area adjoining St Botolph Bishopsgate was known as Petty France, an indication that there was already a foreign colony established. Shakespeare himself lodged with a Huguenot family, the Mountjoys, in the City. By 1629 the industry was sufficiently established for an incorporation of silk weavers to be formed in Spitalfields. Strype Street is a reminder that the historian Strype was born in the area in 1643, the son of Jan Van Stryp from Brabant, one of the early Huguenot textile immigrants.

But it was in the last year of Charles II's reign, 1685, when the French government revoked the Edict of Nantes which had allowed toleration for the Protestants, that the great immigration happened. Fifteen thousand Huguenots settled in London alone. They came from all walks of life but most had established skills; there were clock and instrument makers who congregated in Clerkenwell but the vast majority were in the textile business and joined the earlier immigrant group in the northern part of Whitechapel parish where already the looms were on the go.

In the last years of the century Spitalfields became 'all town' and continued to grow well into the next. Substantial three- and four-storey houses sprang up to house the cottage industry. The families and servants lived on the lower floors and the workshop was usually on the third. The area became world famous for its figured silk and brocade.

Fashion and the silk industry

The flood of Hugueunot refugees in the seventeenth century introduced their special skills and gave extra impetus to a silk industry that existed already in the area. The government encouraged this industry and helped protect it by prohibiting the importation of French silk.

Silk stockings came into fashion in Elizabethan times and were considered degenerate by author Philip Stubbes who argued in 1583 that the English, and particularly Londoners, were 'corrupt, wicked and perverse' in their 'sundrie abuses in Apparell'.

Servants and apprentices were banned from dressing too finely in 1464 and then, in 1582, the Lord Mayor of London and Common Council ordered that 'from henceforth no Apprentice whatsoever should presume to wear any Apparel but what he receives from his Master'.

Puritans regarded bright colours as frivolous but after the Restoration extravagant styles replaced plain ones. Men wore elaborate waistcoats and women light, clinging low-cut gowns.

Many of the silk merchants and master weavers lived in Spital Square, built largely in the 1720s and 1730s. The windows of the attics of houses in Fournier Street were designed so as to allow in the maximum light for weavers to work by.

By the 1830s, the silk weaving had declined and weaving became a 'sweat shop' industry.

When the Huguenots fled France, the silk-weaving industry in the East End was stimulated to new heights by the arrival of fine craftsmen capable of creating exquisite work of many kinds — such as this silk jacket.

Fredrick Owens, one of the last silk weavers, in 1935.

They came from all walks of life; some were poor and regarded by the locals, as will be seen in the Transit Camp chapter, as the 'offal of the earth'. The Bounty Papers at the Huguenot Society have three class divisions: aristos, bourgeois and *les autres* — the others — the 'offal of the earth'.

Mile End New Town

On the eastern side of Leonard Gurle's nursery at the bottom of Brick Lane they built a new town for the immigrant silk workers, where there was open ground available. It was constituted a separate hamlet of Stepney by an agreement of 22 July 1690 between its inhabitants and those of Mile End. It was christened Mile End New Town and thenceforth the original Mile End became known as Mile End Old Town.

The hamlet was two miles in circumference and by 1790 was covered with about 620 houses. The first house went up in what is now Greatorex Street and Hanbury Street and immediately to the east of the nursery. These days few houses dating from earlier than 1800 survive.

Initially, in the 1680s, building was spasmodic and shoddy with jobbing builders raising mortgages to cash in on the demand. In 1675 Thomas Slaymaker was fined for making bad joints and using black mortar, in 1682 for defective tiles and in 1693 for defective bricks. Nicholas Bell and Mr Nicholls, bricklayers, were fined in 1683 for using very bad mortar in eight houses built by them. James Drew and Mr Holles were fined for using bad bricks.

John Holdens

It is interesting, through the court records, to take a look inside a weaver's house which was perhaps in Old Montague Street; the rent owed by the occupant was to a Mistress Montague. In 1693 one John Holden, a weaver, died and there was a lawsuit over his estate. The inventory and account produced to the court show that he lived in a two-storey house with a garret on the top where there were 'two old beds'. On the first floor was a bedroom, a bedstead, two chests of drawers, nine cane chairs and a table, four paintings, bed and table linen and other odds and ends. Next door was the 'shoppe' where he kept four broad looms, weights, scales and other equipment. Below were the kitchen and the parlour. The kitchenware included nine pewter dishes, eighteen plates, two porridge pots, three brass kettles and a silver cup. In his parlour Holden had twelve chairs, a table, a looking glass and a clock in a case.

Did you know

Spitalfields is set where once were green fields to the east of the medieval priory and hospital of St Mary Spital.

A Roman cemetery was discovered here in the 16th century.

Nicholas Culpepper, the famous doctor and herbalist, lived in Red Lion Square in the 17th century.

Brick Lane was once a thoroughfare for the carts carrying bricks from the local brick kiln in the fields.

Spitalfields is a hamlet of Whitechapel — an area that became notorious when Jack the Ripper killed at least six victims in the vicinity in 1888.

Rise and fall

In the eighteenth century, as has been seen, Spitalfields housed a thriving prosperous community; it was a town in itself with an imposing Hawksmoor church, built in 1720 and towering grandly over the gracious streets around. But the industry flowered for a relatively short time; within a hundred years of John Holden's death it was in decline and the weavers started gradually to leave — those that could. The ancestor of the present secretary of the London Huguenot Society took himself up to Macclesfield in the 1790s looking for work. Many of the grandchildren of the successful immigrants moved out into Essex as East Enders have been doing for hundreds of years. It is interesting to note that the membership of the Huguenot Society today is in fact dominated by people from Essex.

By the decade 1820 to 1830 times were really hard for the weaving community and the sort of dire poverty for which the East End became renowned in fifty years' time was already making itself felt in Spitalfields, Mile End New Town and Bethnal Green. A House of Commons Committee reported in 1831-2 that in the three hamlets there were one hundred thousand souls, of whom half were involved in silk manufacture and seventeen thousand were loom weavers; almost all the rest of the population were dependent on it in some way. Weaving collapsed completely in the 1850s and the final death blow came in 1860 when a treaty with France allowed the import of French silk. Into the already run-down area poured the desperately poor Eastern Jews — the 'offal of the earth', as these unfortunate souls were called, were back again.

In 1931 there were still two weaving firms in Bethnal Green and the robes for George VI's Coronation were made by silk produced by Messrs Warner and sons, who had moved to Braintree from Spitalfields some forty years earlier.

MILE END, BOW AND BROMLEY

The commuter belt

Where once penny royal grew in abundance a military parade ground pulsed beneath the march of mustered troops

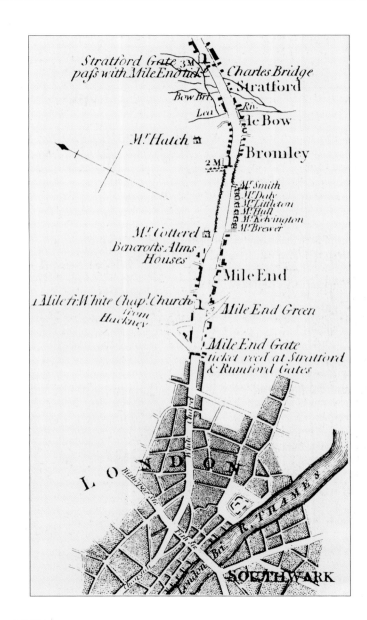

Map of the area in about 1790 when the fine mansions along Mile End Grove were a veritable 'Millionaires' Row'.

Remember the Pickwickians setting off in a coach from The Bull at Aldgate to go to Ipswich? By the time they reached the toll house at Mile End Gate, and the coachman stopped to pay the Mile End Turnpike Trust for the privilege of using their highway, they were in a much more salubrious part than Whitechapel.

The hamlets of Mile End and Bromley, and the larger village of Bow, by virtue of their distance from the City, took longer to become absorbed into the East End proper than the areas considered so far.

Mile End

'... *much more wholesome than the neighbouring places*'
Sir Christopher Wren

M ile End, one of Stepney's hamlets, lay — as its name suggests — one mile from the bars at Aldgate; ribbon development along the Whitechapel Road, it started at Mile End Gate, where the junction with Cambridge Heath Road is now. By the opening of the eighteenth century, from when the first detailed map survives, it was a cluster of houses and market gardens.

The village centre was round about Stepney Green underground station, at the junction of the road down to Stepney village and Broome Lane (Globe Road) which led north up towards the manor house. In medieval times the hamlet was perhaps most associated in the public mind with the leper hospital, later used as a plague hospital and remembered in the 1703 map by the name 'Pest House Lane', now Canal Road. That was Mile End Old Town, not to be confused with Mile End New Town, which lay to the north west, a seventeenth-century development, adjoining Spitalfields, that was built to accommodate the silk weavers.

Wat Tyler

Mile End Green was a large common to the south of the main road, spreading east towards Bow — the City's

'Hampstead Heath'. The Poll Tax riots of 1381, much more severe than their modern counterparts, brought an army of fifty thousand peasants to London, armed with staves and pitchforks, led by Wat Tyler. The young Richard II rode out to confront and reassure the seething mob on Mile End Green — there is a mural at the junction of Copperfield Road and Bow Common Lane to commemorate the event.

The Black Boy Inn
at Mile End in 1870
by J Wilson

Military associations

Mile End Green — where, according to Gerard's *Herbal* of 1597, 'penny royal grew in abundance' — was a place of military associations. Musters were held there and the local militia might be seen being put through their paces in Shakespeare's day. The elderly justice, Shallow, in *Henry IV*, reminising about the

The Plough Inn,
Mile End Road in
about 1870 by J Wilson

glories of his youth, spoke of the common:

> I remember at Mile-End Green (when I lay
> at Clement's Inn) I was then Sir Dagonet in
> Arthur's Show, there was a little quiver fellow,
> and he would manage you his piece thus: and he
> would shout and about, and come you in and
> come you in: 'rah, tah, tah, tah' would he say;
> 'bounce' would he say; and away again would
> he come — I shall never see such a fellow.

Tuesday 13 July 1588 was a day the locals would not easily forget — what a show there was! It was an anxious time, as Philip II's fantastic Armada set sail from Spain on the 'Enterprise of England', to invade and restore 'Popery' to the heretic island. For days the 'home guard', the militia, had been training for the defence of London and a 'fortress' was set up on Mile End Green.

On the morning of the thirteenth there gathered all the forces from the City and the suburbs, including some four hundred and fifty lads from the East End and Clerkenwell, under their colonel, a Mr Robert Wrath, esquire. Between noon and five o'clock a mock battle raged, as the fort was assaulted and defended, watched by a crowd of nobility and aldermen and 'citizens of good account'. The exercise was one of inspired Tudor propaganda, one suspects, rather than a serious war game; the author of the account of it says the audience were 'not a little encouraged against the enemy' as a result.

Pepys, pubs and the Jewish community

It was not just a military parade ground; the common with its fine taverns was a popular place for citizens to go for a day out. Samuel Pepys often went to drink at Mile End and to visit his friend Sir William Penn who had a country house there. On the fourth of July 1668

he noted in his diary that he with his wife and maid had gone to The Rose and Crown and eaten a 'jole of salmon'. From 1666 a market was held on the Green.

The new Sephardic Jewish community, invited back into the country by Oliver Cromwell, settled on the eastern side of the City and chose the pleasant fields of Mile End for their cemetery. It is stll there, dating from 1657, just near Queen Mary and Westfield College, anonymous and enclosed behind high walls. The Dutch and German Jews established a burial ground to the east of the college site in 1773.

A more wholesome place

In 1673 Lady Philadelphia Wentworth applied for a licence to build houses at Mile End to pay off her father-in-law's debts. She intended to develop all along the main road, from the Fort to Globe Road, on the north side, and from Cambridge Heath Road on the south side, as far as Stepney Green itself.

Sir Christopher Wren, as Surveyor General, reported to the Privy Council that it was a convenient spot for the habitation of mariners and manufacturers, who supplied the shipping, and 'much more wholesome than the neighbouring places'. It is doubtful whether all this area (called Westheath) was built on, as on the the 1703 map, the south side of the Mile End Road, between Cambridge Heath Road and Stepney Green, is still shown as open ground.

Almshouses and schools

In the late seventeenth and early eighteenth centuries Mile End became something of a geriatric place. If you had taken a coach at Aldgate or Whitechapel in the eighteenth century, by the time you reached Bow you would have rattled past no less than nine 'old peoples' homes' — almshouses established by local worthies for the poor of the parish and by various livery companies

Brewers' Almshouses in Mile End in 1828.

A crowd poses for the camera outside The Vine Tavern at Mile End in about 1870.

for old and indigent members or their widows — standing alongside the breweries and rope walks.

First you would have passed the Whitechapel parish almshouses (1614) and Meggs' Almshouses (1658) opposite one another just a little to the east of Whitechapel church. The Trinity Almshouses, just beyond the junction with Cambridge Heath Road, built in 1695 for old masters and mates and their widows, are still there. Set back from the road, gracious and elegant, they are mellow three-hundred-year-old brick and white plaster, with lawns and trees and gravel paths, a surprise among the the heartless sprawl and turmoil of modern Mile End.

The other almshouses probably looked much the same; certainly Bancroft's hospital did. It stood where Queen Mary and Westfield college is now, some way beyond the turnpike, established in 1727 to house twenty-four old drapers. The Skinners' (1688) and the Vintners' (1676) almshouses were next to one another, next-door neighbours of the Trinity Almshouses on their western flank. Well set back from the road to the north, just before Stepney Green, were Judge John

Fuller's Almshouses (1592) and just before Bancroft's was Margaret Astill's Charity for the Poor of Cripplegate (1665). Beyond Bancroft's was Captain James Cook's establishment, founded in 1673.

Then there were the schools. Davenant's near the parish almshouses, established in 1686, the Mile End Charity School, set up in 1724, and Bancroft's School, opened in 1735. The 1703 map also shows a boarding school in the village.

From mansions to the 'city of terrible night'

The 1664 Poll Tax records show that Mile End had a far longer list of landowners than did any other part of the East End. A century later Cary's *Survey of the High Roads from London* — a tourist guide to turnpikes,

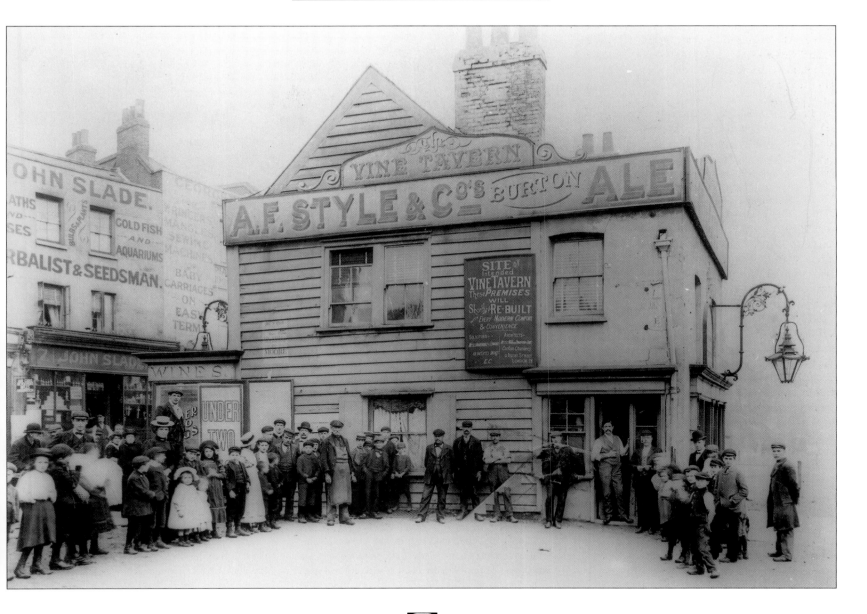

View of the City of London and Tower Hamlets Cemetery at Mile End, framed by Shouters Hill and Greenwich Hill.

'gentlemen's seats' and inns — indicates a row of mansions strung out along the Mile End Road. The Sindall map of 1801 shows them more clearly in a stretch of highway called 'Mile End Grove', a veritable 'Millionaires' Row'. These fine houses, standing in considerable grounds, were situated along the south side of the main road, on either side of the junction with Coborn Road to the north.

Today's Mile End has no charm but at least it is not as bad as it was a hundred years ago. The great road is lined with breweries, with Indian take-aways and chippies, with garages and Edwardian pubs, cheap shops and blocks of shabby flats; off it scuttle rows of mean Victorian dwellings, some prettified, but most not.

Where once the gardens of the Mile End Grove mansions lay, is now the Tower Hamlets cemetery, crammed with the thousands of corpses of men, women and children who lived through the 'city of terrible night', in and out of the horrendous workhouses, in and out of the factories, turning, perhaps, to some chilly castle of a church for comfort.

A nice row of elegant late nineteenth-century houses line the road on its northern side, just before where Millionaires' Row would once have been, and trees were planted along part of Bow Road in the 1840s. But the days when James Gordon's nursery specialized in rhododendrons and carriage wheels crunched up gravel drives is quite lost.

Bow and Bromley

Shaped like a bow, the pretty old stone bridge gave the area its name. Samuel Pepys, accompanied by his wife and maid, often went to take the air there.

Beautiful old Bow Bridge.

From Mile End, travel eastwards along the road to Bow, beautiful Bow. When the Elizabethan actor William Kemp wrote his account of his marathon nine-day morris dance from London to Norwich, he said 'Mile End is no walk without recreation at Stratford Bow with cream and cakes'.

The farthest east of the suburbs, with its picturesque bridge over the Lea, was the most nursery-rhyme sort of place in the eighteenth century, with its comfortable medieval church in the middle of the road, its market gardens and cosy bakehouses. There was Sir John Jolles School for Boys (1613) and Mrs Prisca Coborn's School for Girls (1701), a free school attached to the church, an annual fair (where Fairfield Road is), pretty weatherboard houses and welcoming taverns.

Over to the east at Stratford the famous blue-and-white porcelain was made which became known as 'Bow China'. Alongside the river, a little way out of the village, were calico printing works and a dye house. At the end of the century there were 330 houses in the 465 acres. The poor were well provided for by local charities, among them Mrs Meliora Priestly's trust which allowed for the monthly distribution of twenty sixpenny loaves.

Bow's descent into slum was sudden and came later than its western neighbours; a former resident of eighty remembers conversations with a very old lady who told her that, as a child, she used to go blackberrying in Coborn Road. Coborn Road and Tredegar Road used to be called 'Beerbinder Lane', supposedly after the convolvulus or bearbind which twisted its way through the hedgerows. In the mid-seventeenth century, however, the name appears as 'Beareburden Lane'. A newly built sandy-coloured block of flats at the corner of Tredegar Road and St Stephen's Road has been christened 'Berebinder House' as part of Bow's regeneration as a desirable residential area.

*The toy factory in Roman Road, Bow, was started
in the First World War by Sylvia Pankhurst,
to employ destitute soldiers' wives.*

Bromley, Bow Bridge and the bakehouses

South of Bow village and the main road was the hamlet of Bromley, 'Braembelege' in the eleventh century, a place overgrown with brambles, famous for St Leonard's Priory where Chaucer's Prioress 'spoke the French of Stratford atte Bow'. Before industrialization, railways and the Victorian population explosion, threads of canal and river meandered by clumps of flags and rushes through the wet pastureland down past Bromley Hall to Poplar. Footpads roamed around to ambush the unwary in 'the great field between Poplar and Stepney', according to newspaper reports. Barges ploughed up and down bringing grain from East Anglia to be ground in the local mills.

There is still a Three Mills Lane in Bromley. There used to be a Four Mills Street but it was renamed St Leonard Street, a reduced way running in dirty and hidden, parallel to the great Approach Road to the Blackwall Tunnel.

Stratford Bow, as it used to be known and Old Ford started life as settlements at river crossings. The Old Ford was where the Roman Road crossed the Lea; by the twelfth century it had become dangerous and Henry I's wife, Mathilda, had a bow-shaped bridge built, to the south of Old Ford, where the flyover is now. Tradition says that she was held up by the flooding of the ford one day whilst she was hunting.

The medieval village was London's bakehouse. The wheat that was ground in the Bromley and Poplar mills was made into bread in the ovens of Bow; the Court rolls indicate that many of the bakers were women. In the early morning carts rumbled over the bowed bridge, loaded high with golden loaves bound for the City, where the loaves would be sold by hawkers carrying big round baskets of them.

Some of the earliest records relating to Bow are two little pieces of parchment, tied together with a string to replace the leather thong. They can be read (if you can

read Latin) in the Public Record Office. The larger of the two is the coroner's report, dated 1473, on the body of a baker called David Ashton, killed by a schoolboy, William Norburgh, the son of another baker. The inquest ascertained that the boy was fifteen, that he was related to the deceased, and that he had killed Ashton quite by chance; he threw a dart (worth fourpence) and it caught the unfortunate baker in the head and was the finish of him.

Medieval and Tudor Bow

Medieval Bow probably had more inhabitants than the rest of the East End villages, except possibly Whitechapel. There were enough of them to merit their own chapel of ease by 1311, although it did not break free of Stepney parish until 1719. In 1348 Old Ford and Bow had their own aletasters — at a time when only a few of the Stepney hamlets had these.

By Tudor times Bow was a large and flourishing village. According to the 1548 Chantry Certificate it stood on a 'great thoroughfare and much people there inhabiting'. Bow church was so busy that an extra priest had to be supplied, even though it was only two miles from the mother church at Stepney. In 1591 the King of Portugal, or, rather, the pretender to that title, stayed in Bow's Peter and Paul tavern when he came to visit the Queen!

The case of Elizabeth Barcroft

In April 1640 the Court of High Commission, Charles I's 'moral purge' court, heard accusations levelled against a hosier's wife who lived in Old Ford. The proceedings tell us something about the lives of Bow folk in those far-off days.

Elizabeth Barcroft was the daughter of a Whitechapel silk throwster and when her husband went bankrupt and took himself off to Virginia to trade in

tobacco, she moved from the City to Old Ford and her parents joined her. Unlike many 'Virginia widows' she was maintained still by her husband, who sent tobacco over to an agent in Bow who sold it and gave Elizabeth her share of the profits.

The suit against Elizabeth was brought by one Christopher Medcalfe who claimed that she had become notorious for her adulterous carryings on, and that 'the gentry thereabouts have foreborn her company'. It was common fame that she entertained...

divers young men...at unseasonable hours [who] carried her abroad in coaches oftentimes to playe tavernes and other places.

She dressed in a flamboyant fashion; costly apparel was 'translated by her' and she made her own ornaments. She wore ...

a variety of curious apparel, such as might well befit any Gentleman's wife of one thousand or at least five hundred pounds per annum to weare, being farre beyond the degree either of her said husband's wife or father's daughter.

It sounds as if she was a fun-loving girl, abandoned by her husband, who had turned her hand to making herself pretty clothes — as might be expected from someone who had grown up in the 'rag trade' — and to having a good time. At all events, it emerged that the proceedings had been instituted as revenge by a disappointed suitor. Medcalfe had, apparently, hired a girl called Elizabeth Bludder to lure Mistress Barcroft from her house ...

into a place adjacent unto Beareburden Lane where Mr Medcalfe appointed to be with a coach and two men to carry her off and be merry with him.

She refused to 'be merry with him' and a few weeks later he met her walking home from Bow church, assaulted her in the highway, kicked her and called her 'whore'. He then went round the alehouses and taverns of Whitechapel collecting women to 'give evidence', bribing them with wine and oysters and telling them he was worth one thousand pounds a year.

Today Coborn Road is turning from grim to prim. Take a walk down there and try to imagine how it looked when Elizabeth Barcroft refused to be merry there some three hundred and fifty years ago.

The Queen's Head

The Queen's Head seems to have been Bow's most popular tavern after the time of the Restoration. In the spring and early summer of 1666 and 1667 Pepys often set off with his wife and maid to take the air at Bow and have an evening picnic or eat at The Queen's Head. When his friend Sir William Penn, who lived in Mile End, wanted to alter his will, it was to The Queen's Head that he summoned his lawyers. Lady Pooly, the wife of the Member of Parliament for Bury St Edmunds, had a fine house in Bromley and Pepys was a visitor there just a month before the Great Fire.

Pestilence

The Great Plague was no respector of class; the wealthy folk of Bromley were as prey to its ravages as the poor of Whitechapel. The probate account of the executor of a Bromley sugar merchant's widow, Mary Blacklocke, survives to show how the fine folk dealt with pestilence. The beadle was paid six shillings and ten pence for watching and airing the house with five shillings and ninepence worth of saltpetre and sulphur. Various sums were paid out to nurses, including two pounds and eight shillings to one for six weeks. The 'wash women' earned six guineas.

The doctor who attended Mistress Blacklocke had evidently been carried off by the plague himself, as often happened, and the one pound and eight shillings for medicine was paid to his executor. A Dutch doctor took over and was paid seven pounds for looking after the family in the sickness.

The funeral was some affair. For 'spice to burn the funeral wine and other things' the executor paid ten shillings and seven pence. Coach hire 'to bring the kindred from London' cost seven shillings. Captain Palmer provided the wine at a cost of two pounds and seven shillings and the mourners consumed sixty pounds of Naples Biscuit which cost, together with the

The contrasting faces of Bow in 1986 and as it used to be in 1912.

1921: The Royal bride, Princess Mary, comforts two children lost in Victoria Park.

rosemary and sweet water, £3 19s 9d. Another £3 6s 6d was paid to St Leonard's for ringing the bell, digging the grave and for supplying the coffin and a porter.

The nineteenth century onwards

The transformation of Bow in the nineteenth century was more dramatic than most of the eastern suburbs. The population rose from about two thousand in 1801 to forty-two thousand in 1901. Factories were opened in the 1850s and 60s, producing soap, rubber and, most famously, matches, produced by Bryant and May, using timber brought up the Lea Navigation Canal and employing 5,700 people in 1875. The Match Girls' Strike of 1888 is described below and in chapter twelve we discover some Bow people from the 1920s who would have been astonished to know that convolvulus ever grew in Coborn Road.

Bow was the last of the Tower Hamlets to go quite down into the abyss; there were many streets of dire sodden poverty but even at the turn of the century there were still reasonable residential areas to the

The Match Girls strike

In 1888 over 1000 matchgirls walked out of the Bryant and May factory. Some of them scarcely more than children, they worked incredibly long hours for an average of seven shillings a week, a substantial part of which was subjected to illegal fines — for such crimes as talking. Bullied and working in deplorable conditions, they even ate their meals at their benches contaminated with the omnipresent yellow phosphorus: it burned the skin, caused loss of breath, jaundice and sickness — luminous vomit gathered in the gutters when the girls finished work. Teeth fell out as 'Phossy Jaw' ate away at live bone until pieces of jaw could be simply pulled out, with much pain and disfigurement. Helped by social reformer, Annie Besant, they formed a union and successfully fought for better wages and conditions.

The Strike Committee of the Matchgirls Union, whose courage in resisting the continuation of unjust practices, low wages and dire working conditions led to the renowned strike of 1888. Annie Besant and Herbert Burrows, honorary members, are standing centre back.

Fairfield Works — the Bryant and May match factory in Bow and as it is now — The Bow Quarter.

north of the main road. After the Second World War it was the first part of the East End to start raising its head. The large, cream stucco houses in Tredegar Square — which were the last knockings of Bow's more spacious days, predating the arrival of the Eastern Counties Railway in 1839 by a few years — were the focus of the start of her regeneration in the 1960s.

The square does not look like the East End at all, and is the pride of New Bow, which is really the hamlet of Old Ford. Many of the Victorian artisans' dwellings around have been 'done up' and given tubs of geraniums; lamp-posts, bollards and rubbish bins are painted the smart dark blue and gold of the former Bow Neighbourhood. The market in Roman Road, which started life as a general market for the poverty-stricken newcomers in the middle of last century, has been tidied and cleaned up beyond belief, encased in a blue and gold straight jacket and labelled 'Roman Road Market'; it is rapidly becoming a mecca for women from all over London who like fashionable clothes at cheap prices.

Bow is beautiful again, in parts. The Bryant and May factory in Fairfield Road has been converted into select apartments and calls itself 'The Bow Quarter'. And then there is Victoria Park, up near where the manor house used to be, north of Old Ford Road, with enough greenery to permit a dream of the days not so long ago when Bow featured in a book called *The Beauties of England and Wales* (1816). The old village centre down by St Mary's church and the Bow flyover, like all of Bromley, has been despoiled utterly; carved up by roads and littered with industrial debris. It is presided over by the statue of Gladstone which the poor match girls were forced to subsidize. The medieval church was badly damaged in the war but stands still in the middle of the road, a solitary reminder of the pretty village of bakers and market gardeners. One cannot imagine a Portuguese king, even if he was a pretender, staying in The Little Driver or The Bow Bells.

POPLAR AND THE ISLE OF DOGS

From cattle pasture to Canary Wharf

'And there be yet remaining in that part of the hamlet which bordreth upon Limehouse many old bodies of large poplars standing'

Those who enter into the great maw of the 'ferry boat' tunnel at the eastern end of the Highway, emerge to find themselves in a world of massive pillars, flyovers and skyscrapers. Glittery glassy, new Docklands spreads out before the gaze, dwarfing the sturdy old West India Dock warehouses on the right — practically the only bit of old Docklands that is left in all this strange new town which covers the East End's 'island'.

The tower of Canary Wharf dominates the scene, winking at the centre of a brand new complex, built by Canadians — the East End's departing children have come back, maybe. Until recently it was the highest tower in Europe, as once St Paul's was the tallest church in Christendom. The Docklands Light Railway curves and buzzes colourfully overhead. From it you can see the great lakes made from the docks, all lying empty: no ships these days — just monster buildings, like 'Cascades', the block of flats, a giant, like the

hanging gardens of Babylon without the gardens. A few trace elements remain of the heyday of working-class exploitation when the island was a dense community of workers — a few sad little rows of Edwardian villas straggling and stranded among the new finery. Cuba Street, Manilla Street, Havannah Street and others are still there — or some of them — to remind the new residents of the days when the warehouses overflowed with sugar, tobacco and goodness knows what else, and London was the biggest and busiest port in the world.

Greenwich and the Isle of Dogs in the 18th century, ringed with windmills.

The West India Docks, looking west from Blackwall, painted in 1802 by William Daniell.

Work and poverty

The village of Poplar and the Isle of Dogs have undergone the most dramatic of changes in the last two hundred years, passing from pastureland to a world of ship-building and dockers, and then to the waiting wasteland that it is now. By 1848 there were thirty-eight firms on Millwall, with ship-building and engineering dominating the list. The inhabitants were clerks, coopers, lock-keepers, dock police, engineers, warehousemen, carters, stable boys, smiths, porters, stevedores and dockers, iron founders, blacksmiths, sail-makers, rope-makers and shipwrights.

In the 1860s it has been said that the shipyards and marine engineering firms on the island employed fifteen thousand men and boys. The building of the Great Eastern brought numbers of new workers to the area, including many Scotsmen who built their own Presbyterian chapel, St Paul's, in West Ferry Road.

Meanwhile, on the eastern side of the island, Cubitt Town grew up. The land was leased by a builder called William Cubitt from the Countess of Glengall; there were rows of terraced housing for the workers in the dry docks and engineering works by the river. In 1857 the island acquired a parish church, Christ Church, partly financed by Cubitt.

By 1867 there were thirty thousand people on poor relief in Poplar, following the collapse of the Thames ship-building industry, caused by the competition from the increasingly large and efficient yards in the north. At the turn of the century twenty thousand people lived on the island. It was a strangely isolated community which kept itself to itself, enclosed as it was by the river on three sides, with dock bridges to the north; there were delays of up to half an hour for those unfortunates who 'caught a bridger'.

The islanders worked and played on home ground; there were forty pubs and from 1885 they had their

own football team, Millwall. By 1900 most of the dwellings on the island were at least fifty years old and lay crumbling and neglected by the private landlords. Life was hard for the many dependant on charity and poor relief and — as is usually the case when everyone is fighting for the same crust — there were tensions. The poor and the not-so-poor hated each other; the unskilled workers resented the skilled workers and the members of the Temperance Society despised the hard drinkers.

Nevertheless, when the chips were down, they would present a united front to fight to improve their lot; the Isle of Dogs Progressive Club, founded in the 1890s, helped form the Poplar Labour Party and return Will Crookes to Parliament. Poplarism was soon to become a universally known term when George Lansbury led the local fight against central government. In 1906 and again in the 1920s the left-wing Board of Guardians gave generous relief to the swelling ranks of Poplar poor which could not be paid for out of the rates. Meanwhile prosecutions were brought against anti-centralization protestors and those responsible went to prison for their pains.

But let us just go back a little. The names of Seven Mills School and Millwall remind us that once this was a farming community; gentlemen lived around and there was even a royal palace. Once poplar trees ranged across the skyline; they were still there when Strype wrote in the 1720s: 'and there be yet remaining in that part of the hamlet which bordreth upon Limehouse many old bodies of large poplars standing'.

The Isle of Dogs

Stepney Marsh was the old name for the island, which seems not to have acquired its nickname until the sixteenth century. No one really knows why it came to be called the Isle of Dogs; perhaps it was because the royal hunting dogs from Greenwich Palace were kept here. A tale used to be told of a young nobleman and his bride who lost their lives, drowning in the marshes while they were on a wild boar hunt, with dogs who howled for them after their demise.

Probably the explanation of the name is less romantic, being a corruption of the 'Isle of Dykes'. The fight to keep the Thames out of the salty muddy swamp began long ago; we know little about the early days — there was a manor called Pontefract, presumably after a broken bridge, which had eighty acres and a mill in 1230. Certainly by the fourteenth century the area was criss-crossed with streams, dykes, canals and sea walls; by the time the great flood swamped the East End in 1324 one hundred acres of the island had been drained and there was a ferry to take passengers over the river to Greenwich. The names of some of the inhabitants, discovered from the manor court rolls, are significant: Atgoos, Atwall and Dyke.

The village and the pastureland to its south was a flourishing place in those days; in 1348 there were ale-tasters for the Marsh, while the other East End hamlets had only one each. The Black Prince had a palace in Poplar and there was the little chapel of St Mary, down towards the south of the island where pilgrims, it is said, stopped on their way to Waltham Abbey. This was the island's first heyday; unlike the rest of the East End it fell into decline in the late Middle Ages.

Manor and hamlet

Wild and untamed were the fishermen and cattle farmers of the marsh, inclined to go their own way and, in today's terminology, 'do their own thing'. The Abbot of Tower Hill, who acquired the Manor of Poplar from the Loveyne family in 1396, had a tough time trying to regularize the land ownership there. Often land grabbing went on without any formality. In the fifteenth year of Henry VII's reign Thomas Marowe was prosecuted for holding nine acres in Leamouth without copy or licence.

Sir Gilbert Dethick (Richmond Herald and later Garter King of Arms) was a considerable landowner in Poplar after the Reformation, and he sued one Thomas Whyte in a matter of tithes in 1577. There came to the Court of Exchequer to give evidence various ancient witnesses who could remember the old days; one was the monk who had collected rents for the Abbot of Tower Hill from his tenants in Poplar village and on the marsh.

They remembered the manor house with its rabbit warrens, fish ponds and orchards, hay and corn grown in Birdingebushe Field and Ashfield. In those days eightpence an acre was paid for marsh ground 'not mowed but eaten with cattell'. It was said to be the finest pasture in England.

At the opening of the seventeenth century Poplar was a hamlet of Stepney still and Blackwall, its eastern neighbour, was smaller still, with only 229 inhabitants buried between 1606 and 1610. Not until 1650 did Poplar acquire its own chapel, St Matthias, built by the Dethick family. It was later taken over by the East India Company and in 1817 Poplar had its own parish church, All Saints.

The seventeenth century

A rare pictorial map from about 1600 shows rows of small red-roofed houses lining Poplar High Street and some larger residences in North Street with long gardens. These houses belonged, as did 'Master Garter's Pale', to the Dethick estate. A road ran down

Drawing sugar into bags by hoppers on the West India Docks in the 1930s.

across the marsh to the ferry from the centre of the village and the whole area was patchworked with water channels and locks. Grain was brought down the Lea to be unloaded and ground in the local mills for the baking of Bow bread. A brewery stood in the High Street and a small lock-up at the cross roads.

A 'town book' survives for Poplar from this time. It records, amongst other things, that Widow Spynke

…long dweller amongst us for the space of forty years …a great labourying woman

was past her labouring and was to have the Widow Wyer's room in the almshouses. The Widow Wyer was to have Widow Ashforde's room. Presumably Widow Ashforde was dead.

A contentious will

A suit in the probate court in the year of the Great Fire, allows us a close-up of Poplar life in Pepys' day. John Meeks, a scholarly eccentric gentleman died on St Valentine's Day in 1665. Meeks did not care for women but was 'intimate and familiar friends' with one Jonathon Magwicke, a young tanner. Meeks did:

…show and express a great love and affection to the said Jonathon Magwicke and soe much was generally taken notice of in the hamlet of Poplar.

Magwicke, who was hard up according to the Poll Tax records, made a bid for the dead man's money, even though he was said to have left a will benefitting the poor boys of his old school, King's, in Worcester.

By now the East India Company had become an important presence in Poplar and one of the witnesses was the master of the Company's free school there, and chaplain of their chapel, Thomas Hopkinson. Mary Jones, who did 'make [Meek's] fire and dress his

victuals', told the court that she had made Meeks a posset of stale beer and ale, nutmeg and sugar on Magwicke's orders and, with some embarrassment, explained that 'when nature called' her employer would have none of her help but relied on his friend.

Then came Elizabeth Jones, fifty-seven, of North Street, who 'getteth her living by minding of long sick and knitting'. She tended the death bed. Meeks addresses her as 'Goody Jones', and they would sometimes sit by the fire together. Richard Hillyard, born in Shaftesbury, living in Poplar, a barber surgeon who 'maketh his living by lending out money on parenes', also gave evidence. Edward Evans, a tailor who kept a victualling house came to court to add his pennyworth as did an elderly silk winder, a woman from Devon originally — while a farmer called King reported the local gossip that the gentleman and the tanner had gone to the Isle of Wight on holiday with a view to setting up house there together. Perhaps it was to escape from gossiping neighbours!

Thomas Mills of Stratford, aged fifty-six, told the examiner that he drank with Meeks at Mistress Bromley's house, The George at Bow. It was there that Mills was told by Meeks that he had left one hundred pounds to his old school. Thomas Fletcher, a Bow clerk, was a member of the drinking party. Thomas Cowden, an old friend of the deceased, said he had witnessed the will one Friday morning about eleven o' clock in The Red Lion in Bromley. The hamlet's Head-borough, Nicholas Skelton, born in Shrewsbury, turned up to say that farmer King's evidence should be ignored as he had been arrested for 'deceiving and unjustly carrying away'.

Mary East/James How

A hundred years later Poplar's Headborough was the famous transvestite, Mary East. For thirty-six years she kept The White House Inn, parading as a man and

living with a woman. Using the name James How, she took office as Headborough and Overseer of the Poor in 1744 and 1752. Only when she was nominated as churchwarden was she 'obliged to discover her sex'.

One wonders what the process of election to church-warden involved in those days when mills whirred in great number around the Isle of Dogs and they raised the largest ox in England on the marshes. It weighed 236 stone and was sold at Leadenhall Market in 1720.

The Docks

Towards the end of the century the transformation of the area was starting. The East India Company rebuilt the Garter's old chapel in 1776 and 1792 the Chapel of St Mary was a farmhouse. In the year of the storming of the Bastille the Brunswick Dock was built at Blackwall and thirteen years later the West India Docks opened for business.

The docks covered 295 acres of land at the neck of the island. The river — which generations had been at such pains to keep out — was let in again and two great basins built to hold the water. Like a fortress it was, with high curtain walls, thirty feet high, enclosing the riches of Britain's trading empire. An armed force of militia made sure there would be no pilfering from here, as there had been to a scandalous and damaging degree from the 'legal quays' up in the Pool.

Between 1788 and 1960 London was the biggest port in the world.

In 1805 the London Dock opened and in 1806 the East India Dock. Great roads were built across the East End to service the docks — and then came the railways.

The merchants of the West India trade were multi-millionaires, many of them, owning sugar plantations, slaves and ships. For the locals there was work in abundance and new generations of country East Enders poured into Blood Alley, where the heaving of heavy sugar sacks made them bleed.

*The West India import
dock in Poplar.*

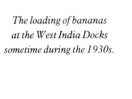

The loading of bananas at the West India Docks sometime during the 1930s.

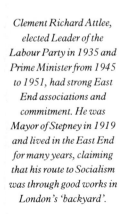

Clement Richard Attlee, elected Leader of the Labour Party in 1935 and Prime Minister from 1945 to 1951, had strong East End associations and commitment. He was Mayor of Stepney in 1919 and lived in the East End for many years, claiming that his route to Socialism was through good works in London's 'backyard'.

Masts of tea clippers blackened the sky. Listen to Henry Mayhew describing Victorian dockland (in an age when his terminology would not have been regarded as offensive):

> The sailors are singing boisterous nigger songs from the yankee ship just entering; the cooper is hammering at the casks on the quay; the chains of the cranes, loosed of their weight, rattle as they fly up again; the ropes splash in the water; some captain shouts his orders through his hands; a goat bleats from a ship in the basin.

In the 1930s one hundred thousand men were employed in the docks, handling thirty-five million tons of cargo.

By 1960 the number had fallen to fifty thousand.

One by one the factories closed down and thousands of dock workers were made redundant as modern cargo handling made the London docks unsuitable. Trade was dwindling anyway. The Dockers' Club in Limehouse today has become a poor runt of a social club with a handful of chaps drinking in a desultory lost sort of way.

The docks were finally closed in 1980 and the London Docklands Development Corporation set about its task of sweeping clean, building Heron Homes and bringing a new sort of life into the old island workshop. Where once the hungry desperate islanders gathered at the dock gates for the 'call on', hoping to get a half-day's work to feed their families, there is a landscaped leisure land.

In 1354 Richard de Vernon, Earl of Chester, and Thomas of Davenport, who held the Bailwick of Sergeantry of the Hundred of Macclesfield came to Poplar to do homage to the Black Prince at his palace. Could they have seen into the future, it is hard to surmise what they might have thought of Canary Wharf some six and a half centuries later.

THE TRANSIT CAMP

A world of strangers: influx and immigration

The Great Synagogue in Brick Lane changed from being a French chapel into a Wesleyan one;
then it became a synagogue and, until recently, was a mosque

Danish church at
Wellclose Square
in 1840.

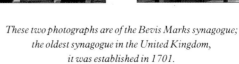

These two photographs are of the Bevis Marks synagogue;
the oldest synagogue in the United Kingdom,
it was established in 1701.

The East End villages grew together irrevocably under the Good Queen Victoria, who gave her name together with her husband's to the latest arriving docks, 'The Royals'. For many hundreds of years, these villages had comprised a world of strangers — strangers who came from the English countryside seeking work, from Flanders (brought in initially by Edward III to improve indigenous cloth-making) and Holland. They arrived in St Katharine's and East Smithfield, in Aldgate and Whitechapel. Italians came on the annual wool and spice run from Genoa and Venice in the Middle Ages and some stayed; 'Lombards and Galymen', they nicknamed them in the Abbot of Tower Hill's patch.

Then, in the terrible Reformation days the religious exiles sought refuge, together with lads and lasses arriving from the shires. Then the French immigrants created 'weaver town'. In the eighteenth century came the Jews and many more were to follow later. The Irish dribbled in and then flocked at the time of the great famine. Lascars and Chinamen settled down by the docks. These days there are mosques where previously there were synagogues.

Always the newcomers were hated and reviled, mocked for their strange way of speaking, resented for their successful businesses and suspect because of their eating habits. In the Peasants' Revolt of 1381:

...many Flemmynges loste here heedes ...
namely they that koude nat say Breede and Chese,
but Case and Brode.

Three-hundred years later Dr Welton, the Jacobite incumbent at Whitechapel Church, (now Itchy Park, opposite the underground station) railed against the Huguenot immigrants, thundering from his pulpit:

This set of rabble are the very offal of the earth, who cannot be content to be safe here from the justice

The river by Tower Bridge, near Irongate Stairs, where the Jews and Irish landed on East End soil a hundred years ago. A notice inviting tourists to play a foreign game is set, coincidentally but very appropriately, at the spot where Irongate stairs led up from the river.

and beggary from which they fled, and to be fattened on what belongs to the poor of our own land and to grow rich at our expense, but must needs rob our religion too.

Up and away they went, as soon as they had made their pile, the East Enders, leaving those behind who could not make it. Another wave of desperate poor refugees, of one sort or another, would take their place.

The Great Synagogue in Brick Lane says it all — it changed from being a French chapel into a Wesleyan one; then it became a synagogue and, until recently, was a mosque.

German sugar bakers, Welsh dairymen, French weavers, Dutch brewers and printers, Spanish pedlars — intermingled with English farm labourers — came to London to seek their fortune or save themselves from starving. Then there were the Irish and the Jews. All was coming and going. All was longing for home and then off they went, at last, to pastures new and better houses with gardens instead of yards and thought nostalgically of the dear old markets, of costers and eel and pie shops.

Under the shadow of Tower Bridge, on the river frontage of the newly built Tower Hotel (where once the Flemings had their own cemetery) a label invites the wealthy tourists to play the foreign game of *Péntanque* (bowls). Appropriately, though unknowingly, it marks the spot where once Irongate Stairs led up from the river. Here many thousands of Irish and Eastern European immigrants took their first weary steps on to English soil, seasick and homesick, storm-tossed and uncertain what would happen next.

Irish immigration

The Irish had been coming for years. Knockfergus, the east end of Cable Street, was full of Irish coal heavers in the nineteenth century, attracted by the name, perhaps, which long predated their arrival. It is thought to have been named by soldiers returning to London after the Irish Wars in the time of the first Elizabeth. The influx of Irish into Spitalfields had led to disturbances in 1736 and during the Gordan (anti-Catholic) riots of 1780, two Irish chapels in Stepney were wrecked.

The Famine immigrants, and those who came later, seem to have made mainly for north London but

Preparing shrines in Poplar's Rook Street (circa 1920)
for the solemn outdoor procession.

enough stayed around in the East End to make a presence felt. In 1851 there were 3,444 Irish in the slum parish of St George's in the East. Dickens, the Uncommercial Traveller, went into an Irish home in Stepney in 1860:

It was a dark street with a dead wall on one side.
Nearly all the outer doors of the house stood
open....The woman of the house had picked up some
strips of wood, about some wharf or barge; and they
had just now been thrust into the otherwise empty
grate to make two iron pots boil. There was some fish
in one and some potatoes in another. The flare of the
burning wood enabled me to see a table, and a broken
chair or so, and some cheap crockery ornaments
about the chimney piece....I saw a horrible brown
heap on the floor in the corner....
'Tis the poor craythur that stays here, sur; and 'tis
very bad she is....Sure 'tis the lead mills, where the
woman gets took on at eighteen pence a day...'tis lead
poisoned she is....'
Better to be ulcerated and paralysed for eighteen
pence a day, while it lasted, than to see the
children starve.
'My husband has walked the streets these four days,
being a labourer, and is walking them now, and is
ready to work, and no work for him, and no fire and
no food but the bit in the pot, and no more than ten
shillings in a fortnight; God be good to us!'

It was the opinion of a one-eyed fish-basket maker who was interviewed in 1884 by Walter Austin for the book, *One Dinner a Week*, that state-assisted emigration would provide no solution to the eternal problem of East End poverty:

It's like this way. The man there goes away, the more
there comes to fill the gaps. See here now, Sir. Last
month about five hundred was shipped off.... Well,

Detail from a Hogarth engraving of a Jewish pedlar.

*Juda and Metka
Fitzer were
immigrant Polish
Jews who opened
their umbrella
shop in Hackney
in 1907, using the
Anglicized name
of Fisher.*

thinks I, a good riddance. There'll be fewer mouths to fill, and fewer hands to work here now. But the last week there come about a thousand from abroad, an' they all landed at the docks, an' here they seem to stick, and its mostly Polish Jews they are.

The Eastern Europeans arrive

Mass immigration from Eastern Europe began with the massacres in Russia in 1881. Between 1870 and 1914 some 120,000 Jews came to England. Most stayed, at first, in East London, mainly in Whitechapel and Spitalfields, and very different they were from the Jews who had come in the previous century to

*Wapping 1881: seamen
of many nations at the
Seamen's Hospital
Dispensary in Well Street
in the London docks.*

I was put on my brother's shoulder, and we led my blind brother by hand, and off we went....Suddenly pandemonium started. The order went out that Jews were to be got rid of, and shooting started.

Later she recalled:

After a rather quiet and unhappy night we woke up to the cries and screams of Jews being pulled out of their houses and beds.

On arrival in London, after arrest by Russian soldiers and horror piled upon horror, they were taken, at first, to the lodgings of an uncle in Ship Alley, a little court in St George's in the East. Those who did not have relatives to take them in went to the Jews temporary shelter in Leman Street and then off to mean lodgings in Brick Lane, Old Montague Street, Fashion Street and the rest, where once the French weavers had started their lives in London.

It was a law-abiding community in the ghetto. There was no drunkenness or licentiousness among them; families clung tenaciously together, protecting one another and always working, working, working to better themselves.

The fact that the invading race gradually settle down and hold their own, superceding the lower class of Londoners, is full of significance.

So wrote Henry Walker in 1896.

The importance of close family ties perhaps rubbed off on the Gentile population and is now what we regard as the East End clan tradition, with Mum at the heart of it all. Not that there was no antipathy between the various groups, Russian, Polish and Lithuanian, but at least they all spoke the same language, Yiddish.

In those days cockerels crowed in Spitalfields. Outside the Rothschild Building in Flower and Dean Street sat the old Russians, Poles and Lithuanians, on

Goodman's Fields. The Whitechapel Spitalfields ghetto was solid and sodden poverty, with some three thousand people to the acre, as opposed to the eight hundred to the acre in the Gentile parts. It sheltered sixteen thousand poor Jews (ironically exactly the number estimated to have been expelled from the country in 1290) and there were twenty thousand more within a half-mile radius.

Lord Rothschild said, 'We have now a new Poland in our hands in East London.'

Some had trades and some country people had none. Most were absorbed into the local 'rag trade' and the Jewish sweat shop became notorious. In 1888 there were 1,015 tailoring workshops in Whitechapel alone.

Others became costers, getting themselves a stall and selling whatever they could — not unlike today's car-boot sales.

It is difficult to imagine how they must have felt, fleeing from persecution, unemployment, war and revolutionary disturbance, humiliated and frightened. Jerry White, in his book on the Rothschild Building in Spitalfields, looked at the Katchinsky family.

The father was a military tailor from Kiev; with his wife and four children, one blind, he settled in Spitalfields in 1911. They had been caught up in the 1905 revolution and Eva, one of the daughters, recalled being taken by her elder brother to one of the revolutionary rallies:

white kitchen chairs in the summer evenings, talking of the days back home. They comforted themselves by keeping chickens as they had done in their farms in the Ukraine and grew potatoes, peas and beans in their window boxes.

It was the old customs, far older than anything observed by their Gentile neighbours, which sustained them — the comfort of the candles flickering in the parlour windows of tenements and cottages as the tailors' cutters and pressers, cabinet makers and milliners came home on a Friday night to the special sacred meal which ushered in the sabbath. In Rothschild Building there was a hushed excitement; 'One could smell and one could feel the impending Sabbath'. A special loaf called a 'challa' was provided and all the family sat round the table.

In 1892 Israel Zangwill wrote in *Children of the Ghetto*:

There was a strange, antique clannishness about these Sons of the Covenant.... They prayed for one another whilst alive, visited one another's bedsides when sick, buried one another when dead. No mercenary hand poured the yolks of egg over their dead faces, and arrayed their corpses in praying shawls. No hired masses were said for the sick or the troubled, for the psalm singing Sons of the Covenant were always available for petitioning the heavens.

All they needed was a synagogue, a ritual bath and a Kosher butcher. Between 1881 and 1914 there was a proliferation of small synagogues or schuls which were places of worship, study centres, social clubs and friendly societies combined. In Princelet Street, under the shadow of the great Christchurch, there is, in one of the old houses, a recently discovered synagogue interior. Untouched for many years it is the very best place to feel the atmosphere of Spitalfields' Jewish years.

Read Israel Zangwill before you go:

The synagogue consisted of two large rooms knocked into one, and the rear partitioned off for the use of the ...women. Its furniture was bare benches, a raised platform with a reading desk at the centre, and a wooden curtained ark at the end, containing two parchment scrolls of the law, each with a silver pointer and silver bells and pomegranates.... The room was badly ventilated, and what little air there was was generally sucked up by a greedy company of wax candles, big and little and stuck in brass holders.

The worshippers dropped in, mostly in their workaday garments and grime, and rumbled and roared and chorused the prayers with zeal which shook the window panes....

In the West End, synagogues are built to eke out the incomes of the poor Minyan men or professional congregants; in the East End rooms are tricked up for prayer. This synagogue was all of a luxury many of its sons could boast. It was their salon and their lecture hall. It supplied them not only with their religion, but their arts and letters, their politics and their public amusements. It was their home as well as the Almighty's, and, on occasions they were familiar, and even a little vulgar with him.

It was a place which they could sit in in their slippers — metaphorically, that is.... They enjoyed themselves in this school of theirs; they shouted and skipped and shook and sang, they wailed and moaned and clenched their fists and thumped their breasts. There is an apocryphal anecdote of one of them being in the act of taking a pinch of snuff, when the Confession caught him unexpectedly. 'We have trespassed' he wailed mechanically, as he spasmodically put the snuff in his bosom and beat his nose with his clenched fist.

Food

Food was an important link with home as well as being part of the religious rite. In 1901 there were fifteen Kosher butchers and poulterers in Wentworth Street alone. Jerry White remembers a chandler's shop run by one Old Mother Wolfe. To the orthodox Jews she was a wicked woman because she defied the dietary laws and sold bacon. Children would run by holding their breath: 'mustn't breathe in the bacon'.

By and large, the immigrant mothers were remarkably competent cooks. Weekend treats of butter and honey cakes or strudels were prepared. Soups were a speciality, made from barley, broad beans, potatoes (*lockshen*) or 'soup greens', which were bunches of small vegetables.

Then there was Borsht and soup with little dough chips in it. For one Austrian family their treat summer meal was tiny Jersey potatoes and curd cheese with radishes and cucumber in yoghurt. Off-cuts of salami were sold cheap at Blooms on the corner of Old Montague Street:

That was delicious. Oh God, you thought you were wealthy if you had some of that!

The observance of Kosher was in decline by 1910 and there was a movement away from the old rituals. After the First World War women started lighting their own fires and gas mantles on the sabbath; the Gentile lads or sabbath goys, who used to come in and light up for a few pence, were dispensed with. One Yom Kippur there was a fight in Thrawl Street when some non-orthodox Jews taunted their neighbours for fasting.

Soon they were up and away — off to Stoke Newington, Stamford Hill, Golders Green — or, following their French predecessors to Chigwell. Even the Museum of East End Jewish Life is tucked away in respectable Finchley. Little trace remains of the

*Catholic shrine in Tobago
Street in about 1930.*

hundred-year Jewish stay; no street name betrays the existance of the old ghetto. Whitechapel library has a Yiddish section and you can buy beigels in a baker's in Commercial Street still but of course nowadays they are available in the most chic West End sandwich bars.

Their words have become a part of our language:

shmaltz - literally, 'dripping'
(meaning something cloying and sentimental)
slep - to drag
chutspa - cheek
Schlemozzle - uproar and confusion.

A solitary Kosher luncheon club in Greatorex Street serves the cheapest of good Jewish lunches and you can still eat chopped liver and hot salt beef at Blooms. But mostly the synagogues have turned into something else now.

Cemeteries

The cemeteries are there, well hidden. On the west side of Alderney Road, just east of Queen Mary and West-field College, behind high walls are the cemeteries of the Sephardic community, opened in 1656 and next to it later Ashkenazi burial ground. Further west in Brady Street, off the Whitechapel Road, is the cemetery for the New and the Great Synagogues where corpses were buried between 1790 and 1858.

More recent immigration

In 1964 a survey showed that the highest concentrations of Pakistanis in East London were in Princelet Street and Old Montague Street. The new generation of the homesick have taken over. A great high mosque towers above the Whitechapel Bell Foundry in the Mile End Road and the cruel zenophobia which made

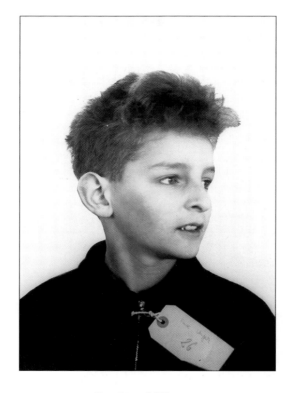

One of some 5,000 young German Jews who arrived in Great Britain in 1938, this boy still has a numbered identification tag tied to his neckline.

Doctor Welton condemn the Huguenots as the offal of the earth, is now visited upon the immigrants from the sub-continent as once it was upon the Jews.

The East End's polygot nature has bred into it a vibrance not found in other parts, maybe, but it has been a sad dislocated sort of place for many many generations, where perhaps half of the families at any given time, English and foreign alike, remembered a home that was very different from the dark alleys now around them.

On an early summer day in 1887, when the cow parsley was waist high in the Suffolk lanes and the Essex countryside was spattered with white lace May flowers, Queen Victoria ventured through the separate and dangerous territory of her capital's eastern slums to Mile End. There she opened the Queen's Hall, all lined with statues of queens, the first part of a 'palace of delights' to educate and elevate the minds of the East Enders:

It gives me great satisfaction to open this fine building provided for the benefit of the people of East London, whose lives of unceasing toil will be cheered by the various opportunities of rational and instructive entertainment, and of artistic enjoyment here afforded to them.

After the Queen had spoken Madame Albani sang:

Mid pleasures and palaces
Though we may roam
Be it ever so humble
There's no place like home.

The Times noted the 'thrilling effect'. Did this rendering thrill or chill the new country East Enders and their neighbours — the poor homesick Irish and the unhappy exiled Jews? It is unlikely that any of them were in the audience anyway.

SLUMS AND DEPRIVATION

'Not a wery nice neighbourhood'

Poverty wore a worse face in East London
than it did in Calcutta.

*Dickens's Pickwickians
suffer a break-down
on their travels.*

*Dr Barnardo awoke public
attention to the plight of the
homeless and orphaned
children whom he set
about rescuing.*

W hen Charles Dickens's Pickwickians went east to take the coach from The Bull at Aldgate to Ipswich, as they rattled along the Whitechapel Road, Sam Weller remarked; 'not a wery nice neighbourhood this, sir.' 'It is not indeed, Sam,' replied Mr Pickwick, surveying the crowded and filthy street through which they were passing.

Tubby Isaacs sells shell fish just a little way along from where The Bull Inn stood — perhaps there was a similar stall when Sam and Mr Pickwick rolled by:

Here's an oyster stall to every half-dozen houses.
The streets lined with 'em.
Blessed if I don't think that ven a man's very poor,
he rushes out of his lodgings, and eats oysters in
reg'lar desperation.

If conditions were bad when the Pickwickians rode out, they became infinitely worse in the following decades. The two chief local industries of ship building and weaving collapsed; then, as we have seen, poverty-stricken immigrants arrived in their thousands. These are the dark days, from the depression of the 1880s, the swirling blanketing, fog days of the 'Autumn of Terror' when girls were so scared that they might be next on Jack the Ripper's list that they took shelter in the dreaded workhouse and the word 'Whitechapel' sent a shiver down every London spine. The East End, they truly called it now; Beatrice Webb described it as the 'bottomless pit of decaying life'.

Charles Booth's survey showed thirty-five per cent of the population living below the poverty line. Doctor Barnado found starving hopeless children sleeping

huddled under railway arches and saved numbers of little girls sold and beaten into prostitution. Henry James saw London as:

an ogress who devours human flesh to keep herself
alive to do her tremendous work.

This East End carried on, with some improvements, until the Second World War. Sid Short, the oil-and-colour man of Roman Road in the Twenties and Thirties, might have made a fortune if he had patented the 'bug blinder' which he created and sold to the local housewives. One of the favoured methods of ridding the insanitary hovels and tenements of bed bugs was to stand the legs of the bed in paraffin. As Bill Fishman says of the 1880s and 1890s:

It was an uncaring and brutalised society. The people down here are a different race from the rest of London, or so it seems. They daren't even call a spade a spade for fear of being overheard and caught out — so they talk in rhyming riddles.

Walter Besant proclaimed it to be …

…a Great Joyless City of two millions of people without a gentleman among them, or a rich man, or a nobleman, or an artist, or an author, or anybody at all lifted above themselves by culture and education — except the clergy.

A perusal of the records of the Whitechapel Board of Guardians for these times reveals that the forbidding registers have a column for 'deaths from starvation'. Lord Beveridge's father, who had lived in India, said that poverty 'wore a worse face' in East London than it did in Calcutta.

The workhouse

Remember the Whitechapel workhouse in the eighteenth century? It is no longer like that in the next century; the number of paupers are now so high that the government has long decided that out-relief is too soft an option and, by and large, the crowds of destitute must be brought within the prison like walls of 'the house' and frightened into becoming respectable working citizens. Never mind if there is no work to be had.

Vallance Road, which runs north of the White-chapel Road near the underground, is a grim reminder of William Vallance, Clerk to the Board of Guardians from 1868 to 1902. In 1888 there were about 1,500 inmates, with similar numbers in the Mile End and St George's workhouses. In 1887 Poplar had an astronomical 3,836. In June 1888 London was providing in-door relief to 55,187 and out-door relief to 33,715.

No time to play: children making sacks in between school hours.
Child labour provided an essential contribution to
family income and survival in the slums.

The casual ward was the worst; it was ancillary to the main workhouse and offered a free night's 'kip on the spike' and some minimal nourishment to the desperate. In Whitechapel they were given a tin containing one half of gruel and eight ounces of bread and a night in a freezing cell, eight foot by four. In the morning each casual had to smash half a ton of stone with a hammer or pick four pounds of oakum.

Bill Fishman, quoting from John Law's *In Darkest London* compares the atmosphere in the Southgrove workhouse in Bow to a Nazi labour camp:

Ringing the workhouse bell, they enter into the forecourt of neat flower beds, closely-shaven grass plots, smooth paths and trees which had been pruned until their branches had reached the legitimate amount of foliage. The Bastille stretched further than

Three illustrations of London by Gustave Doré:

Above left
'Scripture reader in a Night Refuge'.

Above right
A child 'Found in the Streets' and brought into the refuge

Below right
'The Bull's Eye', waifs and strays, thieves and vagabonds huddled in the dark lanes and byeways.

the eye could see, and seemed a standing rebuke to its poverty-stricken surroundings, for it was clean ...not a spot on it, not a stain, nothing to show a trace of sympathy for the misery and sin of people who lived in the neighbourhood.

Life at home

Fear of the workhouse remained a present terror within living memory but what was life like at home?. Walter Austin went out into the homes of 'the people of the abyss' in the 1880s and talked to them, rapping with his knuckles on the doors — no-one had knockers or bells. The standard family accomodation, before the 'model dwellings' arrived, were very small houses, blackened with soot, one-up-one-down and only ten foot square, privately rented at about four shillings a week. Some had the whole house, some shared it with another family.

Down by the canal, perhaps in Bow, living in a 'house of a room ... and one bedroom over it', Walter Austin met a cheery little woman with seven children and some ugly china. Everything was neat and clean and the bedroom was divided into two by a curtain which separated the boys from the girls. By local standards they were doing fine; her husband was a jobbing builder and 'well nigh a croesus':

He'll work from morn to midnight, now, he will, and never grumble not one bit, he won't. And he gives me all he gets, too an' I can feed the children well now, an' keep 'em clothed, an' tidy like. And I never could do that, you know, he was mostly all'ys glumpy afore he took the pledge.

An ancient yellowed gypsy caravan in King's Arms Yard was let out to an old woodcutter and his family for a shilling a week. They survived on what the husband made for selling firewood and reckoned they hadn't

A typical East End cottage
with an outside privy.

eaten two pounds of butcher's meat in a year. He was born off Curtain Road in Shoreditch; 'Ah, 'twere a'most in the country then'.

A docker's family had a four-shillings-a-week house, behind which there was a festering rubbish dump. The only furniture was the beds, with coarse sack cloth for bedding, and an old cracked mirror. The father had been injured in the crush at the dock gates and was in hospital. When in work he earned two shillings a day but would normally only get a full day's work one day in three. The wife complained of the dampness of the house, its leaking ceiling and when it was suggested that the vestry should be told, replied:

They won't do nothing, not if you goes on your knees to 'em … It do smell bad at times but there's no use our complaining. The landlord 'ud soon turn us out if he found us grumbling.

Last April they had lost three of their children in the space of a fortnight:

An' a jolly good cry I had when they was took. An' I've had many many a cry since … poor little souls. Maybe they're happy now they're dead, an' while they lived I know they hadn't much to make 'em happy.

One mother had just lost her only boy from fever:

He's better off where he is, I'm pretty sure of that, sir; and though I were main proud of him, I wouldn't wish him back.

The top floor of one of these hutches was let to a widow and her old mother; there were three children. The two women made hammocks; the canvas was hard to sew and made their hands sore and they had to make regular trips to a workshop to have the eyelets drilled. Mother and Grandmother slept in the one bed, with

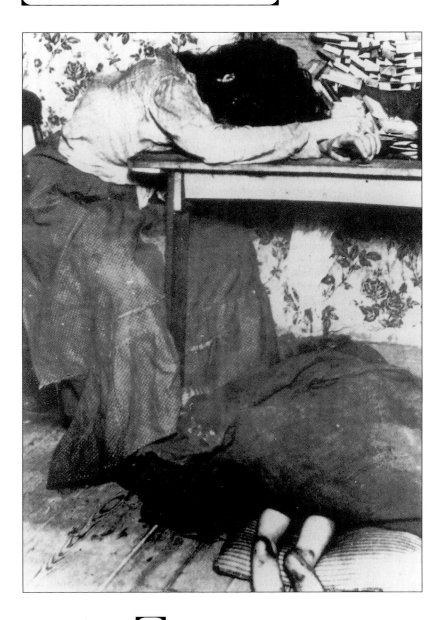

It was a grim existence from which a child's death was sometimes seen as a sad but blessed escape from a harsh world.

Home industry: the whole family help to make brushes.

the thirteen-year-old girls lying across the bottom. The three younger children slept in sacks on the floor.

A tumble-down rotten, wooden corner house with a large yard was rented out at twelve shillings a week to a man who worked 'on the coal' at the Stepney gas works. On a Saturday night a whole crowd would gather in the yard to listen to the man of the house playing his harmonium. 'He plays *The Bells of 'Eaven* beautiful,' boasted his 'woolly-haired ' Creole wife.

This was a palace compared to the rest, chaotic but full of furniture and brightly ornamented, with a whole array of cheap pictures; one was of a clown with a six-foot string of sausages giving a dancing lesson to a little girl dressed as a fairy. Five of their ten children were still at home and they had an old half-blind lodger. Tom, one of the grown-up sons, complained that his mother's house was a pigsty:

Why you papers it and paintes it, you does,
and 'angs your picturs on the walls,
an' there you cosies yourself up,
an' makes believe as you live comfortable.
But it ain't much of a 'ouse for
a family of Christyuns.

For housekeeping the wife had a sovereign a week:

He earns more than that, though,
but he puts it away somewhere.
No, it don't go down his throat now.
He's a tee-tottler, is my husbin'.
When folks begin a borryin',
they mostly ends a buryin'.
Often drinks theirselves to death they
does, cause they keep gettin deeper in,
until they're right down desperate.
They're a deal fonder o' him now that he
don't wallup them. They used to catch it
hot a' times, when he were in drink.

Toshers and mudlarks

In the last century, and indeed up until the 1920s, whole families in the East End were engaged in the unenviable occupations of 'mudlarking' and 'toshing'.

Mudlarks were mainly, but not all, children who roamed up and down the river collecting 'dock droppings' and generally looking for anything thrown up by the tide which might fetch a few pence or more in the local market.

Toshers were a strange clannish breed who haunted the gloom of the stinking sewage network which sprawled beneath the Victorian slums. Here the search was, by and large, for small valuables which had found their way down the waste pipes of London. Coins and jewellery were the most prized items, along with silver tea-spoons, watches and any other trinkets small enough to be lost into this labyrinth.

The foul smell of sewage clung to their clothes and tosher families were forced to keep their distance from their relatively sweet-smelling neighbours.

Marriage into a tosher family was frowned upon.

In the early hours of the morning, before the grey East End dawn fingered its way through the mean streets, those abroad and watchful might have spotted the toshers' descent into the underworld. This was not regarded as women's work and it was likely to be a man and his boy, bundled up in protective clothing, that lifted up the manhole cover (sometimes in their own backyard) to clamber down into the darkness to set about their day's work.

Some of the toshers managed to make a surprisingly good living from their gleanings and there was an unexpected 'perk' for these East Enders. Because of their continual exposure to bacteria, toshers developed immunity to some of the great killer diseases of the time. So, for example, when an outbreak of cholera or typhoid struck their cleaner neighbours above, these smelly pale-faced people busy in the slime were relatively safe from the disease.

Gathering to gossip and take the air outside are a group of Jewesses by their street doors.

Well there, I was a bad'un now, weren't I, Mr Austin? A blessed day it was when your mission chaps got hold o' me, that time I were so mad. An' a 'ardish work you had too, when you first took me in 'and. Many's the time I've ben a lying on t'other, an' both of us so tight as we had to be picked out of it. I often wonder I'd not done for some o' them poor children when I got the drink in me. One time I remember ketchin' up the bilin' kettle and a chucking it bang at 'em, but it missed 'em by good luck.

'East Ending'

With Whitechapel as the 'boldest blotch on the face of the capital' and so to near the thriving hub of a vast and wealthy Empire, the Great Victorian Conscience stirred. The ladies of the leisured classes firmly pinned on their wide-brimmed netted and feathered hats and then off they went 'East Ending'. Meanwhile, the gentlemen with starched shirt fronts and gold watches sat in solemn conclave upon solemn conclave and turned their attention to those alien unhappy beings who rankled and squirmed in the mire on the edge of the city.

In 1883 a penny pamphlet called the *Bitter Cry of Outcast London* sold millions of copies, cashing in on what must have been an eager and ready market.

All that do-gooding which went on! Up where Stepney Manor House had once been, they laid out a park for the poor. It was opened in 1845 and named, inevitably, after the Queen — Victoria Park. Everywhere rose monstrous great buildings, public and private while 'model dwellings', like the Peabody Estates, were built to replace rotten tenements and leaky hovels.

Listen what Ramsay MacDonald, who became the first Labour Prime Minister, has to say about them. The one he lived in, briefly, was in Grays Inn Road but they were all much of a muchness:

The sky could only be seen from the top floor. The staircase was of the kind known as 'enclosed', little air passed up and down it, and in the evening it was haunted by a medley of cooking savours which had been accumulating since morning, and the remnants of which would be carried on until next day. At night when the stair lights were put out, the homeless wanderer made his bed on the cemented landings ....

Parachute Gardens had once been a collection of rotten tenement buildings, abounding in abomination and harbouring the worst thieves and vagabonds in town. But these had been cleared away. A philanthropic company had raised its brick walls there. The thieves had gone. Science had been satisfied. There were no germs there now — only ugliness, squalor, dulness and noise. But these do not send people to hospital and certainly keep them from being discontented.

A few model dwellings are still around. There is a Peabody standing back from the Highway towards its Eastern end, looking more like prison than the South Grove Workhouse. Most have been replaced by high rise — and what, one wonders, would Ramsay have to say about them?

The People's Market, Whitechapel, opened in 1867; a barn of a Victorian building, station-like, with cheap organized food (like Kwik Save). Soup, at tuppence a bowl, was dispensed to five hundred hungry mouths daily. There were sailors' homes down by the docks and temporary shelter and soup kitchens for Jews in Leman Street. Stepney Green had a home for old Jews so they needn't end their days in a Gentile workhouse. There were lunatic asylums, public baths, schools, libraries, orphanages and more and more churches.

The Settlement Movement

The Settlement Movement brought middle-class edu-cated young men down into the abyss to do their bit. Bethnal Green, Whitechapel and Bow were their chief targets. Ramsay MacDonald was doubtful as to their value. In an unpublished novel written in the early 1890s, he describes one such, the ethical Socialist *Fellowhip of the New Life* and catches the posturing nicely.

The settlement ... was one of those that have sprung up by the dozen within recent years in London. Its distinctive feature was that it posited no dogma for the basis of its social work. The men living there had almost without exception gone through a university and were now engaged in professional work. In the evenings they met in the Common Room of the Hall where they found they did not agree on very much except that lectures and concerts and entertainments of various kinds would improve the lives of the poor.... There was not a pagan amongst them. Each one to himself was the centre of a Universe ... he read his metaphysics and attended ethical discourses, and thus became aquainted with a system of principles which to him became immediately a master tailor who treated the devout settler's body as a badly fitting coat.... They all read history in cycles, and graphically pictured Time to the slum boys who had not read philosophy, as ascending a patent spiral iron staircase always coming back to the same point but always reaching higher levels.

At Toynbee Hall, the Universities' settlement in Commercial Street opened on Christmas Eve, 1884. The saintly Canon Barnett and his wife, Henrietta, presided. From their educational activities and social work sprang the Workers' Educational Association and the Workers' Travel Association. It is no chance that Lord Beveridge, the founding father of the welfare state, did a stint at Toynbee.

Church and mission

The ecclesiastical census of 1851 showed that the poor did not go to church. The Oxford Movement, as seen in Bethnal Green and Wapping, did its stuff, offering, as the early church had done, the promise of a comfortable final escape from earthly woes and, in the meantime, warmth, companionship, light and a heavenly palace of a place to come to for a bit on Sundays.

Mostly, East Enders went to church in the evening, having a morning 'lie in'. Nonconformity, which had always been strong in the East End, flourished. It is interesting to call in on the East London Tabernacle in Burdett Road. It is still there, an uncompromisingly ugly post-war, lets-pretend-it's-not-a-church sort of building. In the 1890s, if Henry Walker's contemporary account can be believed, it was a mecca unparalleled in the religious life of East London.

It is a Sunday morning, and streams of well dressed people are setting in from all quarters — from Mile End, Stepney and Bow — towards the Tabernacle. Soon the spacious building with its wide floor and capacious galleries, is well filled.... Morning congregations in East London are almost everywhere at a minimum; yet here every Sunday is gathered, for the eleven o' clock service, a congregation of nearly two thousand persons.
The service is marked by a simplicity which takes us back to the public worship of a former generation. In the musical portion chanting is unknown and there is no organ to accompany the singing. The hymns are sung with impressive congregational fervour, and each verse is read out by the minister before it is taken up by the congregation.

The pastor there, Mr Archibald Brown, was a very important local figure, as anyone who can command an audience of two thousand every lie-a-bed Sunday morning might be. He was not just a good showman; he was a tireless visitor to the poor homes of Bow.

When Frances Short died in her home in Armagh Road just after the century had turned, Pastor Brown was at the death bed. Mr Short was an anxious oil-and-colour-man who drank to keep himself going and left most things, including all the children and all about them, to his wife. Aged fifty-two, she died, exhausted. With her dying breath she recited all seven verses of the hymn *Peace perfect peace*:

It is enough
Earth's struggles soon shall cease
And Jesus call us
To Heaven's perfect peace.

'Your mother's death,' declared the Pastor to Mrs Short's teenage daughter, 'was such as would make the angels weep.'

There was mission upon mission; the George Yard Mission in Whitechapel, the King Edward Mission in Spitalfields, the Nichol Street Mission, the Harley Road Mission and so forth. The 'Out and Out' Mission in Bow is still there, on the east corner of Lefevre Walk estate, open for 'informal worship'. A Sikh lady brings offerings of fruit and bright coloured table cloths.

At the London Cottage Mission at 67, Salmon Lane, two hundred children were fed every Wednesday from November to May. Three times the hall was filled and soup ladled out from vast tureens after grace had been sung to the tune of *The Old Hundredth*. Besant noticed a pretty girl with poppies in her hat 'quite a little lady'. She had eaten only a little bread since last Wednesday; there were three children at home, a mother out-of-work and no father.

A museum was opened to bring culture to the starving, just near the site of the Blind Beggar's mansion; it is still there, calling itself the Toy Museum these days, with a garish 'Toys R Us' sort of a label on its sturdy iron structure encased in brick, a refugee

A soup kitchen for the Jewish poor depicted in 1894.

Façade of the soup kitchen in Brune Street.

from South Kensington. On a sticky Bethnal Green evening in July 1884, the portly fun-loving Prince of Wales and his beautiful Danish princess glittered their royal way through the streets of the abyss to a soirée there. The Prince addressed a crowd of worthies:

For some time past my thoughts ...have been given to
ameliorate the condition of the laborious working
classes of the metropolis ...They like all other, or
above all other classes of the community must have
their recreations and amusements ...so that you may
have, after your toil is over, your concert rooms, your
reading rooms, and, if possible, your gardens, in
which you may enjoy the summer nights, such
as we have had this year.

The occasion was one of many functions held to publicize a scheme for creating a 'Palace of Delights' for the East Enders on the site of the old Bancroft school and almshouses. A wealthy philanthropist called Barber Beaumont, who had made his money by insurance, was the prime mover in the scheme fifty years before.

...being minded and desirous of founding an
Institution for the purpose of affording persons in the
neighbourhood of Beaumont Square ...the means of
meeting together for mental and moral improvement
and amusement in their intervals of business freed
from the baneful excitement of intoxicating liquors
and also for the cultivation of the general
principal of natural theology'.

A dream of charity

In 1882 Walter Besant had published a novel, *All sorts and conditions of men — an impossible story*. The tale is of a clever man and a rich young woman, Angela Messenger, who devote themselves to the East End

and plan a cultural, educational and recreational institution. To quote Angela:

This is our own palace, the club of the ordinary
people; we will not let anybody make money out
of it; we shall use it for ourselves, and we
shall make our enjoyment for ourselves.

Besant's book was a scoop; it rapidly became a best seller, catching the mood of the times.

With royal support, well-orchestrated publicity and private endowment Besant's 'impossible story' turned into reality and a People's Palace rose, comprising a vast concert hall, the Queen's Hall, a technical school and a library — as well as a winter garden (completed in 1892 at a cost of fourteen thousand pounds) for refreshments and music.

There were twice-weekly concerts in the Queen's Hall and religious music on Sundays. The man turned out of doors while his dinner was prepared, according to the Chairman of the Beaumont Trustees, instead of waiting for the pubs to open 'finds the great Queen's Hall, well warmed and lighted, open to him, and excellent recitals of sacred music performed for his benefit'. Audiences were over three thousand on Sundays and between 1,200 and 1,400 people used the library every day! Had you passed along the Mile End Road on a Tuesday or Thursday evening in the 1890s you might have heard the merry sound of a band playing in brilliant electric light of the Winter Garden, with East Enders in their Sunday best sitting among the palms and aspidistras. A reporter from the *Manchester Guardian* was amazed and delighted to see 'hundreds of young men and women dancing a quadrille'.

Perhaps more attention to unemployment or the support of the destitute would have been a more sensible approach but the locals undoubtedly used their Palace of Delights and were very proud of it. Some it lifted out of the abyss, no doubt.

Sid Short — he of the Bug Blinder — had his proudest moment in when his daughter Lily sang before the Duchess of York (the present Queen Mother) at the People's Palace, as it came to be called. As far as its educational function was concerned, by 1932 the East London College which had grown out of it was being criticized; according to a letter to the Charity Commissioners:

The poor of East London do not pass
through its portals.

The college gained recognition as a school of London University and they decided to change its name from the East London College in 1934. The Academic Board thought it...

especially unfortunate to have a local name because
the eastern half of London, perhaps unjustly, is
generally disparaged by those resident in other
quarters of the metropolis.

When a lecturer from the history department there published the seminal history of the East End's medieval past in later years the publishers advised that it should be called *Medieval London Suburbs*, by way of disguise. So it became Queen Mary College and Sid Short's grand-daughter took a first class degree there in due course. Now it is Queen Mary and Westfield College, having joined in an unlikely alliance with the polite ladies' establishment from Hampstead, Queen Mary and Westfield College. Happily the technical and practical bias of its origins is not forgotten — this was once a place of useful instruction for the working end of town. Queen Mary's and Westfield's engineering department excells.

Thousands and thousands of charitable pounds were poured into the East End towards the end of the last century; the Charity Organisation Society started

Instructions in many skills
were available at the
People's Palace, including
woodcarving, carpentry
and joinery, electrics,
dressmaking and tailoring,
modelling in clay and art.

Entertainment was also
provided at the People's
Palace with twice-weekly
concerts — and religious
music on Sundays.

PEOPLE'S PALACE,
MILE END ROAD, E.
A GRAND VARIETY
CONCERT
Will take place at the above
MONDAY, MAY 11,
On behalf of
Mr. W. H. WHEELER,
Who was for many years with the London General Omnibus
Co., and has now been out of employment for the past six
months, and is in great need of assistance, being unable to
regain his employment through the failure of his eyesight.

ARTISTES—
WILL BURTON
The funny man in his funniosities of Gesture and Facial Expression.

HARRY LANE   ALLAN ORR
The Ideal Comic.   The Society Comique.

Professor RENI
In his Ventriloquial and Royal Living Marionette Entertainment.

MISS ADA WRIGHT   J. STUART
Charming Comedienne & Burlesque Artiste.   Musical Comedian.

ALBERT HORNBY
The great Silver-toned Tenor Artiste.

Miss NELLIE RAVEN   WILL DREW
Vocalist and Expert Dancer.   The Up-to-date Comic.

ALF OLDHAM
In his wonderful FEMININE Impersonations.

W. Austin Kennedy   Charles Willacy
The famous Elocutionist.   Comedian.

J.W. CROUESTE
The favourite Character Comedian.

This case is strongly recommended and supported by the
following influential gentlemen:—ERNEST GRAY, Esq.,
M.A., M.P.; ALDERMAN J. H. BETHEL, Esq.; ALDERMAN
C. HARBOTT, Esq., J.P.; COUNCILLOR J. R. HURRY, Esq.;
COUNCILLOR J. FARNIE, Esq., and many others.

Secretary—J. K. UNDERHILL, 34, Vicarage Road, Stratford.
Treasurer—G. OFFLEY, 74, Warwick Road, Stratford.
Chairman of Committee—C. D. KING.   Musical Director—J. STUART.
Pianist Mr. GEORGE LEAVER.

**PRICES OF ADMISSION: Reserved
Seats, 2/-; 1/6 (to admit 2), 1/- & 6d.**
DOORS OPEN AT 7.30, COMMENCE AT 8 SHARP.
Don't look on the Other Side.

From the early 19th century, starvation wages were paid to workers at home in the so-called 'sweated industries': mattress stuffing was one such industry.

to rationalize it all. The problem of the poor, debated since the end of the previous century was at its most acute now in the capital. Margaret Ethel Gladstone, a Kensington girl of genteel birth and non-conformist stock, one of the many brave ladies who went 'East Ending', pondered in her diary in September 1893:

> The rich think themselves of different stuff; it is kind of them to give the tiniest share of their fortune to those less fortunate, a special virtue in giving a sixpence or a ten minutes' visit to a poor person which there is not in the giving of a six pound and six shilling's present or an hour's call to a rich person; and the poor share in the delusion. But the poor are waking up to the fact that this magic gulf between them is imaginary, and unless the rich wake up to it too we shall have a rumpus.

Well — there was a rumpus. There were strikes and demonstrations and the education which those kind old Victorians had brought to the East End 'arabs' gave the workers an articulate voice. Gradually, private charity and missions, soup kitchens and quadrilles for the workers disappeared, and good and wise men decided, for the most part, that redistribution of wealth was the answer, for the time being, at least. The East Ender, along with everyone else, had a real say in government and the working man went to Westminster, led by the 'unsatisfactory man' who Margaret Ethel Gladstone had found and married.

MORE FRIENDLY THAN IT IS NOW

The East End remembered

hings haven't really been the same since bus conductors went — or most of them. They used to sing and make jokes and turn the number eight into a fun run, or, if you were easily embarrassed, a nightmare. There are a few singing conductors left; one can be found on the number twenty-five, which goes to Bow church:

> Here we are at Bunches Wine Bar,
> ladies and gents. Anyone for a snifter?

But, for the most part, buses are now solemn places where you queue up to pay the driver who has too much on his plate to bother with quips.

Reminiscences of the 'Old Days' in the East End, both private and published, conjure up a world 'more friendly that it is now'. It was a world of warmth and

Tram in Jamaica Road in 1951. To begin with trams were horse-drawn. Electric trams arrived in London in the 1890s before electricity was introduced into the home. The first LCOG motor bus service became operational in 1904.

camaraderie, they would have you believe, with all the front doors open with a welcome: 'you must have smelt the teapot!'

> Put your feet on the mantleshelf
> And make yourself at home.

Mum is there smiling by the stove in an apron; Dad pulls on a pipe and puts on his slippers. Everyone gathers around the kitchen table for sausages and mash or a feast of cockles and winkles. Someone may pop in to borrow a cup of sugar or for a chat. There is no telly to keep folk behind closed doors and all is share and share alike.

Nan and aunties, uncles and cousins are within walking distance, if they don't actually share the house, and there are frequent family gatherings. From time to time bunting is hung along the street and all the neighbours join in to load the trestle tables with plates of sandwiches and bottles of beer. Late into the summer night everyone will jollify and dance to celebrate some national event. Shopping, instead of being a lonely trolley push along organized gangways, is an exciting expedition to a colourful market where folk wander from stall to stall, meeting friends and exchanging banter with the 'characters' there. Churches, chapels and synagogues were filled with song and vibrant worship, and children were taught with proper discipline to respect age-old moral values.

Mildred Gordon, the MP for Bow and Poplar, used to live, as a child, in a house just by St Georges in the East. Hers was a Jewish family; she remembers there being a spirit of co-operation among the mixed races; if anyone made a bread pudding, they always made enough for 'next door' to have half.

Jessie Owens and Ivy Ducas remember

Listen to Jessie Owens and her friends, interviewed in 1977 about their experiences of the First World War and the 1920s in Stepney:

Jessie: If you were ill someone said, 'Oh, Mrs Rose is not well, someone will soon come in to help....Have you had you dinner yet? We will keep it ready for.

Ivy: When Mum used to have a baby, the neighbours would say, 'We'll take the children,' and that one [would] take all the washing.

Their recollection of the exciting hot summer nights of an East End youth heart-rend the most.

> Oh the day of the Kerry dancing,
> Oh, the ring of the piper's tune.

The longing for lost happiness is the same, whether it be for sweet nights spent under the stars in an Irish glade or outside a sleazy Limehouse pub after throwing-out time, where the stars cannot penetrate the industrial gloom.

Jessie remembered there were three pubs on the corner of Salmon Lane:

> Saturday night 'course people used to [be] going out,
> and the kids were allowed out late, and there used to
> be a man, I think his name was Charlie Saunders, but
> they used to call him Mutton Eye cause he had a bad
> eye, and he used to have one of those folding organs
> and he used to tramp. Oh, about ten o'clock, and
> sometimes he was joined by a blind woman and
> sometimes her daughter came, and they
> really were smashing singers.
> And when the pubs turned out, everybody used to be
> out, and they used to have lovely nights, and you never
> went indoors till one or two in the morning.
> And they nearly always ended up in a fight.

Ivy: But they'd be happy, didn't they?

Jessie: It all used to be lovely, I always used to love Saturday night.

There is no doubt that, as Jessie said, a neighbourhood support system might swing into action in times of crisis. The Rothschild Building in Spitalfields was full of Russian and Polish Jewish families at the turn of the century. One such was the Morris family: Mum and Dad and seven children, a fellow occupant remembers:

> This Mrs Morris got on to a chair to put a penny
> in the slot for her gas to go on, and she fell and broke
> her leg. Oh, tragedy! She was taken to the London
> Hospital. What should she do with her seven children?
> ... All the neighbours collected around and said they's
> take it in turns each day. One would go in the mornings
> to give them their breakfast to see that they's get off to
> school, and in the evening when the husband comes
> home he'll take in the pot of
> whatever it was and they'll all feed together....
> Now, on the day [Mrs Morris] came home from the
> hospital, the neighbours all collected together and
> washed the children, made them all clean, sat them in
> a row....She was so overwhelmed by the party, they'd
> collected some cakes and things and made it all
> look very nice, that she burst out crying.

*A Bow wedding in 1908:
the oil-and-rag man, Sid
Short marries Lilian who
looks a little glum about
the occasion, an expression
mirrored by Sid's
mother-in-law, sitting
next but one to her
newly-wedded daughter.*

If anyone was really destitute, collections would be made among the neighbours to tide them over.

Back in the Rothschild Building:

Four [families] gave their rooms for the wedding. And every one of them was baking and making things.... Door was open and the band was playing outside ... a violin player and a bugler ... and anybody and everybody was welcome, the door open to come and drink and have a snack.... And they were dancing ... out in the verandah and in the playground.

The Blitz

Forty years after the wedding party party in Spitalfields the East Enders were coping with an enemy more immediate than poverty in the Blitz.

Everything is dimmed by the smoke of burning houses, and thought is confused by the memory of incessant elongated crashes and reverberations from the earth and the sky, and there is flashing in the eyes and the unforgettable smell of fire and a tingling in the fingertips'.

From this mayhem grew a spirit of legendary fortitude and co-operation, enough to bolster and confirm for ever the notion of East Enders sticking together for mutual help and support.

The Mayor wrote in 1939-40:

What is Stepney? Squalid streets, mean houses, great hearts. Great ships unloading, tailoring trade, sweat shops under glaring electric lights, a brisk business in singing birds.

In its 1,903 acres and among its 34,000 buildings and 200,000 inhabitants, there were 40,000 'incid-

Knott Street in 1941. The Blitz began in September 1940 and by the following May London was being subjected to intense raids. 20,000 civilians had been killed and 25,000 badly injured.

ents' during the War. The Mayor remembered the Mile End Road crowded with 'smart little Cockney girls' arm-in-arm with boys, walking along between the smoking skeletons of houses, wearing their Sunday best and singing. They were not down-hearted and they cocked a snoop at Lord Haw Haw's propaganda, ringing out from the wireless sets:

I know the London East End! Those dirty Jews and Cockneys will run like rabbits into their holes.

The 'sky murderers' hummed high overhead and the sirens wailed, and the German agents in Stepney

Christmas decorations in an East End shelter in London's Underground in 1940.

Lydia Street in 1940

30,000 Jews from Stepney attended an anti-Nazi demonstration in July 1933.

spread the word: 'Hitler's new order will clear away your slums'.

Late one day at the beginning of the War the Mayor dragged himself wearily out of Queen Mary College taken over as the council headquarters. Before him stood hundreds of old prams, chipped and broken repaired with string, deserted in the evening light wrapped in the smoke from burning houses. Their owners and their occupants had been called in for emergency evacuation to the country and there was no room on the trains for the prams. 'Tragic old prams'.

East-Enders were made homeless; they were exiled maimed and killed. They lost their livelihoods and their possessions. Bands of them set off nightly for the West End air raid shelters. Pinned to many doors were scrappy notes giving a 'forwarding address' for those who had taken off to stay with friends or relatives in the outer suburbs. The Mayor goes on proudly:

They went jostling, laughing and jeering into the forefront of the battle: Grannies and costers, Jews and Arabs, Indians and Negroes, tailors and trouser-basters, consumptives and fit, Chinamen and Vicars, and school kids and gasmen; and they fought the fire, and they fought panic and disease and sleeplessness, and they used burning incendiary bombs as hand torches by which to do the rescue work — and presently the Luftwaffe reeled back, and the crisis of the war was passed'.

Grove Road during Bethnal Green warship week 21-28 March 1942.

Was it really so lovely and friendly?

I wonder, was it all really so lovely and friendly? Or are those who reminisce recalling only the good things, lent enchantment by being part of a lost youth? They all seem to sing the same tune, it is true, so there must be strong elements of truth in the myth. Crowded together and sharing what they had, the old East Enders seem, from what is remembered, to have stuck close together to combat the authorities, the enemy bombers and acts of God alike.

But this new, near contemporary folk history is of a different order from the stuff woven from a variety of written sources. Never before have ordinary people left for posterity such personal accounts of their experiences of life. If we had working men and women's recollections from the nineteenth-century East End, as we have from the twentieth, perhaps it would seem to us a 'wery nice' neighbourhood. As it is, we have only the gasps of horror of middle-class philanthropists on which to base our understanding.

We do not starve these days and, although there is poverty and suffering, we are, for the most part, closer in our experience of life to the gasping do-gooders than to the children whom Dr Barnardo rescued from the abyss. For us the baths in front of the fire, the gobstoppers and barley sugars, the larks and the street parties must appear as highlights in a drab, weary and harsh existence. Working hours were still very long and people did die of starvation in Whitechapel only eighty years ago. Lord Beveridge's father wrote that poverty wore a 'grimmer aspect in London' than it did in Calcutta. Diseases were rampant in this vast slum where, even in 1945, few houses had any sanitation.

Racial tension

Maybe Gentile shared bread pudding with Jew, but there was a good deal of racial feeling around and tension between the different groups was magnified, as it always is, by poverty. Everyone was fighting for the same crust. The Protestants hated the Catholics and the Catholics hated the Protestants and everybody hated the Jews, as Tom Lehrer used to sing. Little had changed since the old days when everybody hated the Flemings, then the Dutch, then the French Huguenots, not to mention the Irish, Scots and Welsh and anyone who spoke 'funny' or ate strange food.

Lil Daniels and her brothers, who were of Nonconformist persuasion, used to go around in the early years of this century, searching out the Roman Catholic churches in and around Bow and putting soot in the holy water. So when the 'old mickeys' crossed themselves they made a black mark. When Lil had children she warned them that they must run fast by the convent in Tredegar Square, for fear the nuns should 'get' them.

Frank Lewey, writing his *Cockney Campaign* after the War, expressed surprise that the Jewish community had coped with the Blitz as manfully as those of Anglo Saxon stock.

Neighbours and friends might help one another out in time of need but there was a good deal of back stabbing in the market place. Hospitality was on offer, but only close and trusted friends were expected to enter the house without knocking, even if the door was left open or a key put in a letter box attached by a piece of string. (Locking up wasn't important as burglars were unlikely to bother with homes where there was nothing worth 'nicking'.) In spite of the song, if anyone actually put their feet up on the mantlepiece, they would be soon told to 'sling their 'ook'.

Life for the kids: Crisp Street market

Let us take a look at life as it seemed to a few East Enders. How was it for the kids? They emerged from cramped bug-ridden cottages or ran down the smelly staircases of tenements and out into a cruel grey world. Along the monotonous streets clattered the little boots, off to school or on errands for Mum, perhaps to the local market.

At Christmas, in particular, markets must have seemed like fairyland. Listen to Jim Stuart talking about Crisp Street Market in Poplar:

It drew us like a magnet; its smells, its lights, its jolly crowds. Stepping out lively and chatting like monkeys, eager for the good things to come ... we were caught up in the steady stream of late night shoppers making their way over the railway bridge ... into the throng of ... [the] market.
We briefly glanced into Old 'Inky's' little shop at the foot of the bridge, where trays of home-made Toffee Flats, twists of Panagoric, Barley Sugar and Acid Drops, all laid out on tin trays and finely dusted with powdery sugar, tempted us to spend our fortune.
From all sides came the cries of the stall holders, shouting their wares under the glare of naked electric light bulbs, strung out on wires above the wooden stalls, standing in the gutter.
We watched spellbound at the eels being gutted and chopped up, seconds after trying to slither off the block. The man was too quick for them but we stood and watched, hoping they would get away, but they never did: and he sang 'All alive-o'.
Goods were weighed and wrapped in newspaper and passed over to outstretched hands, with a 'Ta luv, g'night dear.
A dark Indian man poured something on a pile of orange rinds, on a plate, then set light to it .... The stuff was supposed to cure coughs and colds, all for sixpence a bottle.
Familiar smells guiding the shopper to sickly sweet combs and rock, sugar-bubbling in a pan ....
Hot chestnuts: we stood toasting our cheeks at the ... vendor's fire.

School life

An eel stall in Petticoat Lane.

You couldn't spend all your time wandering around the streets — you had to go to school.

Truancy was not the problem it subsequently became and East Enders were anxious that their kids should benefit from education. There was no shortage of schools in the East End; Walter Jones, who was Mayor of Stepney in 1913, wrote:

These wretched schools are like a cancer in the place — eating up all the Funds, absorbing all the attention and interest and life.

Charity schools, attached to the livery companies who owned property in the area, had existed for several hundred years, the Coopers' school and the Drapers' school, and those founded by Nicholas and Avis Gibson in the sixteenth century; the Coborn School for Girls founded by the widow of a Bow brewer, Sir John Cass's school and Raines. In the nineteenth century came the ragged schools and then the industrial schools for vagrant children, run by local prison authorities and, after the 1870 Education Act, Board schools and County Council schools.

Like their ex-pupils most of the ancient foundations have now moved out into suburban Essex. Bancrofts is in Woodford, Coopers and Coborn is in Upminster.

For the Jewish community education was, as it had been for thousands of years, respected and venerated. It was also part of the escape plan. The Jewish Free School in Bell Lane, Spitalfields, with its daily roll of over four thousand children, was an important aided voluntary school for East End immigrant children. In time, however, the Jewish Free School followed the migration to north London.

As far as the immigrant children were concerned the main task of the state system was 'to make all the children good English subjects'. At 3.40 pm on the first

Sarsparilla and other hot drinks, from the Italian man, serving from a colourful little cart; his horse tied to a lamp post round the corner, ate damp cabbage leaves.
From a side street came the tinkling notes of a barrel organ, beating out a tune, accompanied by the clickety-clack of the tap dancers, as they tapped and strutted away on their mat of slatted wood.
Music and cries were all around us; 'Aypers, all aypers?'....cards of buttons, hooks and eyes, lengths of ribbon...cost one half-penny. 'Salt, Ma — don't forget your salt!'

The man cut through the great icebergs of salt....
'Your Army Greys at nine — a tanner a pair your Coloureds [socks].'
Cheap jacks selling off crockery, crashing the plates together, making jokes to the ring of upturned faces.
'Now ladies, who'll make a bid for this gozunder?'
The Pie and Eel shop smelled lovely. The cheery ladies behind the counter ladled out rich green gravy, sloshing it over the mountains of potato set beside the tasty steaming pies, on the thick china plates....
Either side of the marble top table, set in pews down the wall of the shop, people were eating their supper.

Empire Day, in 1904, the strains of *The Flag of Britain* could be heard ringing out from the Jewish Free School. There followed a lecture: 'What the Empire does for us and what we should do for the Empire'. Miss Jackson at the Commercial Street School wore a Union Jack apron. As today, the main problem facing the teachers of the Russian and Polish children was one of language. In 1896 forty per cent of the boys admitted to the 'First Standard' of the Commercial Street School spoke only Yiddish.

John Fletcher at school

It was not just the Jews who saw education as a way out of the ghetto.

John Fletcher lived with his parents in St Stephen's Road. They were country people originally; John's mother had been in service at home in a Northamptonshire village and always kept a nice table, insisting on the cutlery being laid out in the proper fashion and carefully rolling crisp linen napkins into ivory rings. In the late summer and autumn there were always three mop-headed chrysanthemums in each of the two blue vases which stood on the floor in the bay window of her cramped Bow house.

For holidays, if they could afford it, they went back home to the farm. Mum remembered the more spacious days of her own childhood, skating on the village pond at Christmas and losing her red mittens, helping with the harvest and going to market in Oundle with her aunt who set the butter prices.

John's father worked in the armaments factory at the end of the road — the building is still there. In 1921, when the boy was ten, his father died and there was no pension and no insurance — except a couple of bob a week from the Gas Light and Coke Company — and a brother had recently been born. Mum had to take in washing and life was a real struggle. Fortunately, John's father had been a Mason and, now that his Mum

John Fletcher

John Fletcher and his mother outside their house in 1916.

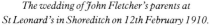

*John Fletcher's mum with the
family in the country, harvesting.*

*The wedding of John Fletcher's parents at
St Leonard's in Shoreditch on 12th February 1910.*

was widowed, his son was entitled to a place at the Masonic School in Bushey.

He remembers the first day —aged eleven, being put on the train in an uncomfortable coarse tweed suit which rubbed his neck. Mum, with sad wispy hair, wearing a brown coat, waved from the platform as he was hurtled away to become a gentleman.

Life was now cold baths and bullying. There were only two East End urchins in the school and the other one was so victimized that he ran away. Lying in the dormitory in those first months, John thought of the familiar streets where he had crawled under the stalls

for specked oranges and raked around for long companionable days with his friend, Mac.

Sunday afternoons, after the walk, the boys had to write home. John wrote, twice: 'Dear Mother, please take me away'. She cried when she received these letters but what could she do? Not only were the Masons giving her son the sort of education which might, with luck, eventually lift him out of the slums, they were also paying for all his clothing and keep, which she could now ill afford.

Life did not improve in Bushey for two seemingly endless terms and when, in his eightieth year, John was

taken back to see the school, it was those first months which came to mind — sobbing in a narrow iron bed, shut in a hot classroom as punishment for his origins while the others played outside. His house master was a persecutor. When Aunt Doll sent him a cake for his brithday John was summoned to the dreadful study and made to watch while the master jumped on the parcel and squashed it into an inedible mess.

John did not run away; he started to fight back. In the second term a chess competition was held. He had never heard of chess, let alone played it and there was much sneering from the master when he announced that he would like to enter. For weeks, with the help of a boy from a suburb superior to Bow, he taught himself the game and practised the odd moves with the high born pieces. He won the competition — check mate and the first step out of the East End.

School life for Violet Beatrice Short

Meanwhile, a few streets away from St Stephen's Road, Violet Beatrice, just five, was setting off for her first day at Malmesbury Road School, oversized for her age, in buttoned boots and clutching a small bag of American cloth made by her Mum. It contained a slate rag, a penny for the 'starving Europeans' and a packet of cold buttered toast for her elevenses. The smell of cold buttered toast still makes her shudder with horror.

At home there was Mum, Dad, Uncle and Aunty, two sisters, Grandad and Omo the cat, tin baths in front of the fire on Friday, Tiger Tim comics, safe and warm.

At school, there was Miss Drayton with a pince-nez and a headmistress who dressed Edwardian style, her hair piled high. If you encountered her in the playground you had to salute. It was bare, bleak and hard, with little except a picture of the coronation and *The Monarch of the Glen* to stimulate a young imagination. There was standing on seats with your hands on your head if you talked, big boys who teased and chased and called her a dunce — because she seemed older than she was. You sat at a double desk and learnt dull stuff by rote, scraping away on slates and soliciting a bit of spit from your nearest neighbours to clean the greasy boards. You had to gallump round in drill trying to 'fall silently like a snowflake…. If you don't stop crying, Violet, you will have to be whipped'.

She howled her way through the infants, nevertheless, finishing the tasks she was given to do quickly, and then sitting red-eyed and frightened at the double desk she shared with a Jewish boy called 'Mossy'. Every morning her family were made to line up and cross

their hearts and swear they would make sure she came home at the end of the day; they had to say 'surficial' (it's official).

In the Junior Mixed things did not improve at once. But the plump white-haired tartar in a black sateen apron who picked on Violet at every opportunity was replaced by Miss Bryant who put her feet up on the desk, sang Welsh songs and told the children tales from *The Water Babies*. Gentle married women appeared on the staff, war widows who came with an aura of glamour to them. A few words of encouragement and school became the little girl's abiding passion.

The sobbing ceased.

As the afternoons grew shorter towards Christmas,
the yellow gas lights were turned up by our teachers,
standing on the nearest desk to each one and applying
a flaming taper; we made paper chains, lanterns and
Christmas cards. As the evenings lengthened after
Christmas, life became more sociable and we stayed to
play the different games as they came in their seasons:
touch, skipping, marbles, hopscotch, please we've
come to learn the trade, grandmother's steps, peg
tops, whipping tops and wooden and metal hoops.

She was one of the two children to pass the scholarship to go to the Coborn School for Girls. To celebrate Mum cooked her favourite meal of fried pork sausages, onions and potatoes baked in their jackets.

Coborn was a genteel oasis in the inter-war East End, where playtime was 'recess', dinner 'lunch' and the girls, attired in navy gym slips and panama hats, sang Wagner's *Spinning Chorus* and *Have you seen but a white lily grow?* There was a prize for the girl who most nearly fitted the description of the virtuous woman from the Book of Proverbs whose price was above rubies. Violet never won it but her sister did.

Violet was made silk-worm monitor and went from strength to strength, eventually becoming head girl for

two years in succession. She remembers representing the school at a League of Nations rally in the Albert Hall where the Prince of Wales talked movingly of peace for all time.

When Dad went to see the head because he was concerned about his daughter's progress in maths, he was firmly told: 'The girls come here not to learn mathematics, but to paint the yellow of a daffodil'.

It was primroses, not daffodils, which set Violet off on her career. Dad was Sid Short, the oil-and-colour man. One spring, Knights, the soap manufacturers, sent him a quantity of artificial primroses to use as a promotion for their product in the shop. Unlike John Fletcher, Violet didn't have any country cousins or, if she did, she never saw them. She had never seen a primrose and was enchanted by the bright masses of tiny pale yellow flowers.

Sitting on the whitened doorstep of their house in Lacey Street, her elder sister dissected a snapdragon and explained about the different parts, the petals, the sepals, the stamen. She decided to be a botantist — perhaps because flowers were a rarity in Bow back yards, perhaps because of Coborn, perhaps because Sid Short had called his daughters Lily, Iris and Violet.

Mum's role

It wasn't only Violet who clung fast to home: families were important, perhaps even more so than in a country village.

In the strange hostile environment that the immigrants found themselves, it was vital to stick together. There was a neighbourliness, as we have seen, an ethnic support group, but the ties of blood and affinity bound the knots of East Enders fastest in a defence against the dangers of poverty, disease and contempt. There was a strong feeling of 'them and us — we were probably slightly better than everyone else and also rather frightened of them all.'

'Dear old Dumps', the clever daughter of the mayor, was banished from her beloved family in Wapping for two years to go to college in Brighton at the beginning of the Great War.

She never adjusted. She wrote to her father:

Silly kid that I am! although I am coming home a fortnight tomorrow I can feel quite a lump in my throat when I think of you and Mum at home.

Her father, who had written twice a week all the time she was away, wrote back, with relief that the separation was over, remembering ...

The meetings and partings at dear old London Bridge, and the cups of tea before going away — the slipping into your hand a piece of gold to make both ends meet while you were away — my feelings as the train left the Station and as I walked over London Bridge — Eastcheap — Tower — Highway — Old Gravel Lane and home — picturing your train all the way and guessing mentally where it was until the hour timed for it to reach Brighton and then imagining you making for the College — the Dorm — the greetings with your Pals etc. etc: and now it's nearly all over'.

At the heart of most families was Mum. 'I'm the only onion,' she might complain as she ran around a 'grizzling' and demanding brood — referring to the onion in the stew which is vital to its flavour but taken for granted. But she was not really. 'Few sections of society', write Robert Barltrop and Jim Wolveridge, 'make mothers the object of so much affection and respect as Cockneys do'.

As has been in the East End since Shakespeare's day, women were independent and tough. Sailors' wives, who dominated the area for several hundred years, had

to shift for themselves much of the time, running alehouses and market stalls. Women were always employed in the local 'rag trade'. In the 1890s, if you were lucky, you might see 'Mog the Man' standing outside one of the lodging houses in Flower and Dean Street in her spotless white apron. A local policeman remembered:

When she was drunk she was a 'he-man' and a terror. Stripped bare to the waist, I have seen her fight the worst Amazons of Spitalfields and Whitechapel and ...nearly beat the life out of them.

The celebrated sociological survey done by Michael Young and Peter Wilmott in the Bethnal Green of the late fifties, concluded that it was a matriachal society in the post-war East End. Most East Enders could have told them that.

When a girl married she stuck close to her mother and would see her as much as twelve times a day; they popped in and out of each others' flats for tea and chats, shopping together and sharing the care of the children. The main meal of the day was invariably eaten at Nan's. No wonder the mother-in-law joke was such a popular feature in the music halls.

Mum was at home more than Dad, cooking and controlling. Dad always at work (or play) and her relationship with the children was all important. Jerry White remembers the Jewish mothers of Spitalfields walking arm in arm with their daughters along the naptha-lit stalls of the Whitechapel Road and gazing into the bright shop windows.

Running the home was hard physical work; the lifting of heavy wet sheets out of steaming coppers, the carrying of food home from the market and the continual preparation of meals and servicing the kids:

Wait a minute and I'll dance for you
the other ha'penny

Would you like me to pick you up and sing
for you as well?

What did your last servant die of?'

More burdensome than all this was the juggling of the budget to make ends meet and the Monday trips to 'uncle', the pawnbroker, to keep the family going until next pay day. One summer day in 1915 Walter Jones had a day out in a pawnbroker's house in Croydon:

My word — what a place!
Orchard — Lawn Tennis — Bowls — Billiard Room — Salmon — Roast Beef — Hock — Champagne — port and cigars.

Mum would often not partake of the family meal and, if anyone was to make sacrifices to keep the rest going it would be her. The wife of Sid Short, the Bow oil-and-colour man, had suffered extremes of poverty as a child. She was a proud little body and ran away from Sunday school to avoid having to receive the hand-out of an orange given to the 'poor children'. Her daughters were going to have the best that she could afford. When, in her twenties, Lily Short left her gloves behind in church, the vicar's wife knew they must be her's as they were of such fine leather.

As smart as paint and 'done up regardless' were the East End girls. They still are. It arose from a combination of 'my face is my fortune' and the availability of cheap 'seconds' and clothes which had 'fallen off lorries' locally. The best place to spy the glamorous girls out these day is on Saturday in Roman Road market, Spain-tanned and elegant in gold jewellery and up-to-the-minute fashions. Their great grandmothers, the Match Girls who suffered and struggled at Bryant and Mays in the last century are said to have been brilliant in their style, although it was short lived. If they survived phossyjaw they succumbed to the early ageing brought on by child bearing and hardship.

'Keep your hand on your ha'penny,' Mum would warn when her daughter started courting. There was a rigorous moral code born of necessity; if you 'got into trouble' it could spell economic disaster. Likewise there was no room for grand romance in the kitchen-cuddling which went on after the rest of the family had gone to bed or, in later years, in the back row of The Odeon. You might listen with your eyes full of tears to *Love's Old Sweet Song* in the music hall but perhaps more to the point was:

> At Trinity Church I met my doom
> Now we live in a top back room.

Aggressive banter was the language of love, and probably still is. Listen to Robert Balthrop's couple sitting on a bench near Watney Street market:

Betsy: Thank Gawd for a sit down, my feet are killing me. I wish you wouldn't take me out on these walks.

Bill: Me take you — I like that. You lug me all round the houses, get me to look at half the shops in Stepney — and when you feel tired, who gets the blame? Joe Soap.

Betsy: Well, you wanted to take me out, and walking me round the shops was taking me out. Anyway I'm sitting here for the next hour and I'm not moving; you want to do any more walking you can do it on your own Jack.

Bill: I'm not sure who took who now, but I know one thing and that ain't two — I've seen enough furniture shops to last me a lifetime. I don't know what you women see in furniture, I don't straight.

And so on.

The interest in furniture, 'keeping the place nice', whitening the doorstep, was an important part of keeping your head above water in the slums. As vital a part of life as keeping up appearances in the home was the 'life force' of snobbery. It was part of the way up and out, to ape middle-class manners, and although there was a strong vein of 'who does he think he is?' and a dislike of social pretension, there was even more abhorrence of 'common' behaviour. Lily Short's mother forbad her children to go to the eel-and-pie shop and kids were walloped for not 'talking proper' even though their parents didn't. John Fletcher's mother wouldn't have dreamt of going hop picking in the summer to augment her meagre income, or of letting her children do so. That was something that the lowest of the low did. Fish and chips had to be fetched in a shopping basket so that the neighbours wouldn't spot the tell-tale newspaper bundles.

Housewives shopping at
Roman Road Market.

*Petticoat Lane
(Middlesex Street) market in 1870.*

Shops and markets

Shopping was a very different exercise from what it is now. It was a social occasion, and a frequent one. Nobody had the money to stock up and trips to the market, small shops and casual barrows were a daily, if not twice-daily occurrence. Most shops stayed open until quite late into the evening.

Markets were the main source, supplemented by the corner shops. In Whitechapel there was a six-day market in Wentworth Street and the turnings off it. The 'beloved Lane' they called it; Jews from all over the East End came to buy the cheap wares, exchange gossip and do their courting. The busiest times were Thursday and Friday mornings when the Sabbath buying was done.

Only on Sunday did it turn into the unofficial outlet for the local rag trade; for the rest of the week it furnished day-to-day household needs. You could get a whole variety of food cheap in Petticoat Lane; over a thousand stalls were licenced to sell in the vicinity, selling meat (Kosher), clothes, boots, cakes, fruit, groceries, gas mantles, fried fish, cooking oil from the vats, cracked eggs to take away in your own bowl. Fanny Marks made a fortune selling fish; she started off with just one barrel of herrings.

The small shopkeepers kept their trade by offering credit and the tiny quantities of products that the poor could afford. Mother Wolfe's long narrow strip of a shop on the corner of Brick Lane was always crowded. Her customers came in for penny packets of tea wrapped in a screw of paper, tiny portions of cheese, single slices of ham. Jam was taken out of jars and sold in halfpenny portions in little dishes. Tins of pickled herrings were opened and the fishes sold singly.

For the kids, sweet shops shone like jewelled caverns of delight in the grey streets. They went in with their few pence on the way home from school and chose from the rows of great glass jars. There were milk

Petticoat Lane market in the mid-1930s. A hatless street seller is encircled by men in 'titfers': this term derived from the Cockney slang 'tit for tat' meaning hat (see pages 104-5).

gums, raspberry drops, licorice pipes with red hundreds and thousands glowing in their bowls, chocolate cigarettes, snow balls, gob stoppers, everlasting toffee and sherbet dabs.

Over in Bow, Fan Short (sister of the oil-and-colour man of Roman Road) would recite to her customers if they couldn't remember what they wanted: 'Soap, soda, starch, matches, vinegar', and dole out ha'penny cups of yellow and red pickle to those whose budget didn't run to jars. Meanwhile her brother-in-law, Ned, was for ever on the pump in the greasy black washhouse at the back. He filled cans and sometimes bottles with paraffin to feed the Valor stoves which smoked with comforting warmth in the local kitchens and parlours, throwing golden patterns on to the ceilings.

'Give us a pint of yer bug blinder, Sid,' women would call out to the shopkeeper, standing, handsome and genial in his leather apron and cap, beneath the mops, buckets, brushes, chamber pots and carpet beaters which hung down in a clutter.

'I'm doing out my front room, Sid, what colour d'you reckon?'

For many years a 'nice light stone' paint was recommended, as Sid had acquired an enormous 'job lot' of the same.

Sid was a favourite with the local kids; however full the shop might be of customers, he found time to tell them stories and was ticked off by the mums for selling (or giving) the youngsters staples to put into their catapults. A romantic of the first order, he read poetry and Dickens to sweeten the world of pickled onions and paraffin. Children, he truly believed, came 'trailing clouds of glory — even Jewish ones.'

Next door the Millets sold clothes. They were a deeply religious family and Old Father Millet was never to be seen without his prayer cap. During Yom Kippur and following the fast, a feast had been prepared by Mrs Millet and the couple had gone off to the synagogue. The son of the house, young Bob, told

Selling glass at Petticoat Lane in 1936.

Sid Short that he had been accidentally shut out. Sid was not convinced of the truth of this but, nevertheless, let him through his backyard so he could climb over the wall into his own house.

When the parents came home from the synagogue to find the food half eaten all hell let loose, with Sid in the middle of it. Thus Jew and Gentile rubbed along.

As well as the neighbourhood shops and markets there were the street sellers. In Spitalfields a red-haired fishmonger used to wheel a barrow with a couple of boxes and a slab with just a few dabs, plaice or haddocks on it. The cat-meat man sold meat by the skewerful; Harry the banana king would shout, 'Open your pinafore, quick' and 'bung a lot of loose ones in.' There were chairmenders, knife grinders and glaziers,

muffin men with bells, winkle men, watercress men and toffee-apple men. In the very early hours of Sunday morning in the Jewish areas you might encounter a woman selling hot beigels.

Dad features less than mum in the nostalgic memories; the kids didn't know him so well and he spent most of his time out of the house.

Perhaps he worked down the docks, in the tailoring trade, in one of the many factories which peppered the East End, in a brewery, on the railway, like Walter Jones, or ran a shop like Sid Short. Hours were long and, if he was a drinker, which many of them were, evenings would be spent in the pub — except when times were really hard, as they were in the thirties, when pub trade diminished.

The ethnic mix of East End London has been evident throughout its history and is still part of its character today.

1936: these two stall holders at Petticoat Lane are selling ties and kippers on their respective stalls.

Entertainment:
pubs, music halls, the seaside

There are still many East End pubs around with enough of the old about them to permit an imaginative journey back a hundred years or so.

Take Hollands, off the Commercial Road. It was established in the 1840s and, until quite recently, was run by the same family, Holland. Its gas mantles and bar are redolent of the past but its quiet, almost suburban demeanour might seem a quite modern overlay until you read Charles Booth's account of the East End pub, written at the turn of the century.

> Anyone who frequents public houses will know that actual drunkenness is very much the exception.... Go into any of these houses — the ordinary public house at the corner of any ordinary East End street — there, standing at the counter, or seated on the benches against wall or partition, will be perhaps half a dozen people, men and women, chatting together over their beer — more often beer than spirits — or you may see a few men come in with no time to lose, briskly drink their glass and go.
>
> Behind the bar will be a decent middle-aged woman, something above her customers in class, very decently dressed, respecting herself and respected by them. The whole scene is comfortable and quiet and orderly. To these houses those who live nearby send their children with a jug as readily as they would send them to any other shop.

Threatened by the Temperance Movement, by the Band of Hope and the cocoa rooms, by Booth's day most pubs offered soft drinks, especially ginger beer, early morning coffee and, at lunch time, bread and cheese or 'sausages and mashed'. They had 'friendly draws' and benefit clubs became increasingly a combination of restaurant, social club and music hall.

Before the Great War, tuppence would buy Dad, or anyone else in the family, an evening of escape and delight in the gallery of a true music hall. There was a good number to choose from: Wilton's, off Cable Street, the Paragon Theatre of Varieties in the Mile End Road, the Cambridge Theatre in Commercial Street, Forester's Music Hall in Cambridge Heath Road, the London and Olympia in Shoreditch, the Queen's Palace in Poplar and many more. For the Jewish immigrants there were Yiddish theatres where Sunday-night audiences might wallow in emotional tales of their homeland. When the Pavilion, at the corner of Whitechapel Road and Vallance Road, put on a melodrama of Jewish life in Austria called *Father's and Mother's Sorrows*, they had to turn people away.

Once a year there might be a chance to go to the seaside. Churches and pubs had annual outings. All dressed up and in a charabanc the regulars from The Salmon and Ball, The Queen Victoria, The Waterman's Arms and the rest, would rattle down to Ramsgate, Margate or Southend, beery and singing. They used to go to Bognor from St Peter's, London Dock; when Theydon Bois was substituted in 1915 Walter Jones of Wapping decided not to go: 'Not in the same street as Bognor, is it, for a day's outing?'.

Southend these days is a most restrained place, with an educational 'Sea Life' on the front and an astonishing brilliance of hanging baskets sprouting from parades of elegant houses. The fish-and-chip shops, funfares and 'china boot from Southend' shops are still there, but are rather overwhelmed. In the nice, dark, lacey-windowed pubs which are strung along the front and among the rows of Edwardian villas which sidle down from the hill above, there is some sense of the atmosphere of the old days. Out they poured into the bathing machines and climbed into the trams which took them along the longest pier in the world. They put their pennies in the slot to watch the 'dear little French cook' undress; they drank beer and ate winkles and cockles. There are still cockle sheds in Leigh, Southend's neighbour.

The only thing resembling a holiday for the really poor was 'hopping', unless there were country relatives to visit and the fare could be scraped together.

Boozey outings to the seaside were frowned upon by the workers in the Settlement Movement and the Temperance organizations so alternatives were laid on. Lil Daniels, who put the soot in the holy water (see page 171), used, as a child, to go on the outings arranged by Bow's Out and Out Mission. On 11 August 1906 (Lil was grown up by then) there was an astonishing sight in Fairfield Road. Crowds gathered to watch as fifty-three 'brakes' drew up. These were great lumbering vehicles, like overgrown stage coaches, needing three horses to pull their heavy load of thirty people. Ragged little 'pot 'erbs' (as the East Enders called the kids), Mums and Nans in wide hats and shawls, Dads buttoned up in their best — if they had any — clambered up into the brakes. There were 'three coach-loads of cripples'.

It took a good half hour to get everybody aboard and settled and then off they went, up into the Mile End Road and eastwards to Epping Forest. The destination was Fox Barrow Farm, in the woods round Hainault, the London County Council resort for excursions, a safe distance from any hostelry selling alcoholic liquor. There, after a sustaining lunch, they rambled about or just had a good sleep in the fresh air. For the children there were donkey rides, coconut shies and sports. After a lavish tea and more games, they set off for home again. As the parade of tired happy East Enders swung and rattled through the warm twilight of Leyton, Mile End and Whitechapel, the Out and Out band played *Onward Christian Soldiers*.

A Yiddish theatre, the Pavilion Theatre in Whitechapel in about 1895.

Hop picking was the nearest many East Enders came to having a holiday. Even the smallest children went along to help.

Hopping

Every August, from the late nineteenth century to the 1950s, there was a mass exodus from the grimy streets, as the mothers and children of the poorest families took themselves off to the Kentish hop fields. Fathers came down for the weekends. Many people still have rosy memories of these long summer days, the nearest they ever came to having a holiday. They lived in huts which were neatly furnished and decorated. In the evening they would go off to the village pub and exchange the tokens their employers gave them for frothy beer.

It was hard work, picking the hops, and even the smallest children were expected to help, throwing the fruit into vast baskets. It was a private world where all sorts of special customs grew up, like 'hop marriages' which involved jumping over a pole and goodness-knows what besides. They had the time of their lives. The Stepney Historical Trust still crowns a hop queen in September.

Escape from the slums

So were these really 'the good old days'? Would any East Enders want to go back to how things were? Largely, in fact, despite nostalgic reminiscences, the East End dream was of an escape from the slums: 'Let's get a nice new place in a leafy part — no bugs, no smoke — somewhere fit to bring kids up.'

Even in Walter Jones's family, so happy in Wapping, there were those who got away. His son, Alban, moved out to Southend when he married. He and his wife toyed with the idea of 'coming home' after their daughter was born in 1915, but were now 'rather afraid of Wapping for Phyllis's sake', and went house-hunting in Upminster instead. And so it was with many, many East End families.

Flower and Dean Street, says Aunt Esther, in Arnold Wesker's *I'm Talking about Jerusalem* was a prison with iron railings. It was her one ambition to break away from that prison. Aunt Esther was a successful entrepreneur; the Jews worked hard to escape. They were artisans and business men with the skills and enterprise and, most of all, the motive to 'get on' and improve their lifestyles.

It took longer than a generation for the community to shift themselves clear of the slums. The drift to Hackney, Stoke Newington, Clapton and Stamford Hill started after the First World War and was a flood by the 1920s. By 1929 it is thought that as many as one third of East End Jewry was gone, the really successful to Golders Green and Finchley, where the museum of East End Jewish life is now.

Eva Katchinsky, who was living in Kiev with her blind brother, finally left Whitechapel in 1964.

Most of the people who had been drawn or driven

Memories of the evenings, the dancing and the hop marriages — the social aspects of hop-picking — overshadow memories of the work aspects.

into the morass left when they could — if they had enough money, making for the outer eastern suburbs, where commuter land trims Epping Forest.

Sid Short took his family to a rented 'semi' out at Woodford and had a long garden and a greenhouse where he stored his geraniums over the winter.

John Fletcher, the East End urchin who was bullied at school, bought a house in Buckhurst Hill when he married, moved later to Worcestershire and eventually retired to a Somerset farm.

Such was the pattern as people moved from the East End to the country or abroad in two generations or so.

Violet, the infant sobbing her heart out at Malmesbury Road School, managed, against all odds, to procure a place at university; she never admitted to her fellow students that she came from the East End. The rest of her life has been spent in Suffolk with real primroses. Like Violet, in the last few decades many have gone out to the Home Counties — to New Towns. 'Essex man' they are called; pale pampered shadows of their highly coloured parents and grandparents.

A hundred years ago homesick Irish children sang in Paradise Row in Bethnal Green (or so the song writer would have us believe):

The cobble stones were a meadow sweet to Nelly and me
The smoky chimney on the house top was a beautiful tree.

Now all is turn and turn about — in the houses of Harlow and Thamesmead, where the air is clean and the meadows are not far away, where the front doors are kept shut and there are no steps to be whitened.

It's all different now they say

That dear old safe place that made you feel good when Mum was alive, where everyone was 'friendly and easily pleased', is good to recall. It's all different now, they say. Certainly much of it looks different; some parts are scarcely recognizable. Commercial Road still growls muckily out in search of the docks but they are no longer there. Shoreditch is as sad and grimy as ever, and as full of workshops and Victorian and Edwardian factory buildings.

Poor immigrants are around in the same streets, by and large, that the French refugees came to three hundred years ago and the Russian and Polish Jews two hundred years later. Brick Lane is still coloured bright with strangers, busy with foreign names and shops and dark skinned gossipers gathered in knots. The newcomers from Bangladesh have turned synagogues into mosques and built new ones. The Jewish sweat shops and Kosher shops have been replaced by shops full of things labelled in Bengali, not Yiddish. Curry is eaten instead of beigels. They celebrate Divali instead of Yom Kippur.

There are signs of gentrification around. Petunias and busy lizzies hang in neat baskets from the elegant blue and gold lamposts in Bow's Roman Road; St John at Bethnal Green has now an advertisement for weight watchers on its notice board. How strange that would seem to grandmothers who once eked out their husband's paltry wages to keep their children from starvation. A fat child was a healthy child then.

The work started by the Blitz and slum clearance has been carried on by the death of the docks and the clean sweeping undertaken by the London Docklands Development Corporation. 'Down by the docks', in the Isle of Dogs sheets of empty leisured water lap, landscaped, around vast blocks of offices and flats, glittering with hope. From miles around the light can be seen sparkling on the top of the tower at the new Docklands city of Canary Wharf, winking out to Hampstead Heath and up the M11 the message; 'Come East, young man'.

Some do, or rather did, before the recent recession called a halt to 'the City moves East'. Catch them on a Sunday morning, jogging along Wapping Wall in their pink tracksuits. They live in nicely arranged jumbles of brand new houses and maisonettes, with antique-looking pitched rooves and miniscule walled gardens. Glossy cars slide into garages, that are firmly padlocked against the old East End, where once you might have seen a rusty bike leaning up against an iron railing. Quaint it is, in Watermen's Walk and the rest, and most desirable.

Garden centres are springing up to supply the new style 'backyards' with clematis for their walls and lobelia for their tubs. The 'spit and sawdust' of the riverside pubs has given way to polished tables and appropriately local prints, aged, and in rather too shiny frames. Old tales of pirates and historical associations are dug up and refurbished. Perhaps the Americans and Japanese will come in coach loads?

Along the riverside in Tower Hamlets there is very little standing from the past. Most of the incoming rich East Enders are housed in those brand new properties specially built for them, with avocado wash basins large enough to accommodate only one hand at a time. The really rich, however, have snapped up the few treasured buildings which have survived both bombing and the developers.

Some have carved enormous apartments out of the few remaining Victorian warehouses, laying Persian carpets across acres of floor, stretching out to balconies overhanging the sweep of the river. In Limehouse's Narrow Street a row of eighteenth-century houses with a prized river view has been restored. At the west end of Cable Street, the old houses which, within living memory were as shamshackle as they could be and as disreputable in occupation, are now pristine in their antique elegance; there is even a 'Hawksmoor Mews' among them.

The most desirable of residences hereabouts must surely be those on Wapping Pier Head. When they opened the London Docks, in the years between the battles of Trafalgar and Waterloo, substantial houses were built for the dock master and his workers. They are still there, standing in a stately enclave by the river, with lawns and trees to dress their classical superiority. Stand in front of them and look to the right for the best view of Tower Bridge that is on offer.

In the north of the borough and in Spitalfields much more remains; eighteenth-century weavers' houses, lovingly restored, seventeenth-century houses on Stepney Green and row upon row of good solid Victorian and Edwardian artisans cottages in Bow, Bethnal Green and Mile End, with a scattering of big houses, like those in Tredegar Square.

Tredegar Square is getting back the 'posh' people for whom it was built at the turn of the century and more and more of the mean little houses are blossoming into cared-for cottages.

Don't think that the whole area has been painted up and invaded by people who are all stripping their woodwork down to the original and scouring antique markets for period fireplaces. It is not overwhelmed by the pink-tracksuit brigade. The East End is still the East End and it should be remembered, with all this talk of foreign immigrants and the exciting mix of cultures, that the majority of the population are, and always have been indigenous. Not pure Anglo Saxon stock (who is in this country?) or anything like that — but people whose families have been in this country for a couple of generations, at least, probably still make up over half the population.

Most East Enders are still quite hard up by modern European standards. Most live in blocks of council flats or houses. They watch the telly instead of going to the music hall, maybe, but they still jollify in the pubs. Generally, East End pubs continue to serve as the usual social centre — as a glance through the pages of *The East End Advertiser* will reveal. There's bingo now and Sunday schools no longer parade their hundreds of children through the streets; they'd be lucky to have five youngsters to march along. People go to super-markets these days but corner shops are still used for emergencies or 'tick' as they always were. Just as in the old days, there isn't the sort of 'stocking up' that occurs in the suburbs. The markets are still there, for the most part, even if they have changed in character and the old ways can still be traced, interwoven into the present.

Women go out to work, most of them, as many have done round here for hundreds of years. There are still nans to look after the kids; the difference is they are no longer down-at-heel wispy-haired, worn-out souls; if anything they are more stylishly coiffured and smarter than their daughters. Listen to one of those 'over the push chair' inter-generation conversations among the stalls of Roman Road or Watney Street, and you will undoubtedly discover that the matriachal society is alive and well — and living in East London.

Long Gone
by Patricia Craven

Memories cluster of bright childhood days
Pre-war in London's East End;
Ha'penny Snofrutes, while street organs played
And Helen next door, my best friend.

The dark blue-cool dairy, the chonk of its churns.
Twisted cough candy, a red apple sharp;
Pattern for hopscotch, a skipping rope burn,
The nightlight glowed gold in the dark.

Practising scales while my mother made tea.
Bread thick with Virol or jam;
The occasional Saturday trip to the sea.
My favourite doll and tin pram.

Carrying shopping in woven straw bags.
The overhead cash loop in Wickhams;
Riding my trike over sun-glinted flags,
Whitechapel Waste and boiled chickens.

Pushchairs, fawn gaiters and ABC Teas,
Open-topped prams made me queasy;
Liberty bodices — double grazed knees,
Adverts for Brighton so breezy.

Blessed to be born when my world lay at ease,
A foundation to cope with life's pains;
All people friendly and easily pleased,
How I'd love to see them again.

BIBLIOGRAPHY

Abbreviations

CLRO
Corporation of
London Record Office

GL
Guildhall Library

GLRO
Greater London Record Office

PRO
Public Record Office

GENERAL

Reconstructions

In describing the various different areas in detail I have drawn on the following:

Poll Tax and Hearth Tax records in the PRO, E 179 (17th century); Assessment Records in the CLRO (17th and 18th century); Land Tax Records in the GL 18th century); printed street and trade directories for London (from 1677); a variety of maps, the most important being those printed in:

The A to Z of Elizabethan London A. Procter and R. Taylor, London Topographical Society, 1979

The A to Z of Restoration London R. Hyde, using the Ogilby and Morgan map of 1676, London Topographical Society, 1981

The A to Z of Georgian London R. Hyde, using John Rogers map of 1746, London Topographical Society, 1981

The A to Z of Regency London Paula Laxton, using Richard Horwood's map, 1799-1819, London Topographical Society, 1985

The A to Z of Victorian London R. Hyde, using the George Bacon atlases, London Topographical Society, 1987

Joel Gascoyne's map of 1703

Population

For population assessments and statistics I have used K. J. Kitching ed. *London and Middlesex Chantry Certificates* 1548, London Record Society, 1980, census population tables (19th Century), the figures cited by Lysons (see below), Llewellyn-Smith (see below) and in the compilation by Beier and Finlay (see below).

I have also used for this purpose, and for locating occupational and ethnic groups and individuals, the original parish registers listed below:

Christchurch, Spitalfields (GLRO)
St Anne, Limehouse (GLRO)
St Botolph, Aldgate (GL)
St Botolph, Bishopsgate (GL) (GLRO)
St Dunstan and All Saints, Stepney (GLRO)
St John, Wapping (GLRO)
St Leonard, Shoreditch (GL)
St Mary, Bow (GLRO)
St Matthew, Bethnal Green (GLRO)
St Paul, Shadwell (GLRO)

Journals

Extensive use has been made of the following:

East London Papers 1958-1973

East London Record the journal of the East London History Society, from 1978

The Cockney Ancestor the journal of the East of London Family History Society, from 1978

Names: topographical

For the derivation of names I have relied mainly on the Middlesex volume of the *English Place Name Society* (volume XVII, 1942) supplemented by information from original records

General works on London

A. L. Beier and Roger Finlay ed. *London 1500-1700* Harlow, 1986

P. Cunningham, *Handbook for London* London, 1849 (especially useful)

Steve Jones *London, the Sinister Side* Nottingham, 1986

D Lysons *Environs of London* 2nd ed., 1811 (most useful)

J.P. Malcolm *London Redivivum* London, 1807

Valerie Pearl *London at the Outbreak of the Puritan Revolution* Oxford, 1961

John Stow *Survey of London* Everyman, 1912

Gladys Taylor *Oranges and Lemons* London, 1954

The Growth of London, Victoria and Albert Museum Exhibition catalogue, 1964

H.Walters *London Churches at the Reformation* London, 1939

E Wayland Young *London's Churches* London, 1986

Ben Weinreb and Christopher Hibbert ed. *The London Encyclopaedia* London, 1983

S. Woodburn *Ecclesiastical Topography* London, 1807

General Works on the East End

Walter Besant *East London* London, 1908

Dockland , an illustrated historical survey of life and work in East London North London Polytechnic and Greater London Council, 1986

Colm Kerrigan *A History of Tower Hamlets* London, 1982

Sir Hubert Llewellyn Smith *The History of East London* London, 1939
Kevin McDonnell *Medieval London Suburbs* London, 1978

Alan Palmer *The East End* London, 1989

Tony Phillips *A London Docklands Guide* High Wycombe, 1986

Robert Philpotts *On Foot in the East End* London, 1992

Millicent Rose *The East End of London* London, 1973

Tower Hamlets Borough Guide

I have used some of the material gathered from my own researches for a more detailed history of East London before the Industrial Revolution, to be published by Juliett Gardiner books, entitled provisionally *London's Backyard.*

Legal records

The records of crime and civil litigation are particularly useful for the purpose of recreating the life and speech of ordinary folk before the literate middle classes started taking an interest in the East End in the 19th century. Some are printed, but most have been consulted in the original. The records of the London church courts are especially rich; for a description of them *see* Jane Cox *Hatred Pursued beyond the Grave* HMSO, 1993

Proceedings of the King's Commissioners of the Peace (Old Bailey Trails) 1766-1777

Middlesex Sessions Records in the GLRO

Records of the Prerogative Court of Canterbury (PRO) ref. PROB, the Commissary court of the Bishop of London (GL), the Consistory Court of the Bishop of London (GLRO) and the records of the court of the Archdeacon of London

Other

Charles Dickens:
The Uncommercial Traveller
Our Mutual Friend
Pickwick Papers
The Old Curiosity Shop

Dr David Parker, lecture given to the Stepney Historical Trust, 15 December 1990

ed. R. Latham and W. Matthews *The Diary of Samuel Pepys* London 1970-1983

SOURCES SPECIFIC TO VARIOUS CHAPTERS:

The Early Days

Walter Besant *Early London* London, 1918

Kate Buck *London in the Fourth Century at the coronation of Maxen Wledig (Magnus Maximus) AD 383, as described in the Song of Wayland* London, 1926

T. Johnson, 'A Roman Signal Tower at Shadwell E.1' *Transactions of the London and Middlesex Archaeological Society,* 1975.

Also information from the Museum of London's Archaeological Department

Jenny Hall and Ralph Merrifield *Roman London* HMSO, 1986

The London Archaeologist: reports

Mc Donnell, *Medieval London*

Suburbs cited above

R. Merrifield *London, City of the Romans* Batsford, 1984

Alan Vince *Saxon London* London, 1990

Stepney

C. Bernau's collection of newspaper cuttings, Society of Genealogists, MX/M46

Court rolls for Stepney Manor, from 1318 Guildhall MS 25, 369; 1654-1925, (GLRO) MS 93/1-109

Alan Fea *The Loyal Wentworths* London, 1907

G. W. Hill and W. H. Frere *Memorials of Stepney Parish, 1579-1662* London 1890-91

A. T. Jones, 'Stepney Meeting' *East London Magazine* 1890-1891

Letters and papers of Henry VIII, 1540 HMSO, 1896 (for the burning of William Jerome)

J. H. Lupman *Life of Dean Colet* London 1909

C More *The Life of Sir Thomas More* 1726

Register of the Stepney Meeting, (PRO) RG 4/4414

St Dunstan's parish registers, (GLRO)

Middlesex Pedigrees, Harleian Society Publications 65, 1914

Aldgate and Whitechapel

The Case of the Hamlet of Wapping in answer to Whitechapel concerning highways late 17th century, (GL) broadside 16.95

E. C. Carter *Notes on Whitechapel* (GL) PAM 6630 c. 1906

A. E. Clark Kennedy *London Pride, the Story of a Voluntary Hospital* London 1979

M. M. Crow and Claire Olson *Chaucer's Life Records* Oxford, 1966

Daniel Defoe *A Journal of the Plague Year* first published 1722, Penguin 1986

Devonshire House Meeting, 'Sufferings', 1684-1791, Friends' House

T. E. Endleman *The Jews of Georgian England* Jewish Publication Society of America, 1979

England's Memorable Occurrences, 1642 (for the building of Whitechapel Mound)

John Foxe *The Book of Martyrs* London, 1776 (the martyrdom of Rowland Taylor)

John Harvey *The Nursery Garden* exhibition catalogue, Museum of London, 1990

G. A. J. Hodgett ed. *Cartulary of Holy Trinity, Aldgate* London Record Society, volume 7, 1971

Richard Kemp *Some Notes on the Ward of Aldgate* London, 1904

Land Tax Records, 1733, (GL)

Lansdowne 16 f 90, printed in *Archaeologia* 23 from 1831 (report of 'lewd and idle people harbouring near the City)

London Commissary Court Correction book, 1470-1473, (GL) MS 9064/1

London Commissary Court Depositions, (GL) MS 9065 (for Isabella Newport) MS 9198/2 (for the Talbots)

W. R. Letharby, 'The Priory of Holy Trinity, Aldgate' *Home Counties Magazine* volume II, 1900

London Archaeologist, Spring 1990 volume. 6 no. 6 (for the dog in Houndsditch)

Will of Richard Maddox (PRO) PROB 11/1354 s 151

Middlesex Sessions, 1589, (GLRO)

A. R. Myers *London in the Age of Chaucer* Oklahoma 1972

Charles Pendrill *London Life in the Fourteenth Century* London, 1925

PROB 24/102/7, (PRO) (the affair in Blue Anchor Yard)

D. W. Robertson *Chaucer's London* 1968

St Botolph, Aldgate, Parish registers, (GL)

St Mary, Whitechapel, parish registers, (GLRO)

SP 44/163/99-100, (PRO) (collection for poor weavers, 1698)

SP 29/442/87 (petition from Whitechapel prison)

Tax assessment for March 1694, St Mary Whitechapel, (CLRO) Ass. Box 40.21

E. M. Tomlinson *A History of the Minories* London, 1907

G. F. Tull *North of the Tower, the story of St Botolph near Aldgate* Ashford, Middlesex, 1974

Whitechapel: An account of the Whitechapel Bell Foundry 1985

T. R. Forbes *Chronicle from Aldgate* London, 1971

East of the Tower

Acts of the Privy Council, 1627 (dregs from the King's alum works)

Aliens in London 1523-1625, Huguenot Society

Calendar of Middlesex Sessions, volume I, 1549-1603 (GLRO) 'Recognisances taken of John Wolfe', 1 April 42 Eliz.

A. W. Clapham, 'The Topography of the Cistercian Abbey on Tower Hill' *Archaeologia* volume 66, 1915

Court Rolls for the Manor of East Smithfield, 1421, 1434, 1509, 1529 and 1533, (PRO) SC2/191/55-59

Exchequer depositions in a dispute over the lands of St Mary Graces, (PRO) E 178/1374

C. Jamison *The History of the Royal Hospital of St Katharine by the Tower* Oxford, 1952

H.M. Tower of London Ditchling 1989

M. B. Honeybourne, 'Two Plans of the Precinct and adjoining Property of St Mary Graces': Transactions of the London and Middlesex Archaeological Society, NS VI, 1933, 20

Ben Jonson, *The Devil is an Ass* Act I, Scene I

London Commissary Court Depositions, 1489-1572, (GL) 9065; and 1594-7, (GL) 9065 A/2

Will of Sir Nicholas Loveyn, Lambeth Palace Library, Sudbury, 86

Maps (PRO) MPB 4 A and B

Museum of London travelling exhibition on the Abbey of St Mary Graces, 1990

Stationers' Company records, Archives of the Company Stationers Hall (for Wolfe)

Note and Queries clxii and cliv (Spenser)

Edmund Spenser *The Works*, a *variorum* edition ed. E. Greenlaw, C. G. Osgood and F. M. Padelford, including *The Life of Edmund Spenser* by A. C. Judson, 1932-1949

Return of aliens dwelling in the city and suburbs of London from the reign of Henry VIII to that of James I ed. E. G. and E. F. Kirk *Huguenot Society of London* volume 10, from 1900

Shoreditch

Much of this section is based on the author's researches for her forthcoming book, provisionally entitled *London's Backyard* (see page 188)

J. Q. Adams *Shakespeare's Playhouses* London, 1917

W. W. Braines, 'The Site of the Theatre in Shoreditch' *London Topographical Record XI* 1917

Sir Herbert Berry *The First Public Playhouse* Montreal, 1979

Acts of the Privy Council, 1599-1600, London, 1905

Exchequer depositions, (PRO) E 134/44 and 45 Eliz Mich 18 (Burbage's barn conversion)

Rosemary Linnell *The Curtain Playhouse* London, 1977

S. Schoenbaum *William Shakespeare, A Documentary Life* Oxford, 1975

S. Schoenbaum *William Shakespeare, Records and Images* Oxford, 1981

Survey of London volume VIII, St Leonard Shoreditch, LCC, 1922

Vicar's will, (PRO) PROB 11/21/35

Wapping, Shadwell, Ratcliff and Limehouse

Assessment for Wapping Whitechapel, 1694, (CLRO) Ass. Box 40.21

Assessment for Wapping Stepney, 1694, (CLRO) Ass. Box 40.5

W. Beek and T. F. Ball *London Friends Meetings* London, 1869

J. G. Birch *Limehouse though five centuries* London, 1930

F. Buckley *Old London Glasshouses* London, 1915

Calendars of Middlesex Sessions, for 1659 and 1667, (GLRO)

Chancery Proceedings, (PRO)

C 10/13/63, 1651 (Lady Ivy's marriage)

Collection of the Merchants living in and about the City of London 1677 ('Yellow Pages')

Coopers' Company Accounts, (GL) MS 5606/1

J. Cox *Hatred Pursued beyond the Grave* HMSO, 1993 (for prostitutes' charges to Flemings)

Daily Post 22 September 1736 (hanging at The Bell)

Madge Darby *Waeppa's People* Colchester, 1988

Execution Dock: the location is based on a 1674 map, (PRO) MPE 494, showing the house of one John Shaw, and the depositions in a case in the Prerogative Court of Canterbury (PRO) PROB 24/8f 182 — which states that John Shaw lives at The King's Arms at Execution Dock

Exchequer Depositions (PRO) E 134 31 and 32 Eliz C 18 June, D 27 and 28 October, Mich number 7, Arden v. Warner (John Stepkin builds Wapping Wall)

Exchequer Depositions, (PRO) E 178/1469 (Wapping brewery of St Thomas of Acon)

Exchequer Depositions, E 134/22 Jas I East, 24, Maunsel v Clavell (Sir Robert Maunsell's glass works)

Julia Hunt *From Whitby to Wapping* Stepney Historical Trust, 1991

C. Idle *Some Dates and Events from the Story of Limehouse Parish Church* London, 1987

P. Linebaugh *The London Hanged* Penguin, 1991

London Commissary Court Depositions, (GL) 9189/II, Wharton v Barwicke

The Observator 1681-1684, British Library Burney 88A (dreams of Irish skrims)

Sir Thomas Overbury, Characters, 1614-6 (Watermen 'telling strange news')

Parliamentary survey of Shadwell, 1649 (GL) MS 11, 816 ff 59 - 65. (This gives, amongst other things, the location of the sugar house)

Poll Tax records for Shadwell and Lower Wapping, (PRO) E

179/143/350

M. J. Power: the story of 17th-century Shadwell is based on Dr Power's lecture to the Stepney Historical Trust given in 1991

M. J. Power 'Shadwell, the development of a London suburban community in the 17th century' *London Journal* volume 4, number 1, 1978

Probate inventories: (PRO), PROB 4: Bartlett 17043, Harrison 13584, Hare 13190, Hooper 14755, John Knight (approx. 1666), Mutton 1477, Watts 13470

The Prospect of Whitby: information about this public house is from the researches for Jane Cox *London's Backyard* (cited above)

N. A. M. Rodger: information about the conduct of the press gang is based on Dr Rodger's lecture to the Stepney Historical Trust

St Paul's, Shadwell, a short history of the church (c 1980)

Neville Williams *Captain Outrageous* London, 1961

Bethnal Green, Spitalfields and Mile End New Town

Census (PRO) HO 107/692/13/2-4 (for the mad house in 1841)

Chancery decree establishing Mile End New Town, (PRO) C 78/1640

Court Rolls for Norton Folgate, 1439-94 and 1509-18, (GL) MS 25, 287

Probate inventories: John Holden, 1693, (PRO) PROB 32/5 ff 88-97; Daniel Abbott, brewer, 1754, (PRO) PROB 31/367/279

A. J. Robinson and D. H. B. Chesshyre *The Green* London, 1986

A. K. Sabin *The Silk Weavers of Spitalfields and Bethnal Green* Bethnal Green Museum, 1931

St Botolph Aldgate, parish clerk's notes, 1586 (GL)

The Survey of London volume XXVII, Spitalfields and Mile End New Town, LCC, 1957

Bow, Bromley and Mile End Old Town

Cary's *Survey of the High Roads from London* 1790, reprinted by the Post

Office Archives, 1989

Coroner's inquest on the Bow baker, 1473, (PRO) C 260/152/17

Court of High Commission, 1640, (PRO) SP 16/26 (for the gay hosier's wife of Bow)

W. Kemp *Kemp's nine daies wonder* London, 1600

Prerogative Court of Canterbury Depositions, (PRO) PROB 24/10 f 173 (for Sir William Penn's will making)

Royal MS 18A LXVI f 176, British Library (for the Armada war games)

Sindall map of the Isle of Dogs, 1801, Museum in Docklands Archive, shows the 'gentlemen's residencies' in Mile End

Poplar and the Isle of Dogs

The Black Prince's Register, (PRO) E 36/179

Bob Aspinall, Museum of London tour of docklands, 1989

Court Rolls, Manor of Poplar, (PRO) SC2/191/50-60

Exchequer Depositions, (PRO) E 134/19 Eliz. Hil. 4, Sir Gilbert Deathicke v Thomas Whyte

Eve Hostettler *An Outline History of the Isle of Dogs* Island History Trust, 1988

Inquisition post-mortem, (PRO) 16 Rich II pt I number 130 (Manor of Poplar granted to St Mary Graces)

Map of Poplar 1600, (PRO) MPB 31

Poplar Town Book, 1595, Tower Hamlets Local History Library

Prerogative Court of Canterbury Depositions, (PRO) PROB 24/26, John Meeks deceased

The Transit Camp

W. J. Fishman *East End 1888* London, 1988

Gina Glasman *East End Synagogues* Museum of the Jewish East End, London 1987

B. Inglis: information about Jewry

Charles Tucker; information about Jewry

Henry Walker *East London, Sketches of Christian Work and Workers* London, 1896. Peter Marcan reprint, High Wycombe, 1986

Jerry White *Rothschild Buildings, Life in an East End Tenement Block* 1887-1920, London, 1980

Israel Zangwill *Children of the Ghetto* London, 1987

Slums and deprivation

W. Austin *One Dinner a Week* London, 1884

W Besant, 'Life in a Hospital' *Gentleman's Magazine* April 1883

ed. A. Fried and R. Elman *Charles Booth's London* Harmondsworth, 1969

Jane Cox *A Singular Marriage, A Labour Love Story in Letters and Diaries*, Ramsay and Margaret MacDonald London, 1988

Peter Marcan *An East London Album* High Wycombe, 1992

G. P. Moss and M. V. Saville *From Palace to College, an Illustrated History of Queen Mary College* London, 1992

Judith Walkowitz *City of Dreadful Delight* London 1992

Whitechapel: deaths from starvation, 1906, (GLRO) St BG/SG/107/55

More Friendly than it is Now

Ivy and Augustus Ducas, Jessie Owen and Mary Pawley *Cockney Ancestor* winter 1979/80 (Limehouse memories)

Robert Barltrop and Jim Wolveridge *The Muvver Tongue* London, 1980

Madge Darby ed. *Tender Grace, Wapping Letters and Diaries* volume III, London, 1993

John and Lillian Fletcher: memories

Grace Foakes *My Part of the River* London, 1974

John Hewitt *100 Not Out, The Story of Bridge House* (formerly the Out and Out Mission) London, 1993

Frank Lewey *Cockney Campaign* London

Dorothy Scannell *Mother knew Best* London, 1974

Violet & Sidney Short: memories

Iris Vivian: memories

Michael Young and Peter Wilmott *Family and Kinship in East London* 1957

INDEX

A

Abbey Court 60
Abbey of St Clare 19, 38
Abbey of St Mary Graces 19
Acton 52
Albani, Madame 150
Albert Hall 175
Alderney Rd 150
Aldgate 9-11, 14-15, 17-20, 22, 35-53, 66, 69, 97, 109, 117, 122, 124, 143
Aldgate Bars 37
Aldgate East 20
Aldgate High St 35, 37, 40, 42-3, 46-7
Alie St 46-7, 51-2
All Saints, Poplar 136
Anchor, The 90
Anchor and Hope Alley 83
Approach Rd 34, 129
Armada, the 25-6, 123
Armagh Rd 161
Artillery Lane 25, 113, 116
Artillery Passage 116
Ashfield 136
Ashton, David 129
Astill, Margaret 124
Attlee, Clement 141
Aubrey, John 71
Austin, Walter 145, 155
Ayliffe St 46, 52
Ayliffe St Theatre 52
Aynsworth John 72

B

Babbs Lane 82
Balermino, Lord 55
Balthrop, Robert 177
Bancroft's Hospital 124
Bancroft School 124, 162
Barcroft, Elizabeth 129-30
Barltrop, Robert 175
Barnardo, Dr 45, 152, 171
Barnett, Canon & Henrietta 160
Bartholomew Fair 60
Barwicke, Elizabeth 80-1
Basset, George 94
Bastille 52
Bateman's Row 69, 70

Bateman, William 70
Battersea 13
Batts, Elizabeth 84-6
Batts, Samuel 84
Beareburden Lane 127, 129
Beaumont, Barber 162
Beaumont Sq 162
Bell Dock 52
Bell Lane 172
Bell, The 84-5
Bell Yard 47
Becket, Thomas 38
Bedford, Earl of 25
Beerbinder Lane 127
Beeston, Christopher 71
Bell Alley 40
Bell Yard 47
Ben Jonson Rd 25, 27, 33
Bent, Alice 81
Bentley, Richard 116
Berebinder House 127
Bermondsey 13
Berry, William 89
Besant, Annie 131
Besant, Walter 8, 153, 161, 162
Besse Street 108
Bethlehem mad house 20
Bethnal Green 10-11, 13, 17, 19-20, 22, 25, 27-8, 34, 37-8, 106, 108-12, 160-2, 170, 176, 185-6
Bethnal Green Rd 15, 17-18, 108
Beveridge, Lord 153, 160, 171
Bevis Marks synagogue 142
Bezer, Leonard 81
Big Ben 39-40
Birdingebushe Field, 136
Bishop of London (&Court) 17-8, 20, 38, 61, 81
Bishopsgate (Bishop's Gate) 9-10, 14, 20, 36, 51, 68, 70-1, 106, 116-17
Bishops Hall 19
Black Boy Inn 123
Black Boy and Trumpet 83
Blackburen, John 84
Black Death 55, 97
Black Ditch 22

Black Horse and Crown 52
Black Lion Court 48
Black Lion Yard 38, 48
Blacklocke, Mary 130
Black Prince, the 136, 141
Black Swan, The 62
Blackwall 19, 94, 103, 135-6
Blackwall Tunnel 129
Blanche, Queen of Navarre 20
Bleda 17
Bligh, Captain 86
Blind Beggar 108-9, 112, 161
Blitz 8, 97, 168, 171, 186
Blizzard, Sir William 45
Blood Alley 133
Bloody Mary 14, 34, 102
Blooms 148, 150
Blue Anchor Yard 47, 52
Blue Board, The 38
Boar's Head Tavern 42, 53
Boatswain, The 90
Bonner, Bishop of London 34
Bonner Gate 34
Bonner's Hall 34
Booth, Charles 152, 182
Booty's Wine Bar 102
Boswell 83
Botany Bay 52
Boudicca 17, 97
Bow 10-11, 13, 17, 19-21, 25, 28, 121-2, 124, 127-133, 138, 154-5, 160-1, 166, 171-3, 175, 180
Bow Bells, The 133
Bow Bridge 19, 127, 129
Bow Church 129-30
Bow Common Lane 123
Bowels Crown Glass 94
Bow Quarter 133
Bow Rd 126
Brady St 150
Brandon, Richard 44
Braun and Hogenberg 6
Braybrooke, Bishop 34
Braybrooke House 34
Brazen Serpent, The 62
Brewers' Almshouses 124
Brewer's Arms 90
Brewhouse Lane 84

Brewster, William 116
Brick Lane 37, 43, 45-7, 49, 117, 120, 142, 147, 179, 186
Broad St 82-3
Brodlove Lane 15
Bromley 11, 18-20, 102, 121, 127-133
Bromley Hall 129
Bromley Marsh 19
Brooks, Councillor Tom 111
Brook St 18
Broome Lane 122
Brothers Houses 62
Brown, Archibald 161
Brune St 147
Brunswick Dock 138
Brutus 14
Bryant and May 131-3, 176
Bryant, Miss 175
Bugbyes Hole 81
Bull Inn 37, 121, 152
Bull Lane 25, 27
Bull Lane Chapel 27
Bunches Wine Bar 165
Burbage, James 62, 71-3
Burbage, Richard 71, 73
Burdett Rd 161
Buskyn, Henry 60
Butcher's Row 55, 95

C

Cable St 15, 25, 52, 82, 95, 122, 124, 143, 182, 186
Cambridge Heath Road 109, 122, 124, 182
Cambridge Heath Turnpike 112
Cambridge Theatre 182
Camden Town 75
Canal Rd 122
Canary Wharf 99, 134, 141, 186
Cannon Street Road 95
Canton Street 102
Cardinal Wolsey 25
Cartwright St 62
Cary 124
Cass, Sir John 48, 51, 172
Catherine Wheel Alley 47, 49, 52
Cat's Hole 67
Chapel of St Mary 19

Charity Organization Society 162
Charles I 34, 44, 67, 129,
Charles II 27, 34, 48, 64, 82, 94, 97, 117
Charrington family 92
Charterhouse Square 92
Chaucer, Geoffrey 18-20, 35, 38, 59, 114, 129
Cheapside 45, 76
Chelsea 13, 25, 87
Chinatown 102
Christ Church 135
Christchurch 15, 29, 148, Christ's Hospital 70
Church Lane 51
Church Row 99
Cinnamon Street 85
City of London 8-9, 11, 14-5, 17, 20, 22, 25, 36, 46, 54, 60-2, 64, 94, 97, 108, 114, 121-3, 126, 129
Civil War 26, 34, 40, 45, 48
Clapham 13
Claver, Elene 69
Clerkenwell 67, 117, 123
Cleveland, Earl of 34
Coborn, Prisca 127, 172
Coborn Rd 126-7, 130-1
Coborn School for Girls 127, 172, 175
Coborn Rd 126-7, 130-1
Cockfield, Zachariah 85
Cockney slang 104-5, 179
Colchester Rd 15
Colet Arms 24
Colet house 29
Colet, John 24-6
Colet, Sir Henry 24-5
College of Acon 76
Collier Lane 25
Collier, Thomas 52
Commercial Rd 34, 37, 95, 99, 102-3, 150, 182, 186
Commercial St 160, 182
Commercial St School 173
Compass Ditch 76
Condell, Henry 71
Conrad, Joseph 103
Constable, John 51
Coopers' Almshouses 93

Coopers' Company 93-4
Coopers School 93, 172
Cook, Captain James 85-8, 92, 124
Copperfield Rd 123
Corineus 14-15
Cornell, George 112
Cornhill 14
Coulston St 42
Court of Exchequer 89
Court of Star Chamber 25
Cow Lane 25
Cowley, Richard 71
Cowper, John 69
Crab, Roger 28
Crassh Mills 61, 66, 77
Craven, Patricia 187
Cripplegate 124
Crisp St Market 171
Cromwell, Oliver 46, 90, 124
Cromwell, Thomas 69
Crookes, Will 136
Crown, The 42-3
Cross Keys, The 71
Cross Wall 38
Cuba St 135
Cubitt Town 135
Cubitt, William 135
Culpepper, Nicholas 120
Cunningham 68
Curtain Rd 69-71, 156
Curtain, The 71-2
Custom House 97
Cutler, Alice 42

D

Dallow, Philip 47
D'Alva, Duke of 65
Dame Colet House 24
Dance, George the Elder 38
Daniell, William 135
Daniels, Lil 171
Darcy, Sir Thomas 64
Dark Entry 67
Darnley, Lord 25
Davenant's School 124
Davenant, Sir Ralph 51
Deacon, Mary 52
Defoe, Daniel 37, 46-7
Delaney, Bridget 52-3
Demaza, Solomon 49
Deptford 19, 93
Derrick, hangman 97

Dethick, Dame Thomasina 27
Dethick family 136
Dethick, Sir Gilbert 136
Devonshire House 51
Dickens, Charles 4, 25, 35, 37, 43, 52, 75-6, 83, 93, 95, 97, 99, 145, 152, 180
Dirty Dick's 116
Dissolution, the 59, 64, 70
Docks and Docklands 13, 17, 36-7, 45, 49, 75, 86-7, 92, 99-100, 102, 134, 141, 146, 160
Domesday 18, 20, 22, 29
Donne's, John 25
Doré, Gustave 49, 100, 109, 154
Drayton, Miss 175
Ducas, Ivy 166
Duke's Place 18
Dunbar Wharf 102
Dundee Arms, The 83-4
Dunstan, Lord of Stepney Manor 17
Duke of Monmouth 83
Durward St 40
Dyers' Company 92

E

East India Company 29, 52, 92, 94-5, 136, 138
East India Dock Road 102-3
East India Docks 37, 92, 103
Eastern Dispensary 51
Eastern Hotel 103
East London College 162
East London Tabernacle 161
East, Mary 138
Eastminster 59
East Smithfield 9-10, 17, 19, 20, 40, 44, 54-67, 116, 143
East Walk Exchange 82
Edict of Nantes 117
Edmeston, James 86
Edward III 59, 61, 93, 143
Edward IV 55, 68, 143
Edward VI 34, 70, 93

Edward VII Memorial Park 90
Edward, Earl of Bedford 25
Eleanor, Queen 61
Elizabeth I 38, 44, 64, 80, 143
Elizabeth, Princess 54
Erasmus 25
Essex, Earl of 97
Evesham, battle of 108
Execution Dock 52, 78-9, 82, 84, 86, 97

F

Fairfield Rd 127, 133, 182
Fairfield Works 133
Fallon, James 52
Fashion St 147
Feathers Tavern 45
Fieldgate St 38
First World War 40, 112, 128, 148, 166, 176, 182, 185
Fishman, Bill 152, 154
Fitzer, Juda and Metka 146
Five Bells, The 90, 92
Five Bells and Bladebone 99
Five Foot Alley 82
Fleet, the 13, 25
Fleet Prison 112
Fleet St 14
Fletcher, John and family 172, 175, 177, 185
Flower and Dean St 147, 176, 185
Flower de Luce, The 43, 117
Folgate St 70
Ford, Margaret 48
Forester's Music Hall 182
Forsherie, John 81
Four Mills St 129
Fournier St 113, 118
Free Trade Wharf 92-3, 95
French Revolution 30, 52, 106
Frobisher, Martin 93
Frying Pan, The 90
Frying Pan Alley 38

G

Gardiner, John 25
Garnet, Father 71
Garnet St 76
Garrick, David 52
Gascoyne, Joel 28, 102
Gate, The 90
Geoffrey of Monmouth 14
George, The 42
George, King 84
George VI 120
George Yard Mission 161
Gerbier, Sir Balthazer 109
Gibraltar Row Cemetery 112
Gibson, Nicholas and Avis 93, 172
Gilber, Sir Humphrey 102
Gilded Helmet, The 90
Glamis Estate 89
Gladstone, statue of 133
Gladstone, Margaret Ethel 164
Glasshouse Fields 94
Glengall, Countess of 135
Globe Rd 34, 106, 122, 124
Globe Theatre 71, 73
Glorious Revolution 83
Gog and Gogmagog 10, 14-15
Golden Lane 52
Gondomar 42
Good Friends, The 102
Goodlad, Mistress 28
Goodman, Old Man 42
Goodman, Thomas 42
Goodman's Fields 15, 42, 44, 46-7, 49, 51-2, 109, 147
Goodman's Yard 38, 44, 47
Gordan Riots 143
Gordon, James 126
Gordon, Mildred 166
Goulston St 49
Gracechurch Street 71
Grapes, The 4, 99, 102
Gravesend 94
Grays Inn Rd 60
Great Eastern Railway 68, 135
Great Eastern Street 71
Great Fire 94, 97, 130
Greater London Record Office 34
Greatorex St 47, 120, 150
Great Place 19, 25, 29
Great Plague 42, 45-7, 97, 130
Great Synagogue 138, 143, 150
Green, The 108

H

Green Coat Charity School 32
Greenhill, William 27
Greenwich 19, 135-6
Greenwich Palace 136
Grene, William 60
Gresham, Sir Richard 64
Gresham, Sir Thomas 70
Grocers' Company 93
Grove Rd 175
Guildhall 14-15
Guild of Knights 17
Gun Alley 86
Gunpowder Plot 25
Gurle, Leonard 47-8, 53, 120
Guy Fawkes 54
Gwynne, Nell 94

Hacche, Peter atte 102
Hackney 11, 17-18, 30, 146, 185
Hackney Brook 14, 19
Hackney Rd 112
Hadrian 15
Haggerston 18
Half-Moon Passage 38
Halstead 38
Hampstead Heath 186
Hampton Court 97
Hanbury St 120
Harley Rd Mission 161
Harrington, Lucy 25
Harrison, Brian 82
Harrydance 40
Hartshorn brewery 43
Havannah St 135
Haw Haw, Lord 168
Hawksmoor 99, 102, 120
Hawksmoor Mews 186
Hayes, Curate 40
Hearth Tax 27
Hebblewhite, William H 34
Henrietta Maria, Lady 34
Henry I 129
Henry III 61
Henry V 14
Henry VI 61
Henry VII 24, 136
Henry VIII 25, 40, 43, 60, 64, 70-1, 113, 116
Hermitage Brewery 67, 77, 92
Herryson, John and Alice 116
Hetherington, Samuel 52
Hewlett Street 71
Hicks, Zachariah 86

I

High Court of Admiralty 28, 78, 93
High Rd 48
High St 69, 70-1, 83
Highway, the 10, 12-15, 17, 25, 29, 34, 67, 77, 82, 85-6, 89-90, 93, 95, 134, 160, 176
Hitler, Adolf 170
Hogarth, William 109, 116, 145
Hog Lane 20, 25, 40, 42, 114
Holdens, John 120
Holy Trinity church 11, 38
Holy Trinity Priory 20
Holywell 20, 69, 71
Holywell Lane 69
Honour and Glory Griffiths 28
Hoop and Grapes 38
Hooper, Francis 82
Hough's paper mill 102
Houndsditch 18, 20, 38, 40, 43, 117
Houses of Parliament 40
How, James 138
Howard, Sir Thomas 94
Hoxton 18, 71
Hoy, James 52-3
Huddlestone, Sir Edmund 71
Huffam, Christopher 73, 99

Ingram, John 61
Irish Famine 143
Irish Wars 143
Irongate Stairs 143
Isaacs, Tubby 49, 152
Isle of Dogs 10, 12, 17-18, 59, 93, 134-141, 186
Itchy Park 38, 48, 52, 143
Ivey, Lady 64, 92
Ivey, Sir Thomas 92

J

Jack the Ripper 9, 38, 95, 120, 152
Jamaica Rd 165
James, Henry 152
James, Peter 60
James I 42, 94
James II 34, 83
Jamrachs 12-13
Jefferies, Judge 83
Jefferson, Thomas 92

K

Jennings Rents 117
Jerome, Jerome K 102
Jerome, William 25
Jewish Free School 172-3
Jewry St 18
Jew's Walk 109
Johnson, Dr 28, 83
Jones, Samuel 86
Jones, Walter 172, 181-2, 185
Jonson, Ben 10, 25, 42, 65, 69, 71-2
Jownes, Commander Valentine 81
Judge John Fuller's Almshouses 124

Kemp, William 127
Kilmarnock, Lord 55
King David Lane 82, 94
King Edward's Stairs 97
King John's Palace 19, 26
King's Arms, The 95
King's Arms Yard 38, 155
King's Head, The 43
Kingsland Rd 68
King St 82
Kirby, John 108, 112
Kirby's Castle 109, 112
Knight, John 82
Knighten Guild 17, 38, 59
Knighten St 17
Knockfergus 143
Knott St 168
Knyvett, Dame 93
Kray twins 78, 112
Kutchinsky family 185
Kydd, Captain 78-9

L

Lacey St 1, 175
Lamb Alley 47
Langley, Francis 71
Lansbury, George 136
Law, John 154
Lea Navigation Canal 131
Lea, river 11, 15, 19, 36, 102, 108, 127, 129, 138
Leadenhall market 14, 138
Leamouth 136
Lefevre Walk 161
Leman, Sir William 38, 47
Leman St 17, 38, 46-7, 51-2, 147, 160, 165
Le Waleys, Henry 22
Lewey, Frank 171
Leyton 182

M

MacDonald, Ramsay 160
Machleyn, family 64
Machyn, Henry 70
Maddox family 48, 52
Maddox, Richard 52
Magog 10, 14
Magwicke, Jonathon 138
Maidenhead Alley 65
Malcolm 92
Malmesbury Rd School 175, 185
Mall, the 186
Mansell St 46-7

Liberty of Norton Folgate 69
Lighter, The 90, 92
Limehouse 4, 9, 11, 18-19, 25, 29, 75, 92, 94, 98-103, 134, 136, 141, 155, 166, 186
Limehouse Basin 102
Limehouse Causeway 102
Limehouse Cut 102
Limehouse Hole 102
Lime Kiln Wharf 102
Lincoln Rd 15
Lion Tower 54
Lisland, Thomas 82
Little Alie St 49, 51
Little Driver, The 133
Little Prescott St 51
Little Tower Hill 59-60
Liverpool Street Station 116
Llyndin 10, 12-13
Londinium 13, 16
London, The 51, 182
London Bridge 73, 97, 176
London Buddhist Centre 108
London Cottage Mission 161
London Dock 61-2, 67, 76, 86-7, 92, 138, 186
London Dockland Development Corp 87, 141, 186
London Hospital, 36-7, 43, 45, 50-1, 166
Lord of the Manor 59
Lovat, Lord 55, 97
Lovell, Joan & John 60
Lovel, Sir Thomas 69
Loveyn, family 61, 136
Love Lane 82
Ludgate Hill 14
Lundenwic 17
Lydia St 169

N

Marks, Fanny 129
Marr, Mr 95
Marten, Old Goodwife 44
Martineau Estate 25
Mary Queen of Scots 25
Mary Rose, the 43
Mason, Robert 44-5
Massacre of St Bartholomew 117
Match Girls 131-3, 176
Matfelun family 38
Mathilda Queen 60, 129
Maunsell, Sir Robert 94
Mayhew, Henry 141
Mead, Dr Matthew 27, 90
Medcalfe, Christopher 129
Meeks, John 138
Meeting House Alley 82
Meggs' Almshouses 51, 124
Mendoza, Daniel 52, 109
Mercer's Arms 33
Mercer's Company 22, 27, 94
Mermaid, The 66
Mico, Dame 27
Middlesex St 20, 25, 40, 114, 178
Middleton 25, 69
Mile End 19-20, 25, 28, 46, 51, 85, 120-1, 124, 126, 130, 150, 153, 161, 182, 186
Mile End Gate 121-2
Mile End Green 19, 25, 27, 122-3
Mile End Grove 121, 126
Mile End Leper Hospital 19
Mile End Manor House 19
Mile End New Town 11, 29, 102, 106, 109, 113-20, 122
Mile End Old Town 10-11, 18, 29-30, 86, 106, 120-6
Mile End Rd 15, 17, 22, 34, 112, 150, 162, 168, 182
Mile End Turnpike 121
Millet family 180
Millwall 17, 135-6
Mill Yard 51
Minories 11, 17, 20, 36, 38, 42-4, 55, 117
Mint Pub, The 59, 62, 94
Monmouth, Duke of 34
Montague St 47, 120
Montford House 108-9, 161
Montford, Henry de 108-9, 112
Montford, Simon de 108
Moorfields 45

O

More, Sir Thomas 24, 25, 26
Morgan, Margaret 61
Morley, Lord 25
Mot, Robert 38
Mountjoy family 117
Murdoch, Rupert 82
Museum of London 59
Muswell Hill 17
Mutton, Robert 82

Nankin Street 102
Narrow St 4, 99, 102, 186
Natt, Anthony 109
Neale, Thomas 90, 92
Nelson and Co 94
Nettleswell House 108, 112
Newdegate, Sybil 69
Newell Street 99, 102
New Friends, The 103
Newgate 76, 78, 97-8
Newgate Church 27
New Gravel Lane 76, 82
New Inn Yard 71
Newport, Isabella 38
New Rd 37, 45
New Synagogue 150
Newton, John 86
New Wells 72
Nichol St Mission 161
Nightingale Lane 17, 59, 61-2, 64, 67
Noah's Ark 90
Norman, Prior of Holy Trinity 38
North St 136, 138
Norton Folgate 114-15

Oak Lane 102
Odell's Playhouse 52
Old Bailey 52
Oldfield, Robert 29-30
Old Ford 15, 18-19, 129, 133
Old Ford Rd 34, 108-9, 133
Old Friends, The 103
Old Gravel Lane 12, 76, 176
Old Montague St 47, 147-8, 150
Old St 68-9
Oldys 61
Olympia, The 182
Orchard, The 93-4
Out and Out Mission 161, 182

P

Owens, Fredrick 118
Owens, Jessie 166
Oxford House 112
Oxford Movement 112, 161

Pace, Richard 25
Page, William 89
Palmer, John 116
Pankhurst, Sylvia 128
Parachute Gardens 160
Paradise Row 109, 185
Paragon Theatre 182
Parliament 45, 67, 136
Parr, Katherine 64
Pavilion, The 182-3
Peabody Estates 160
Peabody Sq 91
Peacock Ct 47
Peasants' Revolt 141
Peckover, William 86
Peel, Robert 155
Pekin St 102
Pelican Stairs 81
Pellett, Richard 42
Penn, Sir William 123, 130
Penshurst Place 61
People's Market 160
People's Palace 162-3
Pepys, Samuel 9, 21, 37, 47-8, 52, 81-2, 109, 123, 130, 138
Percy, Thomas 68, 108
Perkin, William 92
Peter and Paul Tavern 129
Pett, family 27
Pett, Phineas 94
Petticoat Lane 10, 34, 38, 42, 46-7, 52, 106, 114, 172, 178-81
Philip II 123
Philippa, Queen 61
Pillory Lane 55
Pittfield St 69
Plague, the 27, 46, 55, 64, 71, 97, 122
    see also Great Plague, the
Plough Inn 123
Poll Tax 27, 82, 123-4, 138
Pompeii 15
Pomfret 18
Pond Alley 40, 117
Pontefract 18
Pontefract Manor 136
Pool, The 138
Pooly, Lady 130
Poor Law 26
Poor Rate 52
Popish Plot 82

Poplar 11, 18, 20, 25, 29, 59, 61, 102-3, 129, 134-141, 153, 171, 182
Poplar High St 136
Poplar Labour Soc 136
Portugal, King of 129, 133
Potter's ferry 19
Pottlepot Alley 65
Prescott St 45, 47, 51
Price, Mary 80
Priestly, Meliora 127
Princelet St 47, 113, 148, 150
Prince of Wales 162, 175
Priory of Holy Trinity 19
Priory of St Mary, Spital 19, 69
Privy Council 89
Prospect of Whitby, The 76, 81, 89
Protector, Lord 81
Providence Place 32
Prusoms Island 77, 82
Public Record Office 52
Pudding Lane 13

Q

Queen's Head Tavern 90, 130
Queen Mary and Westfield College 124, 150, 162, 170
Queen Mother 162
Queen's Hall 150, 162
Queen's Palace 182
Queen Victoria, 143, 150
Queen Victoria, The 182

R

Rackett, Michael 47
Rag Fair 43-4, 46, 52, 65, 67
Railway Arch Works 34
Raines 172
Raleigh, Sir Walter 25, 102
Ramsgate, The 76, 83
Randolph, Isham 92
Randolph, Jane 92
Ratcliff 11-12, 14, 18-19, 22, 25, 29, 75-7, 93-5, 97, 99, 102
Ratcliff Cross 10, 12, 93
Ratcliff Cross St 93
Ratcliff Highway
   see Highway, the
Ratcliff Highway Murders 95
Ratcliff Meeting House 94
Ratcliff Stairs 25

Ratcliff Sugar House 25
Red Cow, The 83
Red Lion Sq 120
Red Lion St 15, 47
Red Lion, The 66, 73
Rednall House 109
Reformation 25, 40, 43, 70, 73, 76, 117, 136
Regents Canal 103
Regent's Park 54, 67
Restoration 27-8, 47, 82, 118, 130
Rhodeswell Rd 33
Richard II 123
Richardson gang 112
Rising Sun, The 34
Roach, Henry 82
Roman occupation 10, 13-17, 36, 68, 108
Roman Rd and market 15, 34, 108-9, 129, 133, 152, 176-7, 180, 186-7
Roman watch tower 10, 13, 14
Rook St 144
Roper, William 52
Rose Alley 40
Rose and Crown 124
Rose, The 66
Rosemary Lane 42-4, 51, 61, 67
Rothschild Building 147-8, 166, 168
Rothschild, Lord 147
Royal College of Surgeons 45
Royal Mint 59, 67, 97
Royal Mint Ct 52, 55
Royal Mint St 20, 40, 43-4, 59
Rubens, Sir Peter P 109
Ryder, Sir William 109

S

St Agnes the Clear 69
St Anne's, Limehouse 29, 98-9, 102
St Anne's passage 102
St Bartholomew's 70
St Botolph's, Aldgate 20, 36-8, 78, 40, 42-4, 46, 48
St Boltolph, Bishopsgate 117
St Clement Danes 17
St Dunstan's Church, Stepney 10, 12, 14, 17, 19-20, 22-3, 25-7, 29, 30, 32-4, 93, 106, 108
St George's in the East 12, 29, 145, 147, 166

St George's Workhouses 153
St Helen, parish 71, 116
St James's Place 52
Seymour, Jane 93
Shadewellefeld 89
St John the Baptist 80
St John the Baptist, Priory 69
St John's, Wapping 37, 84, 86
St Katharine's 10, 17, 54-67, 114
St Katherine's Dock 66
St Katherine's Dock Co 67
St Katherine's Hospital 19-20, 59-60, 62, 64
St Katherine's Marina 20, 59, 60, 67
St Leonard's Church 53, 69-70
St Leonard, convent 20
St Leonard's Priory 19
St Margaret's House 112
St Mary Chapel 136
St Mary Graces 19-20, 59, 61, 64, 70
St Mary Island 94
St Mary Matfelon 19, 42, 48
St Mary's, Bow 19
St Mary's Church 38, 133
St Mary's Hospital 42, 69
St Mary Spital 20, 70, 114, 120
St Mary Whitechapel 80
St Matthew's, Bethnal Green 29, 37, 112
St Matthias 136
St Paul of Shadwell 12, 90, 92
St Paul's 18, 24-5, 76, 89, 97, 116, 134-5
St Paul's Cross 25
St Peter's, London Dock 182
St Stephen's Rd 173, 175
St Thomas of Acon 20, 76, 89
St Thomas's Hospital 70
Salmon and Ball, The 109, 182
Salmon Lane 102, 161, 166
Salt Petre Bank 47
Salter, Robert 81
Salvation Army 112
Saracen's Head, the 38
Saracen Street 102
Scattergood, Thomas 94
School House Lane 93-5
Seamen's Hospital Dispensary 146
Second World War 112, 133, 152, 171

Settlement Movement 160, 182
Seven Mills School 136
Shadewellefeld 89
Shadwell 12, 15, 17-19, 27, 29, 75, 88-92
Shadwell Basin 75
Shadwell signal tower 17
Shakespeare Walk 92
Shakespeare, William 9, 25-6, 38, 40, 43, 62, 64-5, 71-2, 102, 116-17, 123
Shelley, Ann 48
Sherwin, John 52
Ship Alley 83, 147
Ship, The 43
Shoreditch 10-11, 17, 20, 25, 27, 36, 42, 52, 62, 65, 68-73, 116, 156, 182, 186
Shoreditch High St 15, 20, 73, 106
Shore, Jane 68
Short, Francis 161
Short, Iris 1, 175
Short, Lily 1, 162, 166-7, 175, 177
Short, Sid 4, 152, 162, 166-7, 175-6, 180-1, 185
Short, Violet B 1, 175, 185
Shoulder of Mutton Lane 102
Shouters Hill 126
Sir John Cass's School 172
Sir John Jolles School 127
Six Jolly Fellowship Porters 4, 102
Skinners' Almshouses 124
Sly, William 71
Smithfield 20, 34, 60, 82, 97
Smithfield, East 55, 59, 62, 64-5, 67, 69, 78, 80
Smock Alley 42
Somers, Will 71
Somerset, Protector 93
Sovereign Court 12
Southgate Workhouse 154, 160
Southwark 9, 16, 60, 64, 71, 73, 112
Southwark Stews 60
South West india Dock 101
Sparrows Court 40
Spencer, Gabriel 92
Spenser, Edmund 61-2, 67
Spert, Sir Thomas 25
Spital, Shoreditch
   see St Mary, Spital
Spital Cross 70
Spitalfields 10-11, 15, 17, 20, 29, 37, 42, 46, 51, 70,

106, 109, 113-20, 122, 143, 146, 148, 161, 166, 168, 172, 176, 181, 186
Spitalfields market 114
Spital Square 70, 118
Spring Garden Coffee House 29
Steele, Sir Richard 28
Stephen, King 60
Stepkin, John 89, 92
Stepkyn family 64
Stepney 2, 4, 10-12, 18-21, 34, 36, 40, 48, 62, 102, 106, 120, 122, 129, 136, 143, 145, 158, 161, 168
Stepney Church
   see St Dunstan's
Stepney Green 22, 29, 122, 124, 160, 186
Stepney Marsh 19, 59, 136
Stepney Meeting 27
Stepney, the manor of 11, 17, 20-1, 30-1, 34, 160
Stepney Way 27, 34
Stibba 17, 22
Stibba's Hithe 22
Stow, John 15, 40, 42, 55, 77-8, 94, 97
Strand, the 9
Stratford Bow 15, 20, 127, 129, 138
Streete 82
Strype 46, 90, 117, 137
Strype, Jan van 117
Strype St 117
Stuart, Jim 171
Stubbes, Philip 118
Suffolk, Duchess of 24
Sun Tavern Fields 52, 89, 95
Sun Tavern Place 89
Swan Alley 40, 62
Swan's Nest, The 61-2, 92
Swan Theatre, The 71
Swan with Two Necks 90

T

Talbot, Ann & Richard 44
Telford, Thomas 67
Temperance Society & Movement 136, 182
Tenter St 38
Terricus de Aldgate 76
Thames, river 12-13, 17, 54-6, 59, 78, 90, 97, 100, 102, 135-6, 155
Theatre, The 71-3
Thirwall, Thomas 30
Thomas More St 17, 59, 64
Thorney Island 13

Thrawl St 148
Three Foot Alley 82
Three Colts Lane 99, 102, 112
Three Lords, The 55
Three Mariners, The 90
Three Mills Lane 129
Three Nuns, The 38, 43, 52
Tobacco Dock 87
Tooley Street 97
Tower Bridge 55, 57, 59, 143
Tower Ditch 82
Tower Hamlets 11, 13, 30, 55, 83, 112, 131, 186
Tower Hamlets Cemetery 124
Tower Hill 34, 54-5, 59-60, 66, 97, 116
Tower Hill, Abbot of 59, 60, 136, 142
Tower Hill Court 60
Tower Hotel 60, 143
Tower of London 9-10, 14, 19-20, 25, 36, 40, 43, 54-6, 59, 64, 83, 97, 113, 116, 176
Town of Ramsgate, The 83
Toy Museum 161
Toynbee Hall 160
Tredegar Rd 127, 133
Tredegar Sq 171, 186
Trinity Almshouses 124
Trinity House 25
Trumpeter on Horseback, the 90
Turk's Head 79
Turk's Head Bagnio 52
Two Sawyers, The 90
Tyburn 52, 97,
Tyler, Wat 123

U

Underhill, Edward 102
Upper Shadwell 90, 92

V

Vallance Rd 153, 182
Vallance, William 153
Vanderdelft, Cornelius 77, 89
Vayre, Mathilda le 108
Vernon, Richard de 141
Victoria Park 24, 34, 133, 160
Victoria Park Sq 108-9, 131
Victualling House Yard 52

Vine Tavern, The 124
Vintners' Almshouses 124
Vintners' Company 32, 92
Virginia St 82

W

Waeppa 17, 76, 89
Wagner, Wilhelm R 175
Walbrook 13
Walker, Henry 147, 161
Waltham Abbey 136
Walton, Thomas 78
Wapping 9-12, 17-18, 25, 29, 37, 51-2, 64, 75-87, 89, 92, 146, 161, 176, 182, 185
Wapping Dock 75, 80
Wapping High St 17, 76-9, 84, 87
Wapping in the Wose 19, 61, 77, 89
Wapping Lane 12, 76,
Wapping Marsh 19
Wapping New Stairs 97
Wapping Old Stairs 76, 83
Wapping Pier Head 180
Wapping Station 97
Wapping Wall 44, 76, 80-1, 89, 92, 186
Warren, Sir William 81-2
Waterman's Arms, The 182
Waterman's Walk 186
Watney St 177, 186
Watney St Market 177
Watts, Anthony 82
Webb, Beatrice 18, 152
Wellclose Sq 15, 47, 51, 82-3
Well St 146
Welton, Dr 48, 143, 150
Wentworth family 34
Wentworth, Lady Philadelphia 34, 124
Wentworth St 31, 34, 47, 49, 52-3, 179
Wesker, Arnold 185
Wesley, John 92, 108
West End 170
West Ferry Rd 135
Westheath 124
West India Docks 37, 103, 134-7, 138-40
West India Dock Rd 103
Westminster 9, 13, 164
Westminster Abbey 39
Wharton, Mary 80
White Bear Alley 117
White, Jerry 147-8, 176
Whitechapel 10, 12-15, 17-19, 20, 35-53, 62, 69,

73, 80, 106, 112, 117, 120-1, 124, 129-30, 143, 146, 152-4, 160-1, 170, 176, 179, 182-3, 185
Whitechapel Bars 37
Whitechapel Bell Foundry 23, 38-9, 150
Whitechapel Church 143
Whitechapel Mound 45
Whitechapel prison 48
Whitechapel Rd 15, 36, 38-9, 122, 150, 152-3, 176, 182
Whitehorse Lane 22, 27, 29, 34
Whitehorse Rd 25
Whitehouse Inn 138
Whites Yard 47
Whitfield 52
Wilkes St 113
Wilkins, George 72
Williams, Katherine 90
William the Conqueror 17-18, 37, 54
William III 28
William IV 99
Williams, Thomas 82
Willmott, Peter 176
Willoughby, Sir Hugh 93
Wilson, Dr Thomas 64
Wilson, J 123
Wiltons 182
Wolsey, Cardinal 25
Wolfe, John 62, 64,
Wolfe, Mistress 62
Wolfe, Old Mother 148, 179
Wolveridge, John 176
Woolwich 81,
Woolpack, The 43
Worcester, Marquis of 24, 27
Workers Educational & Travel Assocs 160
Worship St 72
Wrath, Robert 123
Wren, Sir Christopher 46-7, 122, 124
Wythers, John 81

Y

Young, Michael 176

Z

Zangwill, Israel 148
Zoological Gardens 54
Zouch, Abraham & son 90